2 0 MAR 2025

WITHDRAWN

Improvising Improvisation

Improvising Improvisation:
From Out of Philosophy, Music, Dance, and Literature

Gary Peters

The University of Chicago Press :: Chicago and London

The University of Chicago Press, Chicago 60637
The University of Chicago Press, Ltd., London
© 2017 by The University of Chicago
Published 2017
Printed in the United States of America

26 25 24 23 22 21 20 19 18 17   1 2 3 4 5

ISBN-13: 978-0-226-45262-3 (cloth)
ISBN-13: 978-0-226-45276-0 (e-book)
DOI: 10.7208/chicago/9780226452760.001.0001

Library of Congress Cataloging-in-Publication Data

Names: Peters, Gary, 1952– author.
Title: Improvising improvisation : from out of philosophy, music, dance, and
    literature / Gary Peters.
Description: Chicago ; London : The University of Chicago Press, 2017. |
    Includes bibliographical references and index.
Identifiers: LCCN 2016052003 | ISBN 9780226452623 (cloth : alk. paper) | ISBN
    9780226452760 (e-book)
Subjects: LCSH: Act (Philosophy) | Improvisation (Acting) in literature. |
    Improvisation (Music) | Improvisation in dance.
Classification: LCC B105.A35 .P39 2017 | DDC 128/.4—dc23 LC record available
    to https://lccn.loc.gov/2016052003

♾ This paper meets the requirements of ANSI/NISO Z39.48-1992 (Permanence
of Paper).

Contents

Preface

. . . there is nothing to express, nothing with which to express, nothing from which to express, no power to express, no desire to express, together with the obligation to express.

Samuel Beckett[1]

To make something out of nothing—indeed, the felt *obligation* to make something out of nothing—is, for me, at the very heart of improvisation and at the very heart of this, my second book on improvisation. Most improvisations make something out of *something else*, as do most academic books, the vast majority of which *speak about* existing things rather than "*from out of,*" as Heidegger says, the thing itself. So one of the main reasons for writing this book was to see if it really is possible to make something out of nothing, and speak *from out of* improvisation itself.

Yes, everything that follows, regardless of its appearance, is completely improvised, written each and every day from scratch. Not from one chapter to the next (if only), not from one section to the next (I wish), but from one sentence, sometimes one word to the next. Needless to say, it took a while. Why? Because, to repeat, it is not a question of improvising with material that is, returning to Heidegger, "ready-to-hand," within an improvised situation that is assumed or given. On the contrary, and as I hope will become clearer as the book progresses, each chapter is first and foremost an attempt to *create*—from out of nothing—a situation that, only then, can be entered into. In other words, the improvisational dimension of the text operates at two levels, sometimes simultaneously, sometimes not. That is to say, at both the *a priori* and the *a posteriori* level: what I will later refer to as *within* and *between* improvised situations.

We tend to think of improvisation as a thing of speed: snap decisions, lightning choices, and quick-fire responses to the moment. No time for thought, no time to agonize over every next move, no time for prolonged contemplation, and certainly no time for the rhetorical repetition already being indulged in here. Everything has to happen *now*, "in the moment." Everything we have learned, practiced, and perfected has to be forgotten in the automatism of habit, where knowledge and memory become *act*, and "mere" theory and theorizing become practice: *practice*, that hallowed word![2]

Try and imagine a form of improvisation that is painfully, agonizingly slow, forever faltering, more error than trial, struggling to even begin, the interminable rehearsal of a decisive but barely graspable origin. To imagine this is to imagine something approximating the glacial genesis of this current book.

Most writers write because they have something to say; beliefs they want others to believe or at least understand and respect, commitments they want others to commit to or at least understand and respect, a story they want others to hear, understand, and respect. Most writers of academic books write because they have something academic to say to other academics. In academia it is knowledge that comes first, while the book comes second, a documentation and/or telling of this *given* knowledge: what is given shall be given again, an act of (peer-reviewed) communicative communion. Here, writing demarcates a contained space, a space that is determined by the knowledge it is required to contain and document. This space is a memorial trace of all that the writer as thinker and accumulator of knowledge *has been*: a monument. Not how *they* came to be what and who *they* are, but how or why they have come to *know* what they *know*: an epistemological monument (or, sometimes, a monumental epistemology).

Not many improvisers write—I assume they're too busy improvising— but most of those who do, *write about* improvisation. They consider the nature of improvisation, they make claims for it, they recall experiences, and they sometimes theorize on the essence of improvisation, its uniqueness, and its potential impact across a wide range of human activity. Such books are very often inspiring, politically formative, and existentially transformative: they are often intended to be just that, and on those terms are, no doubt, very successful.

Try and imagine a writer who has few, if any, "valuable" experiences to share. A writer with no position, stance, perspective on improvisation. Try and imagine a writer who has no theory or philosophy of improvisation,[3] and, what is more, has no desire to promote anything that might "make a contribution" to the personal growth and/or "well-being" of others. That is to say, finally, a writer who is philosophically, theoretically, politically agnostic—(ironic)—and hasn't the faintest idea why anyone would even consider reading a book on improvisation or, most baffling of all, consider *writing* a book on improvisation.

But seriously, although devoid of any particular philosophical, theoretical, political, ethical, spiritual perspective . . . (the list is endless), this book is grounded on/in one fundamental belief, one that is not up for discussion, one that does not figure at all in the overt content of this book, but without which the book would not be as it is: the belief that improvisation is a *predicament*. Not primarily a genre, idiom, style, technique, skill, or talent, improvisation is first and foremost a *predicament*. Clearly such an assertion is not in itself sufficient to produce a viable or "valuable" book on improvisation, nor does it or could it offer much insight into the whys and wherefores of improvisation, which, I imagine, is what most readers want to know or want to "get out of" such books.

Yes, but the fact remains: the recognition that improvisation is not something freely chosen but a predicament within which one *finds oneself* or into which one is "thrown,"' to use Heidegger's vocabulary, demands (if a book really must be written) a very different kind of book; indeed, the very words *demand* and *must* are themselves already revealing, as the chapter on obligation will acknowledge and address. A book that does not celebrate the celebrated choices made by improvisers in the heat of the moment, within the often over-hyped uncertainty of the improvised situation as it unfolds in the "now," but one that recognizes that the performativity of choice, fun though it may be, is ontologically secondary to the *a-priority* of *decision*: improvisers *make* choices, but they are *made by* decisions. That's the predicament.

The essential difference between choice and decision runs, like an ontological wire, right through this book, from beginning to end (if only there were a beginning and end). True, it does rise to the surface occasionally to acknowledge Heidegger's abiding presence in everything that follows; but for the most part, the decisiveness of improvisation, as an originary predicament, remains *sotto voce*, an unspoken-ness (and thus "heard") within the speaking *from out of* the sense of obligation, resoluteness, the habitual, and the creative passivity of *amor fati*: these are the central concerns throughout.

It is, then, not surprisingly, a slightly peculiar book; at times wayward, at times repetitive, insistent, and, yes, resolute—often resolutely wayward!

It is not until we near the end, though, that resoluteness *itself* becomes the subject of discussion, where it is revealed, thanks to Heidegger again, that it is not only the resoluteness of the improviser *within* the situation that is worthy of discussion (the subject of most books on improvisation), but the manner in which resoluteness is, ontologically, *responsible for* the creation of the situation in the first place. As we will see, it is this concern with an unacknowledged (perhaps imaginary) concept of improvisation, where the action takes place either *before* or *between* the actuality/actualities of the performative situation/situations, that opens out onto some different ways of thinking about improvisation.

Acknowledgments

Much of this book is about solitude, sometimes overtly, often beneath the surface. Solitude, as is explained throughout, has nothing to do with loneliness; rather, it has to do with the conversation you have with yourself inside your own head. This book is one product of that interior tête-à-tête. Of course, this internal dialogue sometimes (hopefully quite often) overlaps with and opens up to the external world, and when it does, the input from friends, colleagues, and whoever else is out there can and does leave a trace on, or simply add sustenance to, the ongoing work: either way I am truly grateful. Here are a few names: Dan Brown, Mike Cooper, Wayne Johnson, Dominic Lash, Marc Medwin, Eirini Nedelkopoulou, Matthew Reason, Fiona Thompson, Roger Turner, Bill Washer, Veryan Weston, and Rob Wilsmore. Needless to say, none of them had anything whatever to do with the actual text before you; in fact most of them will probably never even read it.

I would especially like to acknowledge the unwavering support and, more importantly, the inspiration over many years of Steve Purcell: without his encouragement I doubt this book would have been written.

Similarly, the commissioning editor, Elizabeth Branch Dyson, has once again been the absolute bedrock of this project. Without the knowledge that she would be the first person to read my manuscript, I wouldn't have had the guts or bare-faced cheek to write what I did: she is clearly unshockable.

I should also mention the anonymous (and similarly unshockable) reviewers of the original manuscript, whose incredibly detailed, insightful, and highly constructive comments helped me rethink and rework substantial parts of the text in ways that improved it beyond recognition.

As always, this book is for my wife, Fiona, and my children, Isabelle and Francis, all of whom remain utterly unconvinced by my self-proclaimed genius: maybe this book will help change their minds . . . maybe not.

Introduction

Given the genuinely improvisatory nature of this book, perhaps the best way to read it is in the same spirit, just as you
would watch or listen to an improvised performance: in anticipation of the not yet known—the work "still to come."
Of course, now that the book is written, and now that I (for
one) have read it, it would be easy for me to tell the reader
what to expect, what, indeed, is to come. But I have no intention of doing that, as it would destroy the original purpose
of the book, which was precisely to see what happened when
you tried writing "from out of" the predicament of the improviser: a kind of ignorance. I think it is important to retain
as much of this prior unknowingness as is feasible without
completely alienating the reader. So as a minor concession,
here are a few helpful hints that might offer some guidance
along the forking pathways of the text to come.

To begin with, this book, like my last book, is of a philosophical nature but, to be absolutely clear, it is *not* a philosophical text: I am *not* a philosopher; I'm an improviser.
While my thinking on improvisation draws upon philosophers throughout—in particular Kant, Hegel, Heidegger,
Deleuze, and Badiou—there is nothing here intended to clarify, interpret, or (Heaven forbid) critique their philosophies:
I wouldn't know where to start, and barely understand them
myself. Having no philosophical identity of my own, I regard
these philosophers simply as a means to an end rather than

as ends in themselves, although what the end *is*, well, that's anyone's guess. This book is, if anything (inverting Kant), a "kingdom of means:" and I am, at best, a philosophical ventriloquist.

But why these particular philosophers?

All of them, even Kant, might be described as philosophers of the *event*, and it is, above all else, the event of improvisation that is the primary concern of the following pages. It is this, rather than the sometimes rather technical language of the philosophers, that is the real difficulty. The language can and should be ignored: just read through it until you get out the other side, that's what I do, plus I squint. That seems to help. The difficulty of the event is that it has no presence in the present, it cannot be presented, which makes this a rather futile enterprise in some ways. But, then, futility should never be a barrier to writing and doing: just think of Kafka or Beckett. To be honest, this sense of futility was my constant companion over the many years it took to write this loathsome book, but then, as I hope the book itself will explain, the most profound improvisation can be the product of just such futility.

My last book was criticized (only by one critic, it has to be said) for not sufficiently engaging with actual improvised practice, something that I have tried to rectify in the current text. Indeed, this book is positively bursting at the seams with practitioners and their practices; plus, as a bonus, there is also a prolonged discussion of practising itself as a daily regime. Needless to say, I did this to spite the said critic, because nothing I say about practice or improvised practice could possibly satisfy the needs and demands of such a reader—ever eager to have real-life improvisers and their real-life improvisations analyzed, explicated, and critiqued for the sake of . . . what? I have no idea. So, yes, I have much to say about many improvisers across numerous fields, and, yes, some of this does engage with actual performance; but such discussions always serve something outside of the performative situation, something that I am incapable of analyzing, explicating, or critiquing. Instead, I try and *describe* what I see and hear, but in the sense of *de-scribing*: both writing and unwriting at the same time. That's why it took so long. If the reader can get a sense of this double strategy or stratagem, then everything will make a sort of sense. If not, then *that* is where the difficulty lies. That is to say, the difficulty, if there is any, has nothing to do with technicality, philosophy, or complexity; rather, it has to do with changing one's habits of thought, and, to help this along, a large part of the book is concerned with habit.

It has been pointed out to me—I had no idea—that I tend to work with pairs of concepts, and in retrospect this does indeed seem to be the case. But a note of caution: such concepts are never used dialectically. There should be no trace in this book of oppositional, hierarchical, or contradictory thinking, dialectically working toward some unspoken Absolute: the event is neither an origin nor a goal. Instead these pairs should be thought of as co-present, contestational rather than contradictory, and "compossible," to use Leibniz's term. Anyway, below are some of the keywords that run throughout the text: some of them are in pairs, some of them not.

> Start—Beginning. The general idea is that these two terms do not, or do not necessarily, coincide. Part of this has to do with the retrospective nature of the event, which means that it has always already begun before anything can start, and then sensed again before things can begin again. Another issue is the claim that improvisers are particularly adept at bringing this difference into view, by "dramatizing" the beginning. More generally, what might be called the "sense of a beginning" is the focus of the first part of the book, as it should be: it's a beginning, after all.
>
> Origin—Origination—Originality. As will be seen, most of these terms are interlinked. Following Heidegger, the task of thinking what he calls the "other beginning" leads repeatedly to a consideration of origins, not as a past source but as the work of origination necessarily enacted in the present—improvisation being one performative example. The shift away from the valorization of originality toward what might be called "originarity" is one intended consequence of such a perspective.
>
> Certitude—Certainty. The book begins with an extended discussion of Kant and Hegel on the subject of certitude and "sense-certainty" respectively. The upshot of this is that, contrary to what might be expected, confronted with uncertainty, and with no possibility of certainty, an attitude of certitude or a form of artistic "severity" can be the way forward as regards the creation of artworks (or anything else for that matter). Such ideas can tell us a lot about improvisation, but only of a particular type: something to be discussed at great length.
>
> Fixity—Unfixity. The dual themes of improvisation as unfixing the fixed, and fixing the unfixed runs right through this book. This pairing is generally intended to reverse the dominant improvisational paradigm, which

tends to assume an unfixing of the fixed model of improvisation: the jazz standard being the classic example.
While this issue pops up everywhere in the text, there is
one long section right in the middle that homes in on it
as a kind of thought experiment.

Idiomatic—Non–Idiomatic. The improviser/guitarist/
writer Derek Bailey proposed this distinction in his
well-known book on improvisation as a way of avoiding what he considered the problematical category of
"free improvisation." It has to be said, the terminology
hasn't been willingly or widely adopted by the improvising fraternity, and some are openly hostile to it, miser-
able bunch, which is why, perversely, I devote so much
time and space to it here in a super-subtle reconsidera-
tion and refinement of Bailey's original conception. A
quasi-ironic exercise in hyper-nuancing so typical of the
academic world (although without my irony).

Decision—Choice. Another distinction made by Heidegger,
one that saturates the whole text to come. Once again,
it is the concern with the event of improvisation rather
than improvised situations that turns the discussion
away from the "free" choices that are made "in the
moment," toward the *a priori* decisive moment that
grounds the possibility of these choices. Everything in
this book is trying to bring this decisive moment into
view and, even better, into focus: a failure no doubt, but
hopefully a glorious one.

Accuracy—Precision. The discussion of Kant and Hegel on
certitude and "severity" brings, as a consequence, notions of precision and accuracy as elements of improvisation to the fore. Both are the subjects of suspicion
within improvising circles, so a discussion was needed,
a discussion that also brings back into play the paired
concepts of decisiveness and indecisiveness to help
explain the ontological difference between precision and
accuracy. As ever, Heidegger is my guide here.

Loneliness—Solitude. Hannah Arendt is the source of this
distinction. Essentially, loneliness is a social category, a
by-product of interpersonal relations and interaction.
Solitude is a philosophical-aesthetic relation with the
work and the self. In almost every case below, I find

myself claiming that the most powerful improvisation (whatever that means) is conducted in solitude. This might be seen as an antidote to the prevalence of interaction and dialogics within the writing and talking about improvisation. It is part of an anti-empathic position inherited from Heidegger, Deleuze, and my years working among people I found it hard to empathize with.

Difference—Diversity. Speaking of Deleuze, *Difference and Repetition* is undoubtedly the most significant influence on this text. In a nutshell, one of the main threads running through what follows is the suggestion that a great deal of improvisation offers us a form of diversification rather than real difference. An even more important consequence of this line of inquiry is the suspicion that there exists a form of improvisation that, while producing real difference, is secreted within the appearance of the same: what I describe as a "different sameness" to distinguish it from the "same difference" that is everywhere in improvisation: diversity.

Habit. Drawing on the thought of Deleuze and Catherine Malabou, a lot of energy is put into considering the nature of habit as it relates to improvisation. Looking initially at the way improvisers attempt to avoid or outwit their own habitual selves, the discussion turns toward a more positive evaluation, with the discovery that the habitual offers a particular form of what Deleuze calls "passive creativity" and Malabou calls "plasticity," both allowing me to think habit and improvisation together.

Practise—Rehearsal. Trying to answer the question, Why rehearse when improvisers have no work *to* rehearse? The consideration of rehearsal as a form of re-hearsing, that is to say the re-hearing of the event of improvisation itself, is distinguished from practising as that which preserves the origin rather than prepares for the future. That, in essence, is what this whole book strives to be: a rehearsal.

While all of this is admittedly rather cryptic, at least when some of the above terms make an appearance, the reader will have been forewarned that, while clarity and resolution might not always be fully achieved, these are the surface markers for the "secret" improvisations always underway somewhere beneath the text: *sotto voce*. To hear this other voice, to sense its presence, is, as it turns out, the primary aim of this book: although, of course, I didn't know that when I was writing it.

One last point: to read this text will require patience, the ability to resist rushing in and demanding an immediate explanation, clarification, or justification for every assertion made (and there are many). The writing of this book was a search for what I sensed but didn't know, a reaching out for something—a way of improvising—that was always, and remains just beyond my grasp: tantalizing. Patience will be required to await the results of a sometimes painfully slow and labored process of discovery—the same patience (or was it doggedness?) required to write the book in the first place. As Deleuze and Guattari describe their own approach to writing, the only things worth writing about, the only things that need writing about, are precisely the things we *don't* already know about. Those impatient for immediate knowledge or addicted to the sound of "his master's voice" will be disappointed in what follows; but then it is said that a text creates its own readership (just as this one created its own writer), something which, perhaps, offers the most cryptic clue of all to one of this work's primary desires: to grasp that it is *we* who are the *subject of* improvisation, rather than the other way around.

1

I've Started, so I'll Begin: Heidegger's Other Beginning and the Origin of Improvisation

I've Started, So I'll Begin

The desire to improvise a book on improvisation is the same desire that is now searching for a way of completing this sentence: yes, it is that localized. Not the desire to impart knowledge *about* the many practices of improvisation, but the desire to begin something without knowing where it will end, or indeed if there is an end: it is that global. Which is to say, the desire to begin something for the sake of the beginning and not the end.

In the UK there is a very well known quiz show called *Mastermind*, which has run without a break since 1972. The program has five contestants who must answer questions over two rounds, the first on their specialist subject, and the second on general knowledge. All of this is irrelevant except for one detail: at the end of each timed round, where quicker answers mean more questions, a buzzer sounds to warn of the approaching end. At this moment, if the quizmaster has already started the question, he (it has always been a he) interrupts himself and announces: "I've started, so I'll finish," and then continues to the end. So this has become the catchphrase of the program, one that has subsequently entered British culture as an off-the-peg humorous interjection for a multitude of occasions that invite such a display of zaniness, of which there are many. To counter this catchphrase with

"I've started, so I'll begin," might seem even more zany, but the intention is to raise two issues: first, the distinction between the start and the beginning, and, second, the irreversible teleological thrust of the question form.

"I've started, so I'll begin" is an odd thing to say because it relies upon an unfamiliar disjuncture of *starting* and *beginning*, terms that are commonly used synonymously. True, but their separation makes possible an insight that points toward a significant difference between non-improvised and improvised work: namely, that non-improvised work *erases* the difference between the start and the beginning, while improvisation *enacts*, even *dramatizes* it. This is not to suggest for one moment that the writers/composers/choreographers of works are unaware of this difference; on the contrary, they are as aware of it as any improviser, probably more so, given their desire to destroy it. The point to make, however, is that the improvisatory process, the false starts, the trials and errors, the moments of aesthetic judgment and misjudgment, all necessary for a work to come into being, are all erased *prior* to the work's eventual emergence as a finished work. It is only once this process of rendering simultaneous the start and the beginning, by erasing the difference between them, that the finished work can make its start. In other words, it must be finished before it can start. Compare this to an improvisation, where, instead of forgetting, obscuring, or secreting the above prehistory beneath the lustrous sheen of a pristine "work" and the pure virginity of its commencement, the start almost always precedes the beginning (if indeed there *is* a beginning).

Heidegger often speaks of the "other beginning,"[1] which is often interpreted as the desire for a return to the pre-Socratics, prior to the re-origination of thought in the translation of Greek into Latin. But he intends much more than a historical reevaluation; the essential desire being for an ontological shift rather than a historical reversal, whereby a space of origination is illuminated *now* as another beginning within what has already started. As Heidegger affirms in the essay of the same name, the origin of the work of art is not in the past but *now* as that which is always to come.

Translating the above into our own quizmaster terms, and situating such thinking in the experience of improvisation, "I've started, so I'll begin" is by no means intended to mystify or obfuscate the improvisatory act. On the contrary, the aim here is to be as true to the actual experience as possible; improvisers intuitively know when things "start to happen," that is to say, *begin*. These are the moments to "get into," already suggesting a space to be entered and occupied for as long as possible, although in reality such moments are usually quite fleeting. The common view of free improvisation in particular is that from out of nothing, something *happens*, a kind of "magic:"[2] this is very far from being the case. Indeed, thankfully so, as such sorcery would rob us of what improvisation really does offer: the dramatization of the beginning and, with it, the enactment of the delay that separates the originary moment from the point when things simply get started.

But in order to better understand the difference between the two, let us return to the quizmaster's actual interjection—"I've started, so I'll finish"—and what was described earlier, rather grandly, as its irreversible teleological thrust. At issue here is not just the nature of the question form itself, which, in order to be meaningful and answerable, is required to be complete prior to any response; but also the widely held view that artworks are best understood as answers to questions. Hans Georg Gadamer encapsulates this perfectly when he asserts, "A work of art can only be understood if we assume its adequacy as an expression of the artistic idea. Here too we have to discover the question which it answers, if we are to understand it as an answer."[3] Conceived in these (highly questionable) terms, the artwork, at the moment of its emergence, *already* contains within it the completed form of the essential aesthetic question. While, no doubt, the number of "answers" to any such "questions" is infinite, nevertheless the essential *form* of the answer is, like the question, contingent but closed. In fact, formally speaking, even a so-called "open question" is closed, which, in secret recognition of this fact, explains why there is no such thing as an "open answer." Anyway, the important point to make here is that, if we allow the artwork to be locked into the teleological logic of the question, then the start and the beginning of the work will always coincide, just as the start and beginning of an answer always coincide. "I've started, so I'll begin" challenges this by introducing an alternative logic of delay, one without questions or answers, one much closer to the reality of art practice in general and improvisation in particular.

2

With What Must the Improvisation Begin? Kant and Hegel on Certainty

Beginnings: Kant and Hegel

In the famous "With What Must the Science Begin?" section of his *Science of Logic*,[1] Hegel makes a distinction between two beginnings. As he conceives it, the *logical* beginning of the *Science of Logic* presupposes, and is thus mediated by, the sensuous beginning posited at the start (a word used advisedly) of the *Phenomenology of Mind*. Hegel describes the relation as follows:

> Logic, then, has for its *presupposition* the science of manifested spirit [the *Phenomenology*], which contains and demonstrates the necessity, and so the truth, of the standpoint occupied by pure knowing and its mediation. In this science of manifested spirit the beginning is made from empirical, *sensuous* consciousness and this is *immediate* knowledge in the strict sense of the word. . . . In logic, the presupposition is that which has proved itself to be *the result* of that phenomenological consideration.[2]

So, when Hegel states in the *Science of Logic* that to begin, one must "simply take up what is *there before us*,"[3] he is repeating at the level of pure knowing what is stated at the beginning of the *Phenomenology* in relation to immediate sensuous consciousness. What is more, this repetition is only possible once the phenomenological labor necessary for the revelation of knowledge is complete. To translate this into our current terminology: the *Phenomenology* must have started (and finished) before the *Logic* can begin. However, to complicate matters, and perhaps take some improvisatory liberties, the fact that, for Hegel, the starting point remains preserved as a moment of the end point, means that the sensuous immersion in the given, typical of immediate consciousness, is not transcended or overcome in pure knowing but remains as the limited and arbitrary substance from out of which absolute knowledge is revealed; whether fleetingly for non-Hegelians or absolutely for Hegelians. While the relevance of this to improvisation might seem obscure, it is actually quite straightforward: improvisation enacts and thus reveals what is inherent, but often concealed, in *all* art practice—the co-presence and interpenetration of immediate sensuous experience and a mediated pure logic of becoming. Unlike the Hegelian philosopher who, from the vantage point of the Absolute, is able to purify this logic of becoming, relieve it of its sensuous garb, and speak only of "being" and "nothing,"[4] thankfully, the improviser remains "trapped" within the phenomenological limitations of immediate consciousness, where the aesthetic experience of and aesthetic pleasure associated with "taking up what is there before us" remains the primary task and purpose. And, as Hegel confirms, it is *purpose* that, as the prior phenomenological beginning, is responsible for the unfolding of concrete reality in a way that ultimately makes manifest the pure becoming of logical truth. This is how he articulates it in the *Phenomenology*, a complex passage that will need unpacking as it relates to improvisation. It begins by reiterating the essential identity of the beginning and the end, here described as the "result:"

> The result [end] is the same as the beginning solely because the beginning is purpose. Stated otherwise, what is actual and concrete is the same as its inner principle or notion simply because the immediate *qua* purpose contains within it the self or pure actuality. The realized purpose, or concrete actuality, is movement and development unfolded. But this very unrest is the self; and it is one and the same with that immediacy and simplicity characteristic of the beginning just for the reason that it is the result, and has returned upon itself.[5]

Whether one goes with Kant, who famously describes art practice as being purposiveness *without* a purpose,[6] or with Hegel, for whom it clearly *does* have a purpose, what both have in common is a recognition that it is purposiveness which dynamizes the instant, transforming it into a beginning by assuming an end. While the Hegelian philosopher, surveying all from the height of the Absolute, is able to witness the return of the end into the beginning (of pure knowing into sensuous experience), the improviser, without such philosophical privileges, must remain within the limited perspective of what is immediately given, armed only with a sense of purpose or, as we shall say later, *obligation* that is, by its very nature, in excess of and thus capable of problematizing immediate sensuous experience. Can this double sense—sensuousness and purposiveness—responsible for the "unfolding" of concrete reality begin to explain the proposed distinction between the start and the beginning of an improvisation? Would this mean, if it were true, that improvisation, situated as it is within the conditions and conditionality of particular phenomenological configurations of Mind or Spirit, would be unable to make the transition from the start to the beginning argued for at the outset? Put more positively: could the "freedom" associated with, for example, free improvisation be understood as a freeing-from the immediate experience and knowledge associated with the phenomenological in the name of an eventual ontology of improvisation?

In order to attempt a proper answer to these questions, we will first look more closely not only at the opening pages of the *Phenomenology*, where the immediacy necessary for improvisation is introduced by Hegel, but also as the account of the beginning of art as the "severe style" offered in his *Aesthetics*. Only then will it be possible to offer a more considered response to the above questions as well as a more fully articulated model of improvisation understood as the enactment and dramatization of the beginning. In order to do this, though, we must first draw out the significance of Kant's model of aesthetic judgment as a way of demonstrating the deeper entwinement of his and Hegel's thinking on art and their significance for our own discussion of improvisation.

Aesthetic Taste and Improvisation

We might begin by looking more closely at Kant's conception of aesthetic judgment, first as it relates to the creative act and then, more specifically, with regard to what it might bring to a discussion of improvisation. What is apparent from the outset is that Kant makes a clear distinction between the aesthetic judgment of taste and the creative act:

> The artist, having practised and corrected his taste by a variety of examples from nature or art, controls his work and, after many, and often laborious, attempts to satisfy taste, finds the form which

> commends itself to him. Hence this form is not, as it were, a matter
> of inspiration . . . but rather a slow and even painful process of im-
> provement, directed to making the form adequate to his thought . . .
>
> Taste is, however, merely a critical, not a productive faculty;
> and what conforms to it is not, merely on that account, a work of
> fine art.[7]

This, the adequation of form and thought, offers considerable insight into
the process whereby the cultivation of taste, while not productive in itself, is
nonetheless responsible for the control and, indeed, the certainty we might
expect of artists and their creative practice.

To explain, Kant's whole aesthetic is rooted in the certainty of feeling,
the certainty of pleasure that is immune to the judgments of others. One
does not say: "I think this is beautiful" or "This is beautiful for me" (mere
agreeableness), but simply "This *is* beautiful," a judgment that is aesthetic
to the extent that it *demands* universal agreement. It is for this reason that
Kant claims that there cannot be a dialectic of taste,[8] and that in matters of
aesthetic judgment it is not a question of dispute but only of contention.[9]
What is of interest here is that a lack of taste during what might be called
the developmental stage of an aesthetic practice, where an artist's creative
endeavors fail to "satisfy" aesthetic judgment, does not prevent the production of work. Indeed, a peculiarity of aesthetic judgment is that it is *always*
certain of itself regardless of its relative development or undevelopment.
Kant uses the example of a "youthful poet" to illustrate this:

> Hence it is that a youthful poet refuses to allow himself to be dis-
> suaded from the conviction that his poem is beautiful, even by the
> judgment of the public or his friends. . . . It is only in aftertime,
> when his judgment has been sharpened by exercise, that of his own
> free will and accord he deserts his former judgment.[10]

As regards improvisation, there are a number of things suggested by
this distinction between tasteful critique and creative production. First, it is
clear that the development of aesthetic taste does in fact include an essential
improvisatory dimension, one that through a process of "practise and cor-
rection," many "often laborious attempts," and a "painful process of im-
provement" (who said improvisation was fun?) eventually arrives at a form
that "feels" right and adequately communicates that feeling. In this view the
creative act comes *after* the development of an adequate form, where, Kant
believes, the figure of the "genius" (we would say artist) outstrips the mere
criticality of the aesthetic judge. This is a common form of improvisation

that is often ignored, not least because the finished "work" is precisely intended to conceal or obscure the uncertainty and improvisatory nature of its genesis. Thought in terms of youthfulness and maturity, the very *life* of the artist, is conceived here as improvisatory, leading ultimately to the said adequation of form and thought to be found (for Kant) in works of "genius."

The second point to be made returns us to the "peculiar" certitude of aesthetic judgment throughout its developmental stages. It is only "in aftertime" that the youthful poet recognizes the error of his or her earlier work and acknowledges that, in retrospect, such improvisations were necessary as uncertain gropings on the way to the control and mastery normally associated with maturity and mature works of art. But of course, *at the time*, there is no such uncertainty; far from it. The works of youth are often not only forthright but plain arrogant—such is youth!

Improvisation and Choice

But it would, of course, be somewhat bizarre to suggest that earlier works are necessarily more improvisatory than later ones. The real issue is not the work, but the function of the work within the wider existential structure: the "life" of the artist. Looked at in this way, improvisation characterizes not the interior of the form itself but, instead, the mechanism by which one form is *chosen* over another within a contingent context, without absolute criteria, where all outcomes are intrinsically uncertain. It is not the works of youth that are more likely to be improvised so much as the formal choices that are made before the work even begins.

An interesting corollary of the above, where improvisation takes place *between* rather than *within* works, is that such improvisation does not have to be seen as an intentional aesthetic act so much as a response to a particular existential predicament. At the time the choice *feels* right—hence the self-certainty that prevails, and must prevail if a performance is to come into being. In this regard it might be further claimed that essentially there is no such thing as an uncertain piece, work, or performance. Notwithstanding the fact that improvisers habitually valorize unpredictability and uncertainty, nothing could be more certain: there *will* be an improvisation, and on this occasion it's going to be like *this*.

But what does it mean to improvise *between* rather than within works? And in what ways can the choice of one form rather than another be considered improvisatory? To help answer these questions we return now to Hegel's account of two different (but related) beginnings: the beginning of sense experience, as described in *The Phenomenology* and the beginning of art as accounted for in his *Aesthetics*.

Sense, Contingency, and Severity

Summarized briefly: in the first section of the *Phenomenology* Hegel sets about demonstrating dialectically that the apparent certainty offered by the senses represents, in fact, the most uncertain of experiences on account of the essential abstractness and insubstantiality of immediacy confronted as this "this" and this "now." Obscured by the particularity of what is here and now, the universality of "this-ness" and "now-ness," the recognition of which constitutes a first step on the road to absolute truth, remains beyond the grasp of those entrapped within the certitude of sense-certainty. In this regard then, Hegel recognizes that at the level of sensibility, we witness, paradoxically, the greatest degree of certainty *and* simultaneously the greatest degree of contingency.

This contradiction does, in truth, offer considerable insight into human behavior, where it is evident that in situations characterized by uncertainty, obscurity, and incomprehensibility, the best course of action is often the absolute commitment to one singular task or method. As Descartes famously declares, when lost in the woods, don't run hither and thither; commit yourself to a straight line.[11] So, while Hegel is keen to expose the limitations of sense certainty, it would be quite wrong (and philosophically naïve) to interpret this as a rejection of such an admittedly primitive but nonetheless *essential* dimension of human experience. Indeed, as is well known, the real thrust of Hegel's dialectic is as preservative as it is destructive, and what he seeks to preserve in his phenomenological account of human experience in its infancy is precisely the profound embeddedness in and immediate engagement with a sensuous world that is intuitively *felt* as an all-encompassing presence: here and now as this and that.

Notwithstanding this, it is clear that, for Hegel, sense-certainty, in the brute form of pure, intuitive reception of sense data, is utterly devoid of any consciousness of the universality of truth that transcends immediate experience of the given world. It is for this reason that a broader perspective will be now sought, one that encompasses Hegel's parallel account in the *Aesthetics* of mankind's "infancy" within the domain of art. It is here that the desired model of improvisation begins to emerge.

Of relevance is his account of what he calls symbolic art, as distinct from the classical and the romantic. For him, each form of art is characterized by a different relation of meaning and configuration. With symbolic art, it is the obscurity, incomprehensibility, and consequent arbitrariness of its meaning that results in a "severity" of configuration that brings certainty of form in the absence of a comparable certainty at the level of content. Hegel calls this the "severe style," and offers the Egyptian pyramids as one example of where a severity of form conceals a dark ambiguity of meaning.[12]

While music, for Hegel, falls within the realms of the "pleasing" rather than the "severe," being a "romantic" rather than a "symbolic" form of art, he does nevertheless seem to acknowledge a form of musical severity where the mathematical and architectonic dimensions of music become separated from, or are freed from, its expressionistic meaningfulness and purpose.

> Music may be compared more closely to architecture which derives its forms, not from what exists, but from spirit's invention in order to mould them according to *laws* of gravity and the *rules* of symmetry. . . . Music does the same; . . . it follows the harmonic *laws* of sound which rest on quantitative proportions . . . subject in many ways to the forms of regularity and symmetry. Consequently, what dominates in music is at once the soul and its profoundest feeling and the most rigorous mathematical laws so that it unites in itself two extremes which *easily become independent from each other*. When they do, music acquires an especially architectonic character, because freed from expressing emotion.[13]

Such a description resonates well with much European avant-gardist composition, just as it offers insight into the improvised practices of some of the musicians to be discussed later in this book: not least Derek Bailey. But the point to be made at this juncture is that, unlike the phenomenology of sense-certainty, which describes the unwavering acceptance of the given, the severe aesthetic that Hegel associates with symbolic art, while similarly creating the artwork out of what is "there and available,"[14] nevertheless acknowledges, no matter how obliquely, that such a commitment to rigorous form articulates the dim awareness of an Idea that outstrips such form. Thought in Hegelian terms, the manifestation of Absolute Spirit would be accompanied not only by absolute truth but also by absolute law and the *strict* adherence to that law. The "inkling"[15] of this by the artist unable to either fully grasp or adhere to such law finds, nevertheless, an initial expression in the law-*likeness* of the severe style. Unlike strictness, severity is not obedient but committed.

Art, Improvisation, and Dialogue

So, bringing Kant and Hegel together, we have seen that their philosophical engagement with the non-adequation of thought and form, and meaning and configuration, respectively, leads them into an aesthetic domain that, far from being stricken by dis-integration and lawlessness, is, on the contrary, characterized by rigidity and severity. Quite apart from the challenge this poses to the self-image of improvisation that has for so long enjoyed its reputation as being the epitome of playfulness and flexibility, and quite apart from the realization that such an improvisatory commitment to arbitrary forms in uncertain times is profoundly rooted in the immediacy of what is "there and available" rather than the novel and the unwonted, it is also worth noting one further consequence of this line of inquiry: the intended negation (or at least qualification) of dialogics as the predominant model of intersubjectivity assumed and adopted by many improvisers and writers on improvisation. One typical example of the latter is evident in the title of Daniel Fischlin's and Ajay Heble's excellent edited collection *The Other Side of Nowhere: Jazz, Improvisation, and Communities in Dialogue*,[16] where, for example, Dana Reason puts forward the argument that, unlike the practices of European classical music performance, the dialogical community includes both the improvisers and their audiences:

> While all music engages listeners with some degree of interactivity, in improvisation such an interactivity is an essential structural component. . . . The dialogic and interactive aspect of this kind of musical encounter challenges traditional roles. . . . Thus, the interactive nature of musical improvisation encourages both musicians and audiences to rethink traditional expectations about the expression *and* reception of musical meaning.[17]

Such a view not only assumes the primacy of dialogue in improvisation but also, by drawing the audience into this proposed interactive community, promotes what might be described as an *expanded* dialogical field within which improvisations can be staged.

In the same volume drummer Eddie Prevost also acknowledges and wrestles with the dialogical role of the audience, not so much as an expansion of the interactive field but as a disruption of it. He clearly has some misgivings about this challenge to performative dialogics:

> The other important convergent analytical proposition is the degree to which dialogue shapes the performance. . . . Of course, there are other improvising procedures that may appear to counter these analytical propositions. In particular, I refer to the notion of musicians performing individual improvisations alongside others within the same performance space and time frame; . . . what I mean here is that it is evident that some musicians play without any regard

> to their fellow performers. . . . I concede that this may be a tenable
> mode, even if it counters the important thrust of dialogue in the
> music and its attendant philosophy. It offers a kind of "parallelism"
> that in effect posits the audience as the source of compositional
> decisions.[18]

Interesting and insightful though this is, what is considered tenable or un-
tenable is measured against the dominant "thrust of dialogue" and its "attendant philosophy" that remain in place regardless of whether the audience become dialogical "co-creators" or not. But perhaps it is not a question
of restricted or expanded dialogue, of togetherness or alongside-ness ("par-
allelism"), but of a singularity that operates completely outside of these
familiar parameters.

It is commonly assumed that the improviser inevitably adopts a stance
that is profoundly open both to the world and to those significant interac-
tive/dialogical others within that world, whether other performers or the
audience. If, however, improvisation is understood as one possible response,
not only to an otherness or others that is/are known or knowable, but to a
more radical alterity that resists the transparency of the knowledge economy
and the communicative community that it assumes, then questions of dialogue become themselves questionable. Just as Kant's young poet refuses to
acknowledge the advice and judgment of his friends—indeed, the *Critique
of Judgment* goes so far as to recommend that we "stop our ears" and refuse
to listen to the opinions of others when it comes to the judgment of taste—
Hegel's severe artist is similarly unconcerned with the opinions of others.

> The work of the severe style is entirely shut in upon itself without
> wishing to speak to a spectator. . . .[19]
>
> In the severe style . . . it is as if nothing at all were granted to
> the spectator; it is the content's substance which in its presentation
> severely and sharply repulses any subjective judgment.[20]

Unlike sense-certainty, which *passively* accepts the particularity of each
and every contingent sensuous experience and event as absolute, the militant rigidity of the youthful poet or the severe artist/improviser might be
better understood as a form of certitude, a subjective *feeling* of certainty
(in the absence of objective certainty) that must accompany the feeling of
pleasure that, in its turn, must accompany aesthetic judgment. What this
opens up for consideration is the idea that if improvisation is understood
as a process of trial and error, then it makes sense to at least try and offer

a more sophisticated model, one that goes beyond the banality of merely "having a go." That is to say, a model of improvisation that properly confronts both the complex structure of aesthetic judgment, rooted as it is in a particular form of solitude, as well as the enactment of the adjudicatory process in works of art: the conducting of a trial rather than simply "trying things out." Once again this brings us back to a concept of improvisation that is concerned not with the trial and error that takes place *within* an improvised work but, rather, with a process that puts on trial and, perhaps, tests to destruction the work as a whole. And it is the fact that any possible work within any contingent situation could be other than it is that requires an originary felt certitude that leads the artist *on this occasion* to make *this* decision and then stick with it.

In a sense what is being mooted here is an approach to improvisation that breaks with a perspective that is fascinated with uncertainty as played out from moment to moment within the unfolding of a performance. Instead, we are proposing what might be described as a long-distance or slowed-down model that sees completed and often tightly organized works as part of a much larger improvisatory field that has a much greater scope and much longer duration than any individual piece. As such, *a whole life* might be seen as an improvisation, where individual works or groups of works are but components in the much greater aesthetic and existential enterprise of integrating thought and form, or meaning and configuration.

As we have equated the severity of this task with a solitude that is intended to resist the allure of dialogical improvisation, a moment should be spent considering such solitude and its relationship to the nature of aesthetic judgment and, in turn, the role played by judgment within the trial of the work.

Singularity, Solitude, and Otherness

Regarding aesthetic judgment, in the *Critique of Judgment* Kant elucidates the following three "maxims of common human understanding" as fundamental propositions.

- To think for oneself
- To think from the standpoint of everyone else
- Always to think consistently[21]

Broadening these maxims to thinking and *doing* to accommodate the thought and practice of the improviser, when deciding what to do, regarded here as an essential improvisatory gesture, the artist is advised by Kant to ignore the judgments of others and enter into the solitude of the autonomous work: "think for oneself." But the question immediately arises: How can one protect the autonomy of one's own judgment and subsequent work when the next maxim explicitly demands the necessary acknowledgement of the other? Indeed, for Kant, it is precisely this necessary shift into otherness that constitutes judgment proper. While this would seem to contradict his description of the youthful poet, and the ears-tight-shut approach to aesthetic judgment, the situation is more complex. The key is to understand that when speaking of the other, Kant is speaking as a philosopher and not as a social scientist; thus, when describing judgment as a form of "common sense," this commonality is not assumed as a sociological fact. This is how he makes the same point:

> By the name *sensus communis* is to be understood the idea of a *public* sense, i.e., a critical faculty which in its reflective act takes account (*a priori*) of the mode of representation of everyone else, in order, *as it were*, to weigh its judgment with the collective reason of mankind, and thereby avoid the illusion arising from subjective and personal conditions which could readily be taken for objective, an illusion that would exert a prejudicial influence upon its judgment. This is accomplished by weighing the judgment, *not so much with actual*, as rather with the *merely possible*, judgments of others.[22]

When discussing Hannah Arendt's *Lectures on Kant's Political Philosophy*, Ronald Beiner summarizes her position on judgment in almost identical terms:

> The more she reflected on the faculty of judgment, the more she was inclined to regard it as the prerogative of the solitary (though public-spirited) contemplator as opposed to the actor (whose activity is necessarily nonsolitary). On acts with others: one judges by oneself (even though one does so by making present in one's imagination those who are absent). In judging, as understood by Arendt, one weighs the *possible* judgments of an imagined other, not the actual judgments of real interlocutors.[23]

What both Kant and Arendt share here is a deep understanding of thinking and doing, grasping the necessary solitude of judgment while recognizing that such solitude must on the one hand take account of otherness without, on the other, being in thrall to the judgments of "real interlocutors."

We have claimed above that this manner of thinking pulls the discussion away from the dialogism that retains near hegemonic status within many of the discourses on improvisation, and this is true, but with the following proviso. The break with social interaction is not intended to oppose but to *transpose* dialogue into the interiority of the judging subject. Drawing on Kant's *Anthropology*, where he describes thinking as "talking with one-self . . . hence also inwardly listening,"[24] Arendt makes an essential distinction between solitude and loneliness:

> Thinking, existentially speaking, is a solitary but not a lonely business; solitude is the human situation in which I keep myself company. Loneliness comes about when I'm alone without being able to split up into the two-in-one, without being able to keep myself company. . . . It is this *duality* of myself with myself that makes thinking a true activity, in which I am both the one who asks and the one who answers.[25]

Interesting here is a conception of thinking and judging that is improvisatory to the extent that it is structured around and driven by a process of trial and error while, at the same time, containing this dialogue within the interiority of the subject. The result, as Arendt goes on to argue in good Kantian fashion, is not the discovery of truth (objective certainty) but self-consistency (subjective certitude). As she writes of such "Socratic thinking":

> The criterion of the mental dialogue is no longer truth . . . The only criterion of Socratic thinking is agreement, to be consistent with oneself.[26]

This brings us to Kant's third "maxim": the attainment of consistency, in the absence of objective certainty, contributes to our understanding of the severity and inflexibility not only of the developing artist, keen to protect his or her artistic integrity, but also of the improvisations that conceal their provisionality beneath a mask of commitment and certitude.

If we think this existentially, then we can begin to see a model of improvisation emerging that is characterized by *disengagement* rather than the engagement (political, ethical, spiritual) one often associates with this world. Having said that, though, looked at from a different perspective, such withdrawal from the collective space and all of its worldly concerns must be counterposed to the intensification that, as Kant himself recognized, accompanies the pluralization of the self's interiority as outlined above.[27] While he does not make altogether clear what he means by works "involving intensity," we might conjecture that, in the attempt to "enlarge" one's mind by thinking from the position of the other, the danger is not only one of heteronomy but also of *dilution*. This is avoided by ensuring that the notion of "common sense" at the heart of Kant's second maxim is not understood as a sociological concept but as a *philosophical idea*.

Thought thus, the Kantian notion of "common sense" adds something to Hegel's account of "sense-certainty" not only by situating the certitude of the sensing subject in the commonality of phenomenological experience, but also thereby raising the issue of communication and the communicability of aesthetic feeling. As Jay Bernstein has suggested, Kant's *Critique of Judgment* articulates what he describes as a "memorial aesthetics" that, through the memory of a lost *sensus communis*, "mourns" the demise of this communicative community in a manner that resonates well with the fragmentation and yearning that typifies post-romantic and modernist art forms.[28] What Bernstein describes as "mourning" might equally be referred to, in a more affirmative vein, as *intensity*. Where mourning dwells on and works through the experience of *loss*; intensity, while sharing the same predicament of a commonality without community, is more productive in that it is committed to *finding* a universal means of communicating singularity. In a nutshell: the limits of actual social interaction thought ex-tensively necessitate the philosophical idea of an in-tensive communion between self and other (Arendt's "two-in-one") that, through the solitary duality of aesthetic judgment, puts each and every attempt at communication on trial. And, to repeat, such a trial is not concerned with truth (how many trials are?) but with consistency and the degree to which such efforts (works, narratives, performances) make sense: literally *make* sense.

Like any other aesthetic forms, improvisations need to make sense and, indeed, *make* sense—at least at the time. It is not necessary that they make sense to anyone else, except for the improviser of course, and even the improviser might not see any sense in his or her improvisations in "aftertime," but *at the time*, here and now, they must. The greater the uncertainty, and the more that sense (and sense-certainty) needs to be *made*, the greater the intensity and the greater the consistency: that is the peculiarity of aesthetic judgment and the peculiarity of improvisation.

So, while the above thoughts might help explain the commitment of certain aesthetic choices at the formal level, and also begin to open up a discussion of improvisation at the level of performative practice (understood as trial), they might also feed into the critical analysis of improvisation at the level of content at the moment of its production: the "in-the-moment" moment. In this regard an actual improvisation, taking place now in real time, could be considered not only as a microcosmic repetition of what might be called the grand narrative of an individual life, but also an accelerated version of the slow-motion developmental process traced above. Understood thus, the analysis of an individual unfolding improvisation would be less concerned with the experience of uncertainty, expectancy, risk-taking and surprise; the issue here is rather the extraordinary *certainty* of the improviser, the *predictability* of the improvisation, and the *absence* of risk-taking.

Fixing and Unfixing

As Heidegger affirms, erring is essential to human endeavor, and it is the *work* or *working* of erring that takes place between one trial and another.[29] It is this work that, through what might be described as the auto-education of the "two-in-one," ensures that "trying something out" becomes less and less hit and miss as it increasingly takes on the full adjudicatory force of the aesthetic proper and becomes instead a task that gains in consistency and intensity. This process transforms, over time, if not the nature then certainly the feeling of certitude necessary for an improvisation to take place. So if, on the macro level, the choice between one genre or another, one structure or another, one idiom or another contains an improvisational dimension that is obscured by the fixity of the outcome and the apparent fixation of the artist, deaf to criticism or contradiction, then would it be correct to suggest that the same process of fixation is operative at the micro level, between notes, phrases, gestures, marks and so on? On the face of it this would appear to go against the grain of much writing on improvisation, which tends to place the emphasis on the unfixing of fixed structures; indeed, it uses fixity as a necessary foil for the enactment of unfixing, often conceived as liberation. Scott Thomson, referencing John Corbett's notion of "paradoxy," gives a flavor:

> Under these conditions, the group would be invested in an ongoing avoidance of formal or methodological fixity (including fixity at the level of authority-mobility).[30]

But if things were really as unfixed, fluid, and nomadic as Thomson assumes, why is it that so much improvisation is (as Pierre Boulez, reminds us) so *predictable*?[31] Surely the pleasure associated with improvisation has as much to do with the shared certainty that quite strictly prescribed things are likely to happen as it does with the much-heralded uncertainty that so effectively fuels the risk-taking agenda and the edgy virtuosity that accompanies it. If this is accepted, then Boulez's critique does in reality identify an *essential quality* of improvisation, one that is neither positive nor negative but that undoubtedly distinguishes it from all forms of "composed" work: its *certainty* (to say it again).

John Cage states that improvisation cannot operate at the level of structure.[32] But again, this need not be resisted once we recognize that it is precisely the improviser's desire for certainty that actually protects formal structures from any serious disruption or deconstruction: that's the point. To repeat: if you want uncertainty, then stay away from improvisation. In essence, uncertainty is something produced by writers, composers, designers, choreographers, and dramaturges who, having committed to an arbitrary structure, enact their freedom (to create) by bending, dismantling, or destroying whatever structure is at hand, thus ensuring a degree of manufactured uncertainty. There is a particular kind of aesthetic pleasure that can be associated with this process and the witnessing of it by an audience, but it has little or nothing to do with improvisation. In many ways Artaud comes closest to what is being suggested here when, against the "whims and rough and ready inspiration" of improvisers,[33] he insists upon a "cruel" theater that fixes the unfixed, thus imposing an arbitrary structure upon the uncertain play of the aesthetic space and a severe certainty that must be enacted in the moment on the stage during the unfolding of the work. One does not need Artaud to enforce such "cruelty"; this is the very stuff of improvisation and explains why improvisers spend so much of their time practising in preparation for an improvised performance. This is something Gavin Bryars fails to understand when he mocks those performers who practise all day at home in order to "improvise" in the evening. All of this discipline and disciplining, all of this "cruelty," is necessary to the extent that it allows the improviser to begin and sustain a work with a degree of certitude that belies the uncertainty of its origin and gestation. This, the momentary and momentous fixing of arbitrary structures by the improviser "emancipates contingency" (Niklas Luhmann) from its lowly status as ontologically suspect and aesthetically fortuitous,[34] thereby placing it at the heart of the work's unfolding.

Beginning Again

Turning to the moment of the work's unfolding, seen as a microcosmic and accelerated repetition of what might be called the decisive betweenness where the "two-in-one" self goes to work, we might start with the beginning. Following Luhmann, the beginning is the transition from the unmarked to the marked space.[35] We will describe this as the shift from uncertainty to certitude. The improvisation could begin in any number of ways but (to borrow the phenomenological vocabulary of Husserl) the recollection of previous beginnings will inevitably inform the expectations of how this work will begin, at which point retention and protention will bring a form of temporal certitude to its unfolding. An important part of the improviser's endless rehearsal is the trying-out of beginnings, the performative equivalent perhaps of what Heidegger calls the endless task of "inceptual thinking."[36] Obviously, the beginning of an improvisation can be either certain or uncertain, but in either case the degree of certitude will need to be the same if the work is to begin. The more an improviser practises, the more he or she will *feel* secure within the inceptual moment where everything starts again. What gives this initiatory moment intensity is not its uncertainty but the irreducible duality of certainty and certitude: the certainty that the beginning could be other than it is, coupled with the certitude that here and now it *will* begin like this. Something has to happen, something will happen, neither life nor art can await the arrival of certainty, and it is the improviser who, if nothing else, knows how to get things moving.

To begin with, the beginning must keep beginning if the improvisation is not to deteriorate into the certainty of the "work," with all of the manufactured uncertainty this allows. Incidentally, keeping the beginning beginning is not just an empty play on words but, one might argue, the central task of the improviser. The beginning is not the start of the work but the *choice* of a way into that which has *certainly* already started. As Hegel says, everything is "already there and available," but it is the giving and re-giving of what is already there that constitute the true beginning of the work. As said, improvisation dramatizes this moment, but does so in a manner that carries the sense of this beginning over into the continuation of the work beyond the moment of its inception.

But this is where the current discussion takes a counterintuitive turn, arguing that this sense of a beginning is equivalent to Hegel's sense-certainty, which, in truth, is only a felt certitude contradicted by the contingency of its partial and philosophically inadequate perspective. The "inkling" of this infinite otherness and the dim awareness that one's feeling of certitude is in reality limited to the here and now does not, as might be assumed, undermine the conviction of the work or taint it with a provisionality that renders it "improvisatory" in the bad sense: cobbled together, makeshift, off the cuff. On the contrary, it is this aesthetic sense that, as Kant recognizes, initiates "reflection" and enables judgments of taste to be made, not only between one work and another but between one *moment* of a work and another, the productive moment largely ignored by Kant himself. And this is where we get down to the sense-certitude of the improviser.

In the Moment

Improvisers speak of being "in the moment" as the moment of all moments when the improvisation comes into its own as the expression of . . . what exactly? Unfortunately, the discourses surrounding improvisation, so often written by improvisers themselves, are not particularly helpful in trying to respond to this question; most of them remain too bound up within a humanistic language of emotion, expression, communication, and dialogue to fully engage with the "severity" being considered here. If we could put all of this to one side, it might be possible to reevaluate the value of improvisation not as the wondrous enactment of human freedom but, more soberly, as the performative site where the rigors of aesthetic judgment, locked up in the intensive dialogue of the "two-in-one," transform the confrontation with contingency into art. Thought thus, the "in-the-moment" moment is no longer conceived as an ecstatic oneness where self meets self, meets other, meets all, within the warm glow of utopic togetherness, but as the region where the necessary rigidity of judgment arrives at a method of proceeding that places all of the emphasis on discipline, control, and a sureness of touch that, while having the appearance of spontaneity, is the product of endless drill and rote. Deaf to the aesthetic pleasures of others, the "severe" improviser does, nevertheless, provide pleasure to those who witness the unfolding of a work, where it is not passion but *precision* that is offered, not as something to be shared but as the radically singular and solitary exemplification of aesthetic judgment *in action* here and now.

As with the between-ness that separates one work from another, offering an improvisational terrain that is obscured or erased by the work itself, so still we see and hear that same space, now reduced to a speck and to be scrutinized at the level of instantaneity, as the barely perceptible difference between severity and strictness—the improvised and the non-improvised— here sensed at the point of delivery. Among all improvisers and writers on improvisation, Susan Leigh Foster has come closest to capturing this moment, which so effectively reintroduces contingency into the "in-the-moment" moment:

> The performance of any action, regardless of how predetermined it is in the minds of those who perform it and those who witness it, contains an element of improvisation. The moment of wavering while contemplating how, exactly, to execute an action already deeply known, belies the presence of improvised action.[37]

In this moment of hesitation, in this infinitesimal delay between conception and inception (the start and the beginning), contingency remains, a fact and predicament that ensures the certitude of the improviser is never reducible to the certainty of the work. But, above all, it is good to know that, even at the eleventh hour (the eleventh *second*), the work unfolding before us could have been, and can still be, *different*.

3

Memoir: Lol Coxhill (In Memoriam)

"If you can't be yourself, be someone else."

Lol Coxhill[1]

On hearing of Lol Coxhill's death, I dropped everything and wrote this.

I first encountered Lol Coxhill in 1973 when, as a first-year sociology undergraduate at the London School of Economics, I went to a free lunchtime concert in the Old Theatre there. To be honest, I didn't go to see Lol (I'd never heard of him) but Mike Cooper, with whom he was playing. I knew Cooper essentially as a blues guitarist, so blues was what I expected. I was in for a surprise. The knockabout humor and deadpan irony with which the performance began was disarming—Lol was a very funny man—but the moment the music commenced everything changed. All the chat and backchat silenced, the looseness tightened, the informality formalized in an instant. And the same for us; the theatre audience moved from rumbustious music-hall mayhem to the hushed observation of what suddenly seemed more like an exact and exacting aesthetic experiment than the anarchy of a moment before. Absolute attention, absolute concentration, for everyone present, and not just present, but present within the *presence* of the present: a real "in-the-moment" moment: maybe my first. Yes, Lol was a very funny man but a *very* serious musician.

Back to the moment: a *sublime* moment, if one adheres to Kantian principles, wherein the "mathematical sublime" is described as the moment where apprehension outstrips comprehension—this was just such a moment. Before us were two musicians both playing standard instruments (soprano sax/guitar)—this much was apprehensible. But the sound they produced and the manner in which they produced this sound were utterly beyond my comprehension—a painful pleasure, as is often said of the sublime. In fact it would be better described as a painful experience that *became* increasingly pleasurable as the performance continued. I was transfixed by Lol's playing: I *heard* the sound, a disjointed, mildly cacophonous noise, chaotic and (to my ears at that moment) ugly: an insult, outrageous. But, strangely, I *saw* something different. Given his unorthodox appearance, you couldn't help but look at Lol, but for me it was his hands that were the visual lure, those chubby childlike fingers that promised clumsiness but delivered an extraordinary precision that spoke of an incomprehensible order unknown to me,[2] a musical *logic* that was as uncompromising as it was severe and lyrical too: so much for all the fun and games. Yes, for all of the surface jokes, the *precision*, not only of his playing but also of his very concept of performance was staggeringly consistent, something often obscured by the slapstick, which (incidentally) obeyed the very same logic. Of course he was famed for his open-mindedness, extraordinary eclecticism, and eccentric nomadism: almost Zelig-like in his ability to pop up in virtually any performative context. To use Deleuze and Guattari's terminology, he was a "deterritorializing" performer *par excellence*. But, to stick with Deleuze for a moment, all of this movement, the endless interruption of one direction by another, one possibility by another, would have amounted to little more than empty virtuosity and versatility, compromise after compromise, if it hadn't been for a different movement, a movement that Deleuze describes as taking place *on the spot*; this allows a somewhat different image of Lol to emerge. But first the quotation . . . one of my favorites.

> The nomad is not necessarily one who moves: some voyages take place in situ, are trips in intensity; . . . the journey is a motionless one; . . . it occurs on the spot, imperceptible, unexpected, and subterranean.[3]

This takes me straight back to that lunchtime at the London School of Economics, watching Lol, fascinated, he, almost motionless but for those subtle bends of the torso, seemingly necessary to draw out the bent notes he was always so attracted to (a throwback to the fifties?). A stationary, almost frozen intensity that bespeaks an infinite movement that is motionlessly enacted *prior to* the reenactment of this "voyage" in the finite world of genres, styles, bands, and locations, all weird and wonderful no doubt (and we do love our "eccentrics" in England), but secondary. Yes, he could play the blues, jazz, Cuban, reggae, punk, R&B, folk, with Tinguely's autom-atons, funk, minimalism, ambient . . . the list is endless, and this is what made him so endlessly cool for one generation of musicians after another; but what made him much more than cool was the inspired *logic* of his over-all strategy. This sounds overly calculated: to be clear, to have a strategy is to be in two places simultaneously, both here, now, and also where one could or would want to be: the "goal" (normally, to be credible, in the singular). What was incredible about Lol was that he always managed to avoid the temptation to have one singular goal, always entertaining instead a restless multiplicity of different possibilities; and it was precisely this, the simultane-ity in his performances of what he was doing now and what he *could* do in the future or, indeed, just as easily have been doing now: that distinguished him from almost all of his contemporaries. This is something rarely if ever acknowledged by those who commentate on improvisation: improvisation takes place at the macro as well as the micro level.

We are weighed down with commentaries, descriptions, critiques, cel-ebrations by this and that critic of individual performances by individuals and groups, at this or that venue, with this or that personnel; and, within this hegemonic context, it transpires that I am, sad to say, guilty of not being sufficiently engaged with or providing sufficient evidence of actual performances in my own conceptualization of improvisation—an undeni-able truth: please forgive me. Another undeniable truth is that I am more interested in the improvisation that takes place *outside of*, and *prior to* the "performance" itself, the latter being, in my view, only one part of the im-provisation: the part that receives all of the attention to be sure. Anyway, the fact is, wonderful player though he undoubtedly was, his fame had as much to do with his eccentric career path as it had to do with his outstanding musicianship. But, the *logic* of this unconventional pathway is rarely, if ever, properly addressed or identified *as an essential moment of* the unfolding of actual improvisations.

To explain: achieving/producing/inhabiting the "in-the-moment" mo-ment so sought after by improvisers and their critics appears to remain the preeminent singular goal of improvisation, an admirable goal no doubt, and one that has been responsible for producing many wonderful perfor-mances. In fact I have no problem with this model of improvisation and, to be honest, love the feeling of being "in the moment" as much as the next improviser. The problem is not the model but its *dominance*, the fact that *this* model has become *the* model. Achieving such paradigmatic status has not only rendered any serious critical resistance inconceivable (that's what paradigms do), but it has brought in its wake a whole raft of performative prescriptions and proscriptions that have come to dominate the vocabulary, the discourse and, as a consequence, the self-conception of improvisation and improvisers. Thus it is virtually impossible to resist the lure and allure of the emergent improvisatory culture of care and enabling, where listening and dialogue become categorical imperatives, where absolute commitment and authenticity are both political and ethical prerequisites, and where the reduction of otherness to the same in the ecstatic singularity of the shared moment remains the desire. For me, Lol was the perfect antidote to this participatory paradigm, precisely on account of his apparent participation in just about everything: did he ever say no? But is saying yes to just about everything quite the same as participating? That is the question. To participate, to assume the identity of participant, is to willingly subsume oneself (as part) within a whole or a totality. The affirmative spirit of the true participant is, if not a form of servitude, then the sublation of freedom and servitude in the name of universality and a commitment to the universal. As such, it is, in truth, a negative spirit, negating all that would obstruct participation in the One, a singular yes but, with that one exception: a universal *no*. Lol, being a true affirmer rather than a true participant, reversed this. Saying yes provided him with the endless possibility of participation but, to repeat, it was the infinite openness of possibility rather than the finite closure of participation that attracted him. In this way Lol managed to participate in many things, many more than anyone else I know, yet without becoming "a part" of that thing, alongside rather than inside,[4] disengaged as well as engaged, indeed, often engaged precisely with disengagement.

Ben Watson, in his book on Derek Bailey, describes Lol as a "comedian," which he was in part; but he was also an ironist, thus occupying both the worlds of comedy and tragedy. Irony is both a predicament and (having recognized this) a strategy or stratagem. As predicament, it describes the contingency of all aesthetic forms and the infinite possibility such contingency emancipates. As a strategy, irony allows for the management rather than the overcoming of contingency, thus ameliorating the doubt and uncertainty associated with it in a way that allows for the creation of situations where precision, rigor, certitude, and even rigidity become possibilities in a world without truth. Absolute commitment to what is "there and available," while knowing that such certitude is inessential, epitomizes, once torn away from the dialectical knowledge of Absolute knowledge, the engaged-disengaged strategy of the ironist. And Lol was deeply ironic in this sense. An example: on one of the numerous occasions I played with him (Ross on Wye in the early eighties with the multi-instrumentalist Steve Beresford), we started with the familiar "squeaky-bonk" (as Lol described it) typical of free improvisation. All appeared to be going well until Lol decided to commit to an alternative path. Eschewing the usual responsibilities associated with and expected of the collective improviser (attentiveness, responsiveness, engagement, participation, sharing, enabling, sensitivity . . .), he locked onto a rendition of the much-loved children's song "Nellie the Elephant" with a deadpan mercilessness that, beneath the façade of Dada fun often associated with Lol, increasingly sabotaged any attempt at "real" improvisation as the moronic melody was repeated incessantly and insensitively. No questions, no answers; no call no response. In the face of such adversity, Beresford and I eventually responded in typical fashion: we began to improvise variations on a theme of Nellie the Elephant, much to everyone's amusement, thereby salvaging the situation and regaining the sometimes grudging respect of the improv aficionados in the audience. There was an interesting and (for me) important lesson to be learned from this episode.

Whether wittingly or not, Lol's cantankerous intervention effected, *at the level of practice*, a radical re-conceptualization of improvisation as a macro rather than a micro event. While he effectively sabotaged one model of improvisation at the micro level of an ongoing performance, this was not achieved by simply and crudely juxtaposing free improvisation ("squeaky-bonk") with unfree non-improvisation ("Nellie the Elephant") but by interrupting a series of choices and tacit assumptions made within the microstructure of a particular improvisation with another regime of decisions being made at the macro-level, where improvisation operates *across* or *between* idioms, styles, and genres rather than *within* them. Absent from many accounts, Howard S. Becker's remarks on "choice" provide a welcome departure from the norm:

> As someone composes a work or makes a painting, as they perform a work on stage or in the concert hall, everything they do constitutes a choice. The choice could always have been made differently and everyone who works in these trades knows what the range of possibilities was and what might have motivated the particular choice that was finally made.[5]

This is a useful reminder, but it can be pushed further. Becker is still predominantly concerned, if not with the momentary choices of the work's actual emergence, then certainly with the immediate context of this emergence and the possibilities this context offers for things to be both as they are and/or as they might otherwise be. These choices are made in a complicated social context, in an organized world of artistic activity that constrains the range of choices and provides motives for making one or another of them. Sociological analysis of that context is well equipped to explain the constitution of the range of possibilities and the conditions that surround it and thus might explain the actual choices made. But where the sociologist seeks to explain the constraints on and the conditions of improvisation, Lol perfected a method of working that *enacted* existentially as well as aesthetically what Heidegger would called the ontological difference between decision and choice, a distinction we will return to again and again. Whether an improviser or not, the sociologist is required to stand *outside* of the improvisatory process in order to identify and explicate the macro structures of choice available. Lol, on the contrary, revealed performatively the manner in which apparently "free" choices can only be made within a context that has *already been decided upon*. One might say: the more absolute the decision, the more authentic and committed are the choices subsequently made. As the word suggests, *de-cision* describes a process of cutting away, of freeing oneself from all possibilities except for the *one* that is committed to—absolutely.

Decision and limitation go together, as do commitment and constraint, and it was Lol's allergy to all of these that allowed him to deconstruct again and again the tacit assumptions underpinning the world(s) he himself inhabited. Lol could never decide, but, to be clear, the refusal of decisiveness is not indecisiveness, it is *irony*. Indeed, a great definition of irony might be "the act of choosing without deciding." Such a definition might help counter the universal view that the ironist lacks commitment and is thus a pariah in this world of belief systems, moral majorities, and political positioning. In truth, the ironist is *absolutely committed* to the deconstruction of all regimes of choice that (having been decided upon) make commitment possible. And unlike critique, which must always have its Archimedean point *outside* of the object to be attacked, deconstruction, as Derrida never tired of explaining, can only take place from *within*, as a particular form of occupation, one that is characterized by a "mental reservation" which does not preclude commitment but hollows it out from inside. In other words, choices still have to be made, but, without the prior decision to commit to this or that regime of choice, such choices are revealed as essentially contingent.

As Vincent Descombes observes of Derridian deconstruction, it is best understood as a strategy or *stratagem*, in the sense of a double game conducted by a double agent speaking the enemy's language in order not to speak this selfsame language.

> In silence, the strategist has thought what he could and should not say, namely, that the true is not *truly true* (but often *false*), that the

lawful and the arbitrary are often indistinguishable, etc. How did this *arrière-pensée* come to him? In what silent region was the insurgent able to hatch his plot against the Logos while pretending to speak the language of the master? The question of this mental reservation (in the casuistical sense) is decisive, in the first place, as Derrida observes to Levinas, the only way of pretending to speak Chinese when speaking to a Chinese citizen is to address him in *Chinese* . . . . The mental reservation alone, then, distinguishes sincere speech from speech which dissembles. But this reticence must still be able to insinuate itself between the "speaking subject" and his word; the *arrière-pensée* must still be able to secrete itself somewhere in his head outside all language, never to be uttered.[6]

While I have commented on Derrida's "problem" with improvisation elsewhere,[7] and will again later, suffice it to say that, notwithstanding his own misgivings (and confusions), the dissemblance described opens out onto a whole terrain of improvisational possibility that has remained uncharted. It is not difficult to see why: in a world where attention is almost exclusively given to the exhibition of performative prowess, whether improvisatory or not, the reticence described above, secreted in the space of indistinguishable difference, is bound to be overlooked. And again, one has to be *in* the situation to sense that something is awry; you can feel the insinuation, you can smell a rat, just as I suddenly lost my bearings to the accompaniment of "Nellie the Elephant": something is happening, but you don't know what it is. But perhaps this discussion has now overrun the Nellie moment. After all, such an episode can hardly be described in the language of dissemblance used above; the sabotage was pretty obvious. But, having said that, the fact that Lol repeatedly proved himself capable of, and had a reputation for, speaking a different language to those around him in a way that, as a consequence, drew attention to the often-ignored presence of particular vocabularies, styles, and idioms, and all of the tacit assumptions embedded therein, meant that his participation was always questionable. This is far from being a critical comment; in fact it is intended as the greatest of compliments. For me questionableness, like cleanliness, is next to Godliness— and who or what could be more questionable than God?

So, what exactly was questionable about Lol? Certainly not his ability to improvise, nor his commitment to improvising, which, given his irony, might seem an odd thing to say. But, to repeat even more emphatically, irony in its purest and most developed form is not uncommitted; it is *absolutely committed* at any one moment to the choices necessary to produce a work. Indeed, if anything, to make choices *without* the prior decisiveness necessary to ground the process of choosing demands the greatest commitment of all, far in excess of that required of the non-ironist. Why? Because the non-ironic majority—"normal" improvisers (to recycle Thomas Kuhn's use of "normal" to describe those who work within the parameters of the dominant paradigm)[8]—demonstrate a far greater commitment to a prior and often unthought decision than they do to the choices made possible, in the moment, by this buried decisiveness: hence the semi-automatic nature of most improvisation. Without such an *a priori*, Lol's improvisation always functioned on two levels, usually simultaneously. As I have already suggested, his resistance to decisiveness created a space for him to improvise at the macro level, across and between rich and varied terrains. At this level it was not a question of choosing which moves to make in an ongoing performative game but of choosing which game to play: a choosing of choices if you like. And then he played the game, knowing that he could have been playing another, not only in the future but now: a realization that radically changes the nature of the present moment as it emerges within an improvisation. In this way the necessary un-thoughtfulness of decision is transposed into a process of hyper-choice where everything must be thought, everything must be chosen, and everything must be committed to precisely because everything could be, and would be, different without this, the vigilance necessary for irony and the ironist to secrete themselves within the body of the host.

I spoke earlier of Lol's hands and the precision of his playing; I would like to return to that again here. Deaf to the aesthetic pleasures of others, the "severe" improviser does, nevertheless, provide pleasure to those who witness the unfolding of a work, where it is not passion but *precision* that is offered, not as something to be shared but as the radically singular and solitary exemplification of aesthetic judgment *in action* here and now.

Precision here refers to three closely related but different things:

1. Precision at the *micro* level of the performative moment, directly related to a mastery (whether realized or not) of the improvisatory medium: instrument, body, materials, tools, etc. A product of the endless drill and rote (the improviser's day job) of practise and rehearsal, which are not the same thing, as will be proposed later.

2. Precision at the *local* level of the emerging "work," directly related to the production and management of aesthetic structures for the duration of their often fleeting existence. Here the roles of listening, responding, initiating, and supporting are to the fore, albeit underpinned by the technical ability (precision 1) often necessary for the physical realization of such

aesthetic judgments. Put another way, precision 2 is related to the performance rather than the performer, the artwork rather than the artist. It is the product of aesthetic taste rather than habit, as long as one remembers that taste too develops through practise. But, unlike precision 1, it cannot be taught.

3. Precision at the *macro* or *global* level, directly related to the process of situating an emergent improvisation within a potentially infinite number of "incompossible" works, genres, idioms, or aesthetic "worlds."

Each of the above variants of precision have a different relation to decision. Indeed, to be able to claim that the degree of precision displayed by an improviser is a direct function of the *a priori* decisiveness necessary for precise acts of choice to be made would be neat but not altogether convincing. While it might be the case that a dilution of decisiveness results in a higher degree of uncertainty at the point of choice, where the certitude associated with performative precision is paramount, it is not simply a question of quantitatively identifying a diminution of precision at the level of technique. While this might very well be the case, such a quantitative perspective obscures the fact that *at the level of the work* a qualitatively different form of precision becomes identifiable, one liberated from the market-led demand for virtuosity, technical mastery, and performative brilliance. In such situations, where, to fall back on a weary cliché, the whole is more than the sum of its parts—more than the display of private prowess—a qualitatively different kind of precision is required, one that is primarily concerned with a responsibility for the work and a commitment to its continuance for as long as this is performatively feasible or sustainable. Identified here is a distinction that has much to contribute to our earlier discussion of starting and beginning. The vast majority of improvisations are pre-scribed, the apparent starting point is really just a moment in an ongoing process that could be traced back to a prior decision to start again and again from within the terrain marked out in advance by such a decision: decision, pre-scription and precision can all be thought together in this concatenation. But while this allows an improvisation to start, nothing can begin until at least one of the following takes place.

1. A degree of indecisiveness is detected, at least to the extent that a consciousness of decision and its ontological difference from choice is apparent [precision 1].

2. A shift from pre-scription to de-scription is evident, where, to mobilize both meanings of the word, the work begins to be

seen and can be described as a work or, better, the *working* of
a work, to the extent that it is unwritten or, at the very least,
rewritten/reinscribed [precision 2].

3. There develops an awareness of the contingency of this impro-
    visation here and now and an emerging sense or sensation of
    an infinite and excluded alterity that is not absolutely Other
    in the Levinasian sense, but all-too-familiar, only "incompos-
    sible" [precision 3].

While many improvisers have proved themselves capable of making
things "happen," of starting and then beginning with the necessary precision described above in the first two senses, the claim here is that Lol was almost unique in his perfection of a mode of participation that *very precisely*
effected a performative "*espacement*" (to use Derrida's terminology) not
within but *between* "incompossible" worlds [precision 3].

4 Case Study: The Recedents (Lol Coxhill, Roger Turner, and Mike Cooper)

An initial joke: three balding men name a band the Recedents, a celebration of their collectively diminishing hairlines, long before such things were cool. Lol was always good at daft names—he named my band Stinky Winkles—a silliness that, once again, signals a deep-seated aversion both to the seriousness of decision making and the dubious totalities that such "decisiveness" underpins. Once again, this is close to the stratagems of deconstruction: laughter, comedy, or irony require, to be effective, a complete mastery of that which they mock.

> To laugh at philosophy . . . calls for an entire "discipline," an entire "method of meditation" that acknowledges the philosopher's byways, understands his techniques, makes use of his ruses, manipulates his cards, lets him deploy his strategy, appropriates his texts. Then, thanks to this work which has prepared it, but quickly, furtively and unforeseeably breaking with it, as betrayal or as detachment, drily, laughter bursts out . . . A certain burst of laughter exceeds it [philosophy] and destroys its sense, . . . and this can be done only through close scrutiny and full knowledge of what one is laughing at.[1]

So, The Recedents originated in laughter, an admirably questionable origin that, as with all origins, continued to erupt and interrupt its evolution until Lol's death.

Dunois Paris, 1985[2]

> (Above the cacophony being produced by Cooper and Turner, Lol croons an old standard): *"My romance doesn't have to have a moon in the sky"*
>
> (Interrupted by Lol in irritated old woman's voice, shrieking): "That's better now, I hope he's coughed to death."
>
> (Lol, Crooning): *"My romance doesn't need a castle . . ."*
>
> (Lol/Woman Shrieking): *"I think there's something wrong with this record, he's not singing the words properly. I think he's doing it for money, I don't think it sounds sincere. There's been my poor boy up there coughing to death, and I've been worrying about this record. I'll just go and see if he's OK, the poor boy. I feel a bit sorry about it now. I'll just go and see if he's alright. Are you alright?"*
>
> (Lol/Boy, coughing, spluttering and gasping): *"Aaaaarghh!, I need a glass of . . . "* Oh God!
>
> (Lol/Woman shrieking): *"I was feeling sorry for you, but now you're just as bad as you were in the first place, I'm going to try and play my record again."*
>
> (Cacophony crescendos)
>
> (Lol continues crooning): *"My romance doesn't have to have a moon in the sky."*
>
> (Lol/Woman, calmer): *"That's better; I don't know what was wrong with it before."*
>
> (Lol crooning): *"My romance doesn't need a blue lagoon standing by."*
>
> (Lol/Woman): *"I love this record."*

This is funny (although you have to see it), and it works, not because it is comedic but because it is ironic. It is ironic because it perfectly stages the absurd dissonance of "incompossible" worlds, allowing Lol to do what he did best: interrupt one performative regime with another, thus deconstructing both. This is something he did throughout his career with his famous rendering of the BBC radio play "Murder in the Air," albeit with mixed results: it always worked best when his fellow musicians resisted the temptation to add appropriate sound effects to compliment the monologue. As he says in a duet with Roger Turner as he begins to sing another old standard, "I can't do it with backing."[3] The attempt to engage with Lol's interruptions often failed because such responses unwittingly reduced such otherness to the same, thereby transforming the irony into comedy, which is nowhere near as funny or as improvisationally sophisticated. The "My Romance" piece works precisely because it is sophisticated, and it is sophisticated because it so expertly mobilizes all three of the, let us call them, modalities of precision outlined above.

Café Oto, London, 2010[4]

The Recedents arrived, whether consciously or not, at a method of performance that, in a sense, created or produced a situation within which Lol was able to insert himself and the "incompossible" worlds he occupied. This is how it seemed to work: the performance starts, and immediately there is quite a lot going on, something resembling an aural building site. A pulse is quickly established, but not one that swings or flows; rather, the constant but irregular ricochet of construction and the hubbub of physical labor: the "noise of the world," "the clamor of being."[5] Turner does not play the drums in the conventional sense, but there is play, and the "kit" remains the predominant rhythmic source, albeit both radicalized and problematized. This, the problematization of pulse, is both a sonic and a visual experience, one that is heard as a series of discontinuous but precise snaps, crackles, pops, bangs, and crashes, shattering clatters, scudding thuds, and skimming, ringing rims—anarchic-machinic. One that is seen (and, if possible, improvised music should be seen), indeed, *intended* to be seen as a continuous series of decisions, the live enactment of aesthetic judgment. To watch Turner "at play" does have something in common with the earnestness of a child's logic of discovery; the puzzlement and curiosity coupled with a determination to put everything to use in some way or another, no matter how bizarre or surprising, although, of course, being a logic, the result does usually make sense. Surrounded by the ever-shifting accoutrements of his practice, the plethora of objects/things as well as a drum kit in one form or another, he introduces an extraordinary degree of uncertainty into a continuous and often urgent process of decision making that, as is obvious given the earlier discussion, is not really decisive at all and thus not really uncertain (and that's not a criticism). Visually, we observe him inspect or consider everything; every object, every move is subject to the same inquiry: what if I do this? What if I put this here, or there, or back on the floor? What happens when this hits that, when you drop this on this, when you spin something that shouldn't be spun, when you hit something that shouldn't be hit with something not designed for hitting? All of this uncertainty ensures that, from a percussive point of view, the beginning of the work never vanishes into the work's continuity or end but appears to keep beginning, just as radical doubt always remains at its origin. We see, as a visual performance, the contingency of every move, the fact that everything at every moment could be different, we see the trial and error, actions being considered and then withdrawn and then considered again. And yet all of this uncertainty, so fascinating to watch, is belied by what we hear. Turner could hardly be described as reticent; there is no tentativeness in evidence, in spite of his peculiarly investigative improvisatory manner. On the contrary, once he makes a choice, and of necessity he makes them very quickly, the execution displays a certitude and precision that would seem to contradict the uncertainty of its source, but not really if one accepts the view that, above all else, improvisation is the pursuit of certitude in the absence of certainty. Roger Turner is a master of the "severe style," but this severity is not so much sustained as a continuous task throughout the work, but reduced to a multitude of momentary choices, something that resembles Maurice Blanchot's somewhat idiosyncratic concept of "research" where, instead of being intent on always rushing to the end point, the outcome, the "work," what he describes as the "centre," is content to respond to what is there and available, now.

> The centre allows finding and turning, but the centre is not to be found. Research would be, perhaps, that rash seeking determined always to reach the centre instead of being content to act in response to its point of reference.[6]

Every moment becomes a point of reference then, an instant of orientation and reorientation, of attention and attending, where, with attention, it is possible to experience the infinitesimal hesitation that separates certitude from certainty. This recalls Susan Leigh Foster's words again—to repeat, but differently:

> The moment of wavering while contemplating how, *exactly*, to execute an action already deeply known, belies the presence of improvised action.[7]

The keyword here is *exactly*. The very fact that "wavering" accompanies that which is "already deeply known" reminds us that what is known, no matter how deeply, is never certain, and that, in the face of such infinite uncertainty, exactitude, precision, and rigor become the most powerful modes of expressing the certitude necessary for the improvised act to be executed. But, to return to The Recedents, what is the improvised act, and what type of precision or exactitude is at issue?

As already suggested, the majority of performances by The Recedents saw Mike Cooper and Roger Turner busying themselves from the outset with the creation of an improvised structure within which to "house" and support Lol Coxhill's contribution to proceedings. To do this effectively required them both to strive for a degree of precision that functioned at the local level of the emerging work (precision 2) rather than at the micro level of individual technique and the articulation/expression of singularity (precision 1). Where the latter is capable, on a good day, of being delivered with an immediacy that can flow directly from the years of practise, the hesitant certitude of Turner's approach would suggest a different agenda, with a rather different intentionality.

Turning to Mike Cooper, it would be useful to consider the following assertion: where Turner operates with and within a carefully forged *production* aesthetic, Cooper's mode of improvisation is much more focused on the process of *reception*. What is peculiar about this is that Western aesthetics has long been dominated by reception aesthetics and the thought of the nonpractitioner, nonparticipant and, in the case of some of the most important works, the thought of those notably and totally unengaged with art practice. So it is unusual to witness what might be described as the *enactment* of reception from within the improvised becoming of a performance. In retrospect, it was already a bit odd to discuss Turner's improvising in terms of aesthetic judgment, given that, to repeat, such judgments are usually considered to be the preserve of the receivers of the work—the audience, the connoisseur, the art-lover, the critic, the aesthetician. But in a sense, as a producer, Turner's judgments or choices are always just in advance of the work produced, if only by a split second. Hence there is always a pronounced speculative dimension to his playing. With Cooper one witnesses the art of judgment just on the other side of that moment, which of course is why The Recedents are/were such a wonderful trio. Actually, Cooper's improvisation is every bit as speculative as Turner's, but working, as he would appear to, with a concept and process of delay, the outcomes of such speculation are always judged at the moment of reception rather than production. Within the context of The Recedents, it is this performative conjuncture of production and reception which goes some way in explaining how, over so many years, Cooper and Turner have been able to construct—in the moment—a series of sonic situations perfectly designed and tailored not only to realize their own improvisational ambitions, but also to frame the singular contribution of Lol Coxhill.

Looking again at the same footage—Café Oto, London, 2010—but now from the perspective of Cooper rather than Turner, a different improvisational method can be identified, one beautifully captured in one movement of the hand. The performance starts with Cooper creating a whistling sound by blowing into his National guitar, but the performance *begins* when his left arm stretches out with a searching gesture, hovering uncertainly above the electronic modules laid out below. As if blind, he eventually touches upon one of the assorted modules and then begins a delicate process of switching and tweaking that puts in train the electronic effects, which now set about processing the originary whistling. In the excellent video of this performance made by video maker Helen Petts, there is a beautiful hand section where, as a backdrop to Cooper's flitting fingers, Turner's clutching grasp grinds what appears to be a heat sink into the surface of his floor-standing tom with curious insistence that, as always, has the immediacy and instantaneous structural clarity that Cooper's processed delay singularly lacks. This difference is written all over their bodies: Turner in the background, all over the place, restless, unsettled, hitting everything and anything with the demonic virtuosity of a percussion machine on the blink; Cooper in the foreground, arm initially Moses-like, elongated and languid and then agile, but with a grace and precision—a graceful precision—that guides the hand to its appointed place and its appointed tasks. Slowly leaning forward, two fingers working in conjunction to produce the desired sonic transformation; desired but, as desire, something to be awaited, And so he waits, leaning back, listening, considering, judging, all as a form of auto-reception. Once again, instead of allowing himself to settle into the semi-inevitable unfurling of a predictably unpredictable "work," Cooper's mode of reception installs the adventure of waiting into the heart of the improvisation not, as with Turner, through the accelerated decisionism of the instant but as an infinite deferral that absolutizes the beginning in a different way: he never looks satisfied; intrigued, engaged, curious perhaps, but never satisfied. Satisfaction is an end, and improvisers and their improvisations are allergic to ends. The best improvisations don't end, they just stop beginning. Frank Kermode and his over-hyped "sense of an ending"[8] is as far away from improvisation as is imaginable.

So to Lol Coxhill: Cooper and Turner are both extraordinary improvisers: astute, innovative-ish (that's not so important), but above all focused. Focus can take many forms and be directed in very different ways, but, for The Recedents at least, the primary focus has always been concentrated on the mutual creation of a structure, situation, context that supplies a platform for Lol to exercise his own singular, no, plural (and that is the point) manner of improvisatory engagement. The creation of a space for the plu-

CHAPTER FOUR   **44**

ral has nothing whatsoever to do with the wishy-washy pluralism that is
so prevalent in postmodern liberal democracies, one that hides its bland
superficiality behind the self-righteous pseudo-gravitas of right-on contemporary moral relativism. There was nothing relativistic about what might
be called (borrowing Andrew Benjamin's apt book title) the "plural event"
of Lol's improvising. This suggests another great definition of irony—non-
relativistic plurality—that once again places Lol firmly within the quite unfairly besmirched ironic tradition. In fact singularity and plurality, far from
being opposites, are profoundly intertwined, in that each is responsible for
the production of the other. Lol's Recedents' work reveals this intertwinement in an exemplary fashion, as follows.

We have already touched upon the comedic or ironic dimension of Lol's
manner of improvising, and this is a good place to start a consideration of
singularity and plurality. His reputation as an eccentric is testimony to the
fact that he was singular in this regard, but singular in what sense? Certainly this was a much-loved idiosyncrasy that won him many fans, but there
is more to this than just a few laughs, as any review of his performances
will quickly confirm. Most noteworthy perhaps is the degree to which his
comedy was almost completely resistant to the type of response one would
expect from other improvisers during an improvisation, the "Nellie the
Elephant" episode being one case in point: Beresford and I were painfully
unfunny. Another example, mentioned in passing earlier, concerns Roger
Turner, in duo with Lol as opposed to a Recedents performance.[9] The difference is telling. The trio worked best when Turner and Cooper resisted the
temptation to respond directly to Lol's comedic/ironic contribution; in this
performance, however, Turner volunteers some humorous asides himself,
which immediately transforms the interruptive impact of Lol's comedy into
a moment of the improvisation's interiority, something shareable and to be
shared by all present. Lol's comedy was not shareable in this way; it was not
a collective but, to repeat, a singular manner that had efficacy precisely because it originated in an exteriority that was irreducible, not only to this or
that context, but to any communicative community, no matter how healthy
its sense of humor. In this regard Lol was not only singular but also a profoundly solitary improviser, in spite of the rich and varied company he kept,
including, of course, the famous Company gigs arranged by Derek Bailey
and discussed in later in this book. And, as we've seen with Arendt, solitude
can be distinguished from loneliness precisely on account of its plurality.
Here is that same quotation yet again—repetition and difference.

> Thinking, existentially speaking, is a solitary but not a lonely busi-
> ness; solitude is the human situation in which I keep myself com-

> pany. Loneliness comes about when I'm alone without being able
> to split up into the two-in-one, without being able to keep myself
> company. . . . It is this duality of myself with myself that makes
> thinking a true activity.[10]

As long as one allows that this duality is a mobile rather than a static one,
that there are a plurality of other myselves with whom I keep myself company at any one time, then we have something that approximates Lol's sin-
gular/solitary stance. So, to reiterate, the singularity of Lol was precisely
a function of his fugitive plurality. While he was always there, he was also
always elsewhere, and elsewhere again. His ability to occupy plural sites
was precisely what gave him his characteristic, almost defining power of
interruption; there was always an exteriority that breached every continuity, a separation that haunted every new gesture of proximity. The above-
mentioned "Lol Coxhill Sings" duet with Roger Turner is a perfect case in
point. After the unhappy attempt at comedic interaction, Turner returns,
wisely, to the more familiar role of constructing an incredibly fluid and yet
robust percussive terrain for Lol to inhabit. Once up and running this provides Lol with the opportunity to engage in what might best be described
as a performative auto-interruption that both crudely and yet purely enacts
the "two in one." So he alternates between singing and playing in such a
clumsy way that the continuity of both is constantly disrupted, thus exag-
gerating the duality on display. This in turn is exacerbated by the idiomatic
dissonance between the crooning vocal and the super-groovy bluesy sax
interjections that are both, by turn, mocking and celebratory. And the pluralization does not end there: in addition to being radically other to each
other, the singing and playing are each individually other to the sound world
constructed by Turner on percussion, resulting in a complex interplay of
exteriority or exteriorities where everything seems to emanate from a different source.

So, to pick up the thread yet again, what is being described here is a
form of improvisation that, while admirably demonstrating improvisatory
precision at the micro and the local levels (precision 1 and 2), is also characterized by an extraordinary mastery of "incompossible" fields that are
both inhabited and deployed as ironic markers of a multitude of irreducible
differences that, together, become the space or zone of *"espacement"* where
ec-centricity takes on its full improvisatory force. Eccentricity for Lol was
never simply a concatenation of idiosyncratic mannerisms, but the force of
an incompossibility that forever drove him into the essential solitude that
he so carefully concealed beneath his public participatory persona: irony
personified.

5 Precision, Decision, and Accuracy: Heidegger and Arendt on Singularity and Solitude

Precision has a dubious reputation as that which is merely correct, as lacking human warmth. In this sense precision seems to speak against the fuzzy empathic logic that is favored by many improvisers, rooted, as it is often seen to be, in an individual technical prowess that is both self-serving and resistant to the perceived compromises of collective interaction. The main problem is that precision is often confused with accuracy. Heidegger, in a discussion of science, makes a distinction between what he calls: a "sphere of accuracies" (science) and a "zone of truth" (philosophical thinking/art/poetry).

Precision is quite different from accuracy, and to help explain the difference, we can consider the distinction made by Heidegger, one that we have already been utilizing above, between decision and choice. In essence his view is that the promotion of choice fails to account for the more essential *decision* to establish particular regimes of choice. The "task" of thinking for him is to recognize the secondary nature of choice, one that is grounded in an unquestioned, unchosen decision. In this regard, accuracy is measured against a stable reference that is stable precisely by not being questioned. The moment that thought and action become decisive rather than accurate is the moment that precision comes into play. This is because decisive thinking destabilizes, which is why Heidegger understands the "zone of truth" as a space of "withdrawal," where error and erring are the means by which truth is ad-dressed. To err is by no means to be wrong or without truth, it is, rather, to be at a distance from truth, the distance necessary to witness the endless unconcealment/concealment of truth itself. It is here that the concept of pre-cision can be introduced as a way of describing the disciplining of thought and action precisely where accuracy is impossible. Precision is the product of a prior and originary in-decisiveness, an in-decisiveness that is paradoxi-cally dis-closed by such precision. Thus, precision and in-decision need to be thought together. To explain this peculiarity will necessitate (in good Hei-deggerian fashion) the hyphenation of key terms and the transformation of negatives into positives. Thus, indecision becomes in-decision with the consequence that instead of describing a lack of decisiveness the emphasis is now on the positive act of entering into decisiveness and speaking/thinking/acting from within, or as Heidegger says, "from out of" such decisiveness. It is the act of entering into in-decisiveness that is decisive, and, although it is described as prior to the realm of choice and accuracy, this beginning is also understood as the inceptual dimension of the "now." Indeed, for Hei-degger, it is what he calls "inceptual thinking" that is decisive, a thinking of beginnings that preserves the origin, not through the memorialization of the historical past, but through the endless destruction and de-stabilization of re-origination.

Back to the point: a great deal of improvisation might be described as operating within a "zone of accuracies." While it is true that much improvi-sation is intended as the articulation, expression, and celebration of a cer-tain freedom, it is clear that, at best, this is a negative freedom, a freedom-from that is primarily engaged in unfixing the fixed.

There is an interesting and very fruitful duality in the meaning of the German word *Streng* that can be considered here: it can mean both "strict" and "severe." The difference is that strictness assumes adherence/obedience to a fixed law/model/standard, whereas severity, as we have already seen, is a form of discipline in the *absence* of the law. While accepting that these two polarities form part of a much more nuanced spectrum of possibilities—all improvisations have elements of fixity and unfixity—nevertheless, in order to make a point, we might identify two different models of improvisation here: the unfixing of the fixed (idiomatic improvisation) and the fixing of the unfixed (free improvisation or non-idiomatic). The former demands ac-curacy, the latter precision. Accuracy is reproductive; precision is productive and, of course, the former is the familiar and predominant model. Both of the proposed models have a place for singularity, but they are different. Within idiomatic or strict improvisation, the singular emerges out of the collective, the already-given. In this sense, the familiar valorization of individual expression/experimentation/innovation/virtuosity can and does obscure the fact that what counts as singularity here is a product of the collective. As a consequence, the collective does not need to be a key feature in such improvisation, and where it does figure, there is a tendency to strive toward an organic unicity or wholeness that naturalizes and eternalizes, while effectively concealing/forgetting the decisive originary moment that makes such an impressive display possible: as improvisatory "choice." Freedom, here understood as the freedom to choose, is underpinned by the certainty that strictness allows, and by the sureness of touch and clarity of vision that is celebrated within such improvisation. Within severe improvisation the collective emerges out of the singular, not as the realization of a potential or possible communality but as the actualization of an originary, virtual commonality. The result is a commonality without community, as distinct from the community without commonality more typical of strict idiomatic improvisation; and, to reiterate, an improvisation of fixing rather than unfixing.

To make better sense of the above, we will now need to root Heidegger's thinking in the work of Kant. What both have in common is the view that subjectivity is always already rooted in a commonality: Heidegger describes all being as being-with (*Mitsein*) while Kant relies upon the notion of *sensus communis* to forge links between singularity and universality. For Kant, the commonality of singularity is played out in the art of judgment (the judgment necessary for art). What is important to emphasize here is that aesthetic judgment is inherently unfixed, because not grounded in conceptual knowledge. Aesthetic judgment is, rather, enabled by a feeling of pleasure or, more neutrally, rightness that accompanies the play of the human faculties and their mutual attunement. *Play* is the key word here, but it should be made absolutely clear that play is not here referring to the "playfulness" that is often associated with improvisation, but rather the *a priori* play of the imagination and the understanding that cannot be resolved, but is fixed by the act of aesthetic judgment necessary to produce any art, whether improvised or not.

It is this singular act of fixing that produces not only the artwork but also the collectivity that the artist, as judge, assumes, indeed *demands* (as Kant has it), when making an aesthetic judgment. The fact that this demand is rooted in an assumed universality of "common sense," however, does not guarantee the creation of a communicative community, precisely because the act of fixing is singular and thus always open to "contestation," as Kant describes it. What is more, the act of fixing, driven by the art of aesthetic judgment, is also unfixed because the contestatory collective that emerges out of it is nothing more than the actualization of the plural originary event of judgment itself. Put another way, singularity is contestational so, thought in Kantian terms, Heidegger's being-with can be thought as describing an *a priori* critical dialogue where the fixer and the judge together arrive at a judgment that makes possible the creative act: a collective act that takes place outside of the social. Hannah Arendt captures this perfectly in her distinction between loneliness and solitude—or singularity, as we are describing it here. We have seen this passage before:

> Thinking . . . is a solitary but not a lonely business; solitude is that human condition in which I keep myself company. Loneliness comes about when I am alone without being able to split up into the two-in-one, without being able to keep myself company. . . . Nothing perhaps indicates more strongly that man exists essentially in the plural than that his solitude actualizes his merely being conscious of himself . . . into a duality during the thinking activity. It is this duality of myself with myself that makes thinking a true activity, in which I am both the one who asks and who answers. Thinking can become dialectical and critical because it goes through this questioning and answering process.[1]
>
> Critical thinking, while still a solitary business, does not cut itself off from "all others." To be sure, it still goes on in isolation, but by the force of imagination it makes the others present and thus moves in a space that is potentially public, open to all sides.[2]

Yes, Arendt is here talking about thinking rather than doing, but the same holds for the creative act, and such an act, even the freest, most improvised act, cannot be separated from the essential solitude of thought.[3] Thus, the question/answer—call/response model of collectivity popular within some improvisation is not the transcendence of a singularity too quickly and easily confused with the cult of the individual and the dubious "individualism" that accompanies it, but the actualization of the *a priori* question and answer that Arendt mentions.

So, precision, unlike accuracy, is required at the decisive moment where decisionism falters, where there is nothing to measure accuracy against, no model, benchmark, or standard. Where decisive thinking renders all thought and action in-decisive, precision is needed to fix the movement of "erring" that characterizes such in-decision. What Heidegger calls "erring," Kant describes as "trial and error," and we should note the judicial terminology he uses, as it related to the figure of the judge in the solitary question-answer described by Arendt and necessary for aesthetic judgment to arrive at the precision necessary to make the judgment. Precision, unlike accuracy, does not point back to an origin that it realizes or approximates; precision, as the word suggests, precedes the moment of origination; it is, in a sense, always ahead of itself. Where accuracy strives to reduce and ultimately eliminate the distance between an origin and its representation or reproduction, precision denotes the separation of one element and another through a prior cutting (pre-cision) of what might be called the materiality of thought and action: a de-structive process quite different from the con-structive ambitions of accuracy. And the collectivity that emerges out of this singular act of separation itself bears the marks of this prior de-struction: to repeat, a commonality without community.

Improvisation is a solitary business, whether or not it is done in the company of others. The performative moment of an improvisation is not its actual beginning, and while it might be true to say, with Niklas Luhmann, that art (and particularly improvised art as the dramatization of this) is the "marking of an unmarked space," the moment of this marking is not the start of the improvised performance or action but the beginning marked by the prior initiation of a process of trial and error, erring and pre-cision described above. Now of course this can also be a lonely business: the hours and hours of practise and training, the endless repetition of often banal acts, the punishing drill required to master the rhetoric necessary to start anything at all, but such a self-imposed psycho-social predicament is not the point at issue here. Instead, it is the entry into the solitude described by Arendt that signifies the marking of the unmarked space and, thus, the beginning of the improvisation. While we normally think of precision as a quality of the act itself, and thus, by implication, a quality of the individual responsible for this act and their technical prowess, it could be suggested that it is the solitary questioning and answering described by Arendt that separates one possible choice from another, one possible mark from another, one possible mode of fixing from another, prior to this fixing/marking; that is the more essential location of precision. A corollary of this shift of perspective is that precision can now be distinguished from mere technical ability—a form of accuracy—and brought into relation with the true expression of its essence: certitude. Not certainty, which only inhabits the "zone of accuracies," but certitude. As already proposed, for all of the talk of uncertainty and surprise, the most essential quality of improvisation is its certitude. And again, certitude is not merely a psychological trait of the artist/improviser but, rather, a consequence of the assumed commonality at the heart of aesthetic judgment. In this regard solitude does not describe the existential predicament of the self but the structure of judgment itself and the work that it produces: the solitude of the work not the self. As Kant recognized, the certitude of aesthetic judgment, the refusal to be persuaded by the taste of others, is not due to individual arrogance but, on the contrary, a consequence of the fact that "my" judgment and "my" work are never mine alone or even mine at all, but the (forever failed) articulation of a commonality that itself bespeaks a universality that is assumed, albeit as eternally absent. The primary task of the individual improviser, whether alone or in the company of others, is to enact or, perhaps, re-enact "in the moment" the entry and re-entry into the solitude that allows the work to begin prior to the secondary starting of the "work" that is always in danger of obscuring the beginning by promoting itself as an end.

The question now is: To what extent does this model of improvisation "speak against" collective improvisation? Well, the short answer is that it doesn't. Where there is a clear difference, however, is in the consideration of a model of collectivity that is not "the celebration of *collective* politically significant action."[4] This, the expectation, assumption, or even demand that collective improvisation be politically significant, suggests a latent "decisionism" that is in danger of transforming the commonality without community already discussed into what Adorno describes as a "dubious totality," where improvisation itself is in danger of being reduced to the caricature that he himself critiques so mercilessly—a world of pseudo-individualism and tyrannical collectivism. It is because of the extent to which we share some of Adorno's views that we have sought to protect collective improvisation from his charges by attempting to imagine a different model of individualism and totality.

We can begin by acknowledging that there is indeed something worth celebrating in collective improvisation, something other than political action or the warm organic glow of empathy, which have been celebrated enough already. But what is it? Interestingly and, on the face of it, paradoxically, collective improvisation should be celebrated for what might be called its enactment of singularity and solitude. Actually, it can do this much better than solo improvisation, which is too easily appropriated by the discourses of loneliness and the cult of the individual. Throughout his work Heidegger insists that solitude is not a characteristic of the artist but of the artwork. Similarly, and as we shall see in our discussion of Jimi Hendrix and others below, Maurice Blanchot describes the "essential solitude" as the process of being "cast aside" by the work, rendering the artist "workless." Solitude, for him, is not to be without the other (loneliness) but without work. But, strangely, this "worklessness" has to be worked at by the artist: a kind of auto-redundancy, self-created obsolescence or erasure. For Heidegger, art is an event, and recent English Heidegger translations of the very complex and allusive German word for "event" (*Ereignis*) have used the not-altogether-elegant neologism "Enowning" to try and capture the peculiar sense of possession and dispossession being suggested here. This is how the translators of his *Contributions to Philosophy* express it:

> Above all it is the prefix en-in this word [enowning] . . . that conveys the sense of "enabling," "bringing into the condition of," or "welling up of." Thus, in conjunction with owning, this prefix is capable of getting across a sense of an "owning" that is not an "owning of a something." We can think this owning as an un-possessive owning . . . In this sense owning does not have an appropriatable content.[5]

The claim to be made here is that, as opposed to non-improvised art, all improvisation, whether solo or collective, represents a more essential engagement with the event of the work in the terms just described. In particular, it is the improviser's problematization of the concept of the "work," through the prioritization of the working of the work that shifts the emphasis away from ownership and the celebrity culture that often accompanies it. But, having said that, there is still a danger that either the improviser as action figure could, and often does, obscure the dispossession at the heart of this work, or, conversely, that the improviser as the figure "cast aside" by the work mystifies art and the artist, who is seen as simultaneously dispossessed and possessed by this aesthetic alterity. The advantage of collective improvisation is that it can avoid such obscurantism. The "sum is greater than its parts," to return to our cliché, is a mystification; the sum is not greater, it is *different* from its parts, and it is this difference that allows us to speak of such collective action as the enactment of singularity and solitude. Improvisers often speak of creating "space," and there certainly exists a collective ethics of performance committed to ensuring that all have their say/space. But actually this is not the same as the reserve (*Gelassenheit*) encouraged by Heidegger, where the demand is that, by "letting-be," it is not the other individual interlocutor who is offered space, but the alterity of the work itself, unowned by all collaborators. The spectacle of this collective exile should remind us of the fact that "being-with" is the epitome of *unsociability* for Heidegger; so behind the familiar mask of community and alongside the celebration of "politically significant action," collective improvisation can present us with a performative space that, while it is the product of collective thinking, willing, and doing, is by no means the expression or embodiment of an assumed communicative community. Of course, there is communication, but its goal is more related to precision than to empathy. Empathy ultimately seeks unity and totality (to speak with "one voice," one "authentic" voice); precision requires the separation of one voice

from another (a multiplicity of rhetorics). It is precisely the absence of community that can only be demonstrated collectively and which best expresses
the in-decisive essence of singularity itself. The precision of the singular
act, within or without a collective improvisation, buries the prehistory of
its actualization in the certitude of its gesture and fixity of its articulation.
But the precision of the collective or collaborative act, enacted "before our
eyes," puts on view the pre-cision necessary to unfix everything, thereby
allowing an improvisatory fixing to take place. Only in this way can the
performative nature of singularity, forever contested, be grasped as the originary movement of the improvisatory act.

6 Decentered Center/Displaced Periphery: A Deleuzian Perspective

I make, remake and unmake my concepts along a moving horizon, from an always decentered center, from an always displaced periphery which repeats and differentiates them.

Gilles Deleuze[1]

Making, remaking, unmaking; movement, becoming, decentering; this is all stock-in-trade for the improviser, but why does Deleuze repeat the word "from?" Why, instead of saying "from-to" does he say instead "from-from," thereby destroying the linearity and teleology of most improvisation? Yes, improvisation already has, thanks to Keith Johnstone, a concept of "tilting,"[2] one that militantly decenters the formation of centers in an effort to combat boredom in all of its forms; but this remains a linear/teleological model, albeit of an unstable kind, that still aspires to a telos of hyper-tilted, non-boringness that is not half as radical as it sounds: who wants to be bored anyway? Well, actually some people do, or at least accept the fact that boredom, as Heidegger recognized,[3] might be a revelatory moment as regards improvisation. Anyway, what would a from-from improvisation be like?

To begin with, we have to go back to beginnings again. The first "from" would normally be considered the beginning, but not here; any more than could the displaced periphery be radicalized as a non-originary origin—an alternative "from" so to speak. No, as Deleuze continues:

> Following Samuel Butler, we discover Erewhon, signifying at once the originary "nowhere" and the displaced, disguised, modified and always recreated "here and now."[4]

Center or periphery—then and there/here and now/origin and repetition—none are truly the beginning; there *is* no beginning as regards a singular point of origin, whether central or peripheral, only the movement along an horizon that cannot simply be seen in terms of becoming but, rather, must be seen as the ever-transient point or moment of intersection which "repeats and differentiates them." Thus, movement is not understood here as becoming or development but as the repetitive differentiation of two radically pluralized sources: the center and the periphery—decentered and displaced.

The dual origins of center and periphery can both be understood as *starting* points and, as such, always underway prior to the possibility of any *beginning*: the former incessantly withdrawing into an originary absence, the latter approaching incessantly the always disguised presence of a here and now intent upon arriving at an originary moment promised by the repetition of the same (of resemblance). Here the origin becomes the end, albeit unattainable, given the essential absence or "nowhere" of the origin. Clearly, this describes a great deal of what passes as free improvisation, where we can witness both individual and collective attempts to re-originate a lost origin; *origin* not understood either spatially or temporally as place or time but as the *transition* from the start to the beginning—the *decisive* moment prior to all choices. Here we see the ecstasy and intensity of improvisation, but for all of the turmoil associated with it, it remains trapped within a model of repetition that can ultimately only produce diversity rather than difference, the repetition of the same difference rather than a different sameness.

> One is bare, the other clothed: one is repetition of parts, the other of the whole; one involves succession, the other coexistence; one is actual, the other virtual; one is horizontal, the other vertical.[5]

As before when discussing Mike Cooper and Roger Turner, the model of improvisation described above can be mapped onto the first of the couplets Deleuze itemizes. And yet the complexity of the relation between the de-centered center and the displaced periphery would seem to suggest a greater degree of intertwinement than was first thought, or than we may have suggested. On closer inspection, it does seem apparent that the first binary—bare/clothed—is difficult if not impossible to disentangle in *any* improvisation, good or bad, free or not. Many improvisers probably do desire a bare repetition of the originary moment, the ecstatic experience of a pure beginning, and Miles Davis certainly appears to have such a desire when he writes in the prologue to his autobiography,

> Listen. The greatest feeling I ever had in my life—with my clothes on—was when I first heard Diz and Bird together in St Louis in 1944. . . . Anyway, I've come close to matching the feeling of that night, . . . but I've never quite got there. I've gotten close, but not all the way there. I'm always looking for it, listening and feeling for it, though, trying to always feel it in and through the music I play every day.[6]

Nevertheless, the underlying dynamic of improvisation—its becoming-ness—is precisely a function of the "disguise" that contingent, limited forms or situations always impose on the here and now, creating a restlessness and infinite irresolution that marks a crucial difference between improvised and non-improvised work. The "clothes" never fit or suit and thus have to be constantly altered, but they can only be altered in response to the concealed body that incessantly withdraws behind its very medium of display. It is this fundamental dualism that not only drives forward improvisation but which also determines its nature, correctly captured by Deleuze: partial, successive, actual, and horizontal. This provides us with an excellent template by means of which it is possible to identify with some precision the performative character and shape of many improvisations, no matter how varied they might appear on the surface. But the crucial thing to grasp at the outset is that it is the interrelation of the first binary—bare/clothed—that is responsible for propelling improvised repetition into a mode of infinite becoming. If one can, with Deleuze, of course, think outside of this particular, overly dialectical dynamic, then a different template becomes available, one that we have already been groping toward in the account of Lol Coxhill's singularity, and to which we will return in due course. For now though, let us flesh out a little more the suggested connections between improvisation and Deleuze's concept of the repetition of the same: partiality, successiveness, actuality, and horizontality.

Partiality/Participation

By the "repetition of parts" Deleuze points toward a representational logic that is both external to and yet governed by an overarching concept that ensures a consistent diversity (or diverse consistency) rather than pure difference.

> The difference is taken to be only external to the concept; it is a
> difference between objects represented by the same concept, falling
> into the indifference of space and time.[7]

Here, the externalization of a given and regulatory concept is responsible
for the production and proliferation of an infinite number of parts that are
diverse but not different. As regards improvisation, this makes perfect sense,
especially where the governing concept (the standard, "head arrangement,"
the choreography, the script, and so on) permits—even encourages—a diversification of externalization that only has real impact to the extent that
it is performed within the "indifference of space and time." Put another
way, improvisation is here concerned with the production of a diversity that
is not only governed by an originary concept, but also received and judged
within a space/time similarly regulated by the homogeneity of the origin,
against which the differencing of the improviser is measured: diversity is a
product of the same. Should free improvisation be distinguished from this
view, given the proclaimed absence of an originary model that would de-
limit the autonomy of both production and reception of the work? Actually
no: free improvisation, far from being anticonceptual, is overdetermined
by extraordinarily powerful and voluminous concepts of both "freedom"
and "improvisation," which similarly necessitate an externalization that
again produces diversity rather than difference. To be clear, though, there
is nothing inherently wrong with diversity, any more than there is anything
particularly wonderful about difference. Having said that, the aim here is
indeed to disentangle very different modes of improvisation, not for the sake
of difference, but for the sake of clarity.

If we put to one side the familiar concept of improvisation as infinite
becoming, as the eternal flow of the new from out of the old, and consider
instead the movement whereby it is the de-centeredness of the center and
the displacement of the periphery that produce the dual dislocation and
consequent ontological absence that is behind the successive production of
parts, then a different perspective immediately becomes evident. Instead of
relating, as is normal, parts to the whole (as origin/center or telos/periph-
ery), here the partial externalization of a de-centered origin and a displaced
telos promotes a regime of repetition that can be more appropriately linked
to *participation*: participation in the part as well participation in the participatory itself, both essential ingredients of improvisation.

Decentered, displaced or not, the whole is difficult to participate in without risking the submergence of the partial in the absolute un-differentiation
of the totality. That is a danger, but another problem is that improvisation is not normally thought to take place at the level of the whole; but,

rather, the variation and extrapolation of parts. This is certainly true of what Derek Bailey calls "idiomatic improvisation," where improvisation does not take place at the idiomatic level but within specific parts of that idiom (individual works), and then only within specific parts of those parts (individual phrases, gestures, and so on). But then we find that the afore-mentioned danger of submergence in the totality is replaced by another risk, an inversion of the first: the dissolution of the whole in an anarchy of fragmentation. Participation and the participatory culture that accom-panies it play a crucial role in forestalling this double danger—individual submergence/total dissolution—by situating the improviser within the mo-ment of repetition in such a way that "playing one's part," "becoming one's part," even just "taking part" take on enormous significance as the means by which the whole, part, and participant do not collapse into each other. In this regard it is worth stating that, in spite of the fact that the language of commitment is ubiquitous in the world of improvisation, it is not com-mitment *to* the part played but participation *in* the part played that is the crucial issue here. Commitment always comes from the outside and, once attained, obliterates difference in the name of the same and, admittedly, the diversity this allows. Participation, on the other hand, requires entry into the interiority of the part, seeking an immersion in the part-icular manner of repetitive externalization: and immersion and submersion are quite different concepts. Like immersion, participation in the part, in the part to be played, allows the improviser to both "go with the flow" and to retain an awareness of where the flow is flowing; however, and this is the essential point that will ultimately lead us back to the non-participatory participation suggested by Lol Coxhill's work, this awareness remains at the micro and the local rather than at the macro level.

At the micro level the part is not the direct repetition of an existing con-cept, but the repetition of the technical and improvisational skills acquired during the hours of solitary practise, and it is those hours that are primarily governed by the twin concepts of freedom and improvisation. It is the latter concepts that are committed to, and not the former skills, which, as noted, are participated in to the degree that they produce parts. This prior com-mitment (*decision*) ensures that the subsequent *choices* made at the moment of performance within the micro-space of the part must be understood as diversification rather than differentiation, the latter being the product of *in-decision*. Participation in the part—"getting into it"—is a necessary component of the centripetal intensity commonly sought for in improvised performance. But alongside this we must also acknowledge the ex-tensive, centrifugal force of participation which drives the participant and his or her parts not out into the whole but out toward other participants and their parts. Thus, this intersubjective moment and movement does not, as is often assumed, create a whole; rather, it creates a participatory culture that, to be sure, can be participated in as an end in itself, as long as it is remembered that the concept of an end in no way implies a concept of wholeness. This is precisely why we have claimed that a primary task, and thus an important goal or end of improvisation, is the *avoidance* of a "work" and the dubious dream of wholeness that frequently accompanies it.

At the local level, then, there is a different set of skills required to manage not only the emergent work, what we have been calling "precision 2," but also the participatory culture that, in the case of collective improvisation, is a crucial component of this emergence. Where the work of participation replaces the "work" itself as end, and indeed *works against it* in the pursuit of an openness associated with freedom and improvisation, it can do so only to the extent that it conceals or obscures the fact that it remains a partial externalization of an originary concept or concepts that it can only repeat in the same, albeit diversified way. In other words, the whole is at the beginning rather than the end, and it is because of the fact that it is only ever repeated in part, through singular parts and collective participation, that it remains largely unrecognized, and its impact on the manner of repetition, necessary for externalization, is left unaccounted for. Needless to say, it is necessary for this repetition of the same to be obscured if the self-understanding of improvisation, particularly free improvisation, is to remain unchallenged, and there is no particular reason why it *should* be challenged; misrecognition is certainly no barrier to great improvisation.

Succession

To have a part to play, to want to play a part—such a participatory desire and subsequent culture are at the heart of improvisation in most of its forms across a multitude of disciplines. The need to be part of something, to belong, and to contribute are all, no doubt, essential parts of being human, social beings. Strange then that improvised performance is such a minority interest; maybe we're not as human as we like to think we are. Or maybe most of us just don't like that kind of belonging: such hard work. This is a serious point: to be part of a whole and to belong somewhere is a common desire, one that is evident in the world of improvisation (is it a world?), and particularly evident in the widespread use of the concept of "space," not understood as something preexistent and to be occupied but as something to be created performatively for the duration of an improvisation, or at least for part—the "happening" part—of it. But it is precisely this productive moment that makes this form of improvised belonging such hard work for all those involved—hard in a fun sense, of course. Why is this? Part of the reason has already been addressed above: the relation of part to whole is mediated by a participatory culture that, in becoming an end in itself, draws participants into a flow that endlessly carries them away from the ground and grounding that would establish a totality. In this regard Derrida's notion of *"espacement"*—of spacing rather than space—might better capture the way in which improvisers utilize the concept of "space" when discussing particularly intense or particularly successful moments of performance. This of course partly relates to the de-centered and displaced origin of improvisation as understood within the current "Deleuzian" context, but it is also the result of the *successive* nature of the repetition of the same that he also identifies, and which comes into conflict with, or at least neutralizes, the creation of a stable or static space that might be occupied or belonged to.

Where the division of repetition into parts refers to *spatiality*, albeit temporalized by the introduction of participation above, succession introduces *temporality* proper, and in a particularly discontinuous, even destructive form—one that is not unique to improvisation but which here reaches its apotheosis. Critics of improvisation such as Pierre Boulez draw attention to the episodic character of most improvised performances, allowing him to take a rather condescending pleasure in predicting what is going to happen from moment to moment. For him, it is not so much the successive nature of performance at the micro level of the individual parts that is the issue, which is something shared by all time-based art, including his own, but the *episodic* nature of the local participatory economy that sustains an improvisation for the duration of its very temporary life. Here succession has less to do with the forging of a work from out of what Adorno calls the "artistic material"[8] available to the participants at the level of their technique (precision 1) than it does with the more general *characterization* of performative temporality obeying either a dialectical logic of contradictions and their resolutions or a nondialectical, chiasmal logic of irresolvable binaries. Either way, albeit with different outcomes, the result is almost inevitably a linear series of improvisatory gestures oscillating between some or all of the following: loud-quiet, fast-slow, frenetic-contemplative, dense-sparse, dissonant-consonant, intense-chilled, tragic-comic, continuous-discontinuous, sublime-ridiculous . . . the list is a long one. Obviously, the dialectical logic that dominates Western Eurocentric aesthetics will always be favored by the creators of "works," Boulez being no exception. Within this tradition, success is measured against the *elimination* of succession as a performative mode, indeed, for a work to be success-full it must achieve an aesthetic outcome that reveals apparent succession to be, in truth, the revelation of an immanent fullness that ultimately ties the beginning and the end

of the work together, thus sublating the episodic into the unchanging order
of the absolute and participation in successive parts into the whole—a Wagnerian vision of totality that persisted throughout much superficial anti-
Wagnerianism witnessed during the modernist period. But that's another
story; for now it is enough to note, with Boulez, that improvisation is indeed
successive in form and nature, and that the "problems" associated with this,
rather than being the subject of denial, should be both better understood
and, perhaps then more knowingly deployed.

> Our problem concerns the essence of repetition. It is a question of
> knowing why repetition cannot be explained by the form of identity
> in concepts or representations; in what sense it demands a superior
> "positive" principle. This enquiry must embrace all the concepts
> of nature and freedom. Consider, on the border between these two
> cases, the repetition of a decorative motif: a figure is reproduced,
> while the concept remains the absolutely identical. . . . However,
> this is not how artists proceed in reality. They do not juxtapose
> instances of the figure, but rather each time combine an element of
> one instance with *another* element of a following instance. They in-
> troduce a disequilibrium into the dynamic process of construction,
> an instability, dissymmetry or gap of some kind which disappears
> only in the overall effect.[9]

Deleuze's explication of repetition and difference unwaveringly hits the
bull's-eye when it comes to the essential principles of improvised practice,
regardless of his own apparent unconcern for the topic. So, continuing the
discussion of succession, Deleuze here challenges the negativity of dialectical logic in the name of a "positivity" that works against the desire to forge
an identity between concepts and representations such that repetition *succeeds* in producing a "work." For him it is not a question of, Hegel-fashion,
sublating nature and freedom in a spiraling differentiation that works to
reveal the same, but, closer to Kant, embracing *both* simultaneously with
all of the "disequilibrium" this entails, so expertly described in the above
quotation. To all intents and purposes, Deleuze's "artist" can be our improviser, except for one proviso: in the world of improvisation the dissymmetry
does not *necessarily* disappear in "the overall effect," although the most
"profound" form of improvisation, like the most "profound" form of repetition, does take place in "secret" and thus is indeed invisible (to the untrained
eye/ear): our Cyndi Lauper case study (chapter 23) will struggle with this.

At both the micro and the local levels, we here begin to witness the discontinuous and destructive dimension of succession as it unfolds at the level

of performance, not only through the diversification of parts at the point of delivery, but also as a consequence of an episodic logic which, however predictable it might be to some, actually militates against the attainment by improvised performance of the kind of equilibrium that is always there to tempt those improvisers who are not sufficiently vigilant. And anyway, do episodes have to be so predictable?

7

Memoir: San Sebastian Jazz Festival, July 20–25, 1980

Something I touched on in my last book is the often forgotten or, indeed, often repressed element of competition in improvisation. On that occasion I referenced, among other things, the tap-dance competitions in the 1930s, where it was the pitching of one dancer against another that drove the improvisations on to ever greater heights of invention and intensity.[1] The intention was (as was the intention of the book as a whole) to introduce a note of skepticism into the dominant narrative of improvisation, one that consistently overplays an ethic of altruism and dialogical generosity while downplaying the egotistical competitiveness that, like it or not, is ever-present. And it is not just one player testing himself or herself against another, it is one band up against another, a "battle of the bands," as the rock world puts it, more honestly and more blatantly. In the world of jazz, of course, such vulgarity is generally frowned upon as being deeply uncool: uncool-ness being a cardinal sin (I blame Miles Davis). But the fact remains that competition does not simply lurk undetected as the unsavory underbelly of jazz; it is, or certainly was "in my day," an integral part of the very structure of the international jazz festival circuit.

"My day?"

In 1976 I formed, with the pianist Veryan Weston, the jazz-funk band Stinky Winkles.[2] From the outset, the band performed its own material, initially influenced by, among others, Herbie Hancock, The Crusaders, Weather Report, and rock bands such as Steely Dan (more on them, or part of them, later). Thanks to the experience and input of Veryan Weston in particular, the band quite quickly developed into a far more sophisticated and, indeed, innovative ensemble, combining increasingly complex compositions with extended free improvisations, weaving solo, duo, and group work in and out of the compositional structure.

The first, what one might call, "formal" acknowledgment of the effectiveness or "success" of this peculiarly hybrid form of improvised music was (and this is the point at last) at a jazz *competition*: the Greater London Arts Association "Young Jazz Musicians of the Year," 1979. Winning this competition against twelve other bands in front of a panel of eminent jazz players and journalists at the London Roundhouse launched Stinky Winkles into a series of such competitions at jazz festivals across Europe: Dunkirk, France (1980); San Sebastian, Spain (1980); Wroclaw, Poland (1981). For the record, we won all of them (there were even trophies). So, before returning to my particular memories of San Sebastian in order to set up the case study of the drummer Bernard Purdie to follow, I would like to dwell for a moment on the slightly bizarre, although somehow deeply attractive, notion of being a "winning" improviser.[3] If, as Walter Benjamin suggests, the history we have is the history of the victors rather than the vanquished, then the next question has to be why were the victors victorious? Or, why were Stinky Winkles the best? It's a nice problem to have.

One of the anonymous "reader's reports" for the first draft of this book encouraged me to add some additional sections offering up some judgments on what might distinguish a "successful" from an "unsuccessful" improvisation. Obviously, the last thing they intended was for me to rely not on my own judgment but on actual panels of "judges" across Europe, but it is worth asking the question, Why *did* we win? Obviously, I can't ask the judges themselves; they are all long gone or living in old folks homes (it was the early eighties, remember). But I did seek the views of the other members of Stinky Winkles themselves, none of whom are in sheltered accommodation as we speak: something of a miracle!

Veryan Weston (piano) was the first to respond. His view is that a major part of our success was due to the fact that the members of the band were drawn from very different musical genres (rock and blues; pop/rock and punk; jazz-rock; funk; free jazz, and avant-gardist), resulting in an increasingly complex amalgam of idioms played out both in the compositional content and structure and the unfixed-ness of the improvisation, frequently moving across idiomatic boundaries and also frequently colliding them. He, of course, being a musician rather than an academic who needs to fill up pages of a book, puts it more succinctly:

> Why were the Winkles successful?
> Strange mix of people helped . . . so made the music eclectic . . . post modern even . . . pre Zorn . . . blah blah . . .[4]

We were young (officially "*young* jazz musicians"; and how many people have actual proof of being young?) and, for the most part, pretty ingenuous (I was anyway), certainly too much so to adopt the postmodern know-ingness of, for example, John Zorn's Cobra mash-ups or Bill Laswell's "collision music" that, not unlike Bailey's *Company Weeks*, were hyper-intentional projects specifically designed to create eclectic improvisational situations. With Stinky Winkles this happened largely by accident, a series of chance encounters that, through affirmation and fidelity, took on a certain idiosyncratic necessity over the six years or so of the band's existence. At a time when European jazz competitions were stuffed full of jazz hope-fuls churning out highly skilled but idiomatically mono-logical improvised set pieces (I remember so well listening to them, over and over again, from the side of the stage, waiting to go on), it's no wonder Stinky Winkles cleaned-up.

So, now Dan Brown the bass player has replied (this is all in real time you understand): here is his response.

We kept on winning because of the following:

- a good mix between accessible and challenging music;
- [a] high standard of musicianship;
- [an] interesting blend of jazz, rock, and contemporary classical;
- [a] varied blend of written, free improv, and structured improv;
- the other contestants weren't very good;
- [we were] great-looking young guys (that should be the number one reason, but just trying to be modest)!

OK, enough's enough.

All of this lengthy detour brings me, at last, to my memories of the 1980 San Sebastian Jazz Festival. Interestingly, I seem to be the only one who can

remember anything of this, something to be returned to later in relation
to the vanishing nature of Jimi Hendrix's improvisation. Anyway, having
won the "amateur competition," Stinky Winkles were hanging out, going
to some of the festival gigs, and playing a few gigs ourselves in adjoining
towns and villages (part of the "prize" for winning). Late afternoon or very
early evening on the day that the great Argentinean saxophonist Gato Barbieri and his band were headlining at the Velodrome, we received a rather
desperate call from the festival organizers asking us if we could get down to
the stadium immediately and fill in for an hour, as Barbieri's bus had been
delayed, and he was still in the Bordeaux area of France, a few hours away.
We rushed to the stadium, which contained an all-time record audience of
twelve thousand: Gato Barbieri is huge in Spain, and this is by far the biggest audience I have ever played in front of (my previous personal best was
twenty-seven). We quickly set up and played our set, which, as the Spanish
newspaper *El Pais* reports, was "much appreciated" by the audience, but,
as the report continues in a similarly understated vein, "we were not what
the audience expected"[5] (the story of my life, so far). This became evident
as time passed without Barbieri, although by this time his sidemen were
there backstage, ready and waiting; a band that included one of my heroes:
the drummer Bernard "Pretty" Purdie (more to follow). Another announcement to the increasingly restless crowd assured them Gato was on his way,[6]
and then, unbeknownst to his awaiting fans, Barbieri suddenly appeared
backstage, a minder on each side holding him upright by his armpits: he
was completely wasted.[7] He slumped into an awaiting chair, oblivious to
virtually everything, even where he was (when he did eventually stagger onto
the stage around two hours late, he greeted the audience with "Hello Barce-
lona or wherever I am"; never a good idea in the Basque country!). Anyway,
as the slow handclapping started it was obvious that something had to be
done. After an anxious discussion among the members of Barbieri's band
(Bernard Purdie, drums; Bill Washer, guitar; Lincoln Goines, bass; Edy Mar-
tinez, piano: Stratton Howlett, percussion), the decision was made to get
started without their inebriated and disoriented leader (a causal relation if
ever there was one).

   The only thing I can remember about the "jam" that followed was the extraordinary playing of Purdie. I was standing immediately behind and below
him, just to one side, and could see his every move. Having been watching
many jazz drummers at the festival for a few days (I always watch the drummer if there is one), with all of the associated busyness, malleability, and
shimmering surface activity, the first contrast was that there was very little to
watch; Purdie appeared to do virtually nothing except hold down the beat,
that was it. Fills were rare, no flamboyant tricks, no overt (although many

covert) polyrhythms, no obvious improvisatory flourishes: just "time," the beat, the groove, one might say in his case, the thrust; Purdie himself calls it the "locomotion." Yes, he literally *propelled* the band in a way that, while radically understated, was, simultaneously, utterly dominant.

In trying to recapture the unfolding events of that night, Bill Washer reveals, if little else, the irrefutable authority of Purdie:

> Purdie pretty much took over by setting up the grooves, and we dug in behind him.
>
> Of course, having Bernard on drums was crucial. He's controlling the grooves, the form, and the concept. The crowd didn't get what it wanted, but at least we got out of there alive!

As the most recorded drummer in history, longtime drummer with Aretha Franklin, Roberta Flack, B. B. King, and an almost endless list of others (that he himself so likes to repeat on every possible occasion; . . . he's a great self-publicist), and responsible for some of Steely Dan's most transcendent moments, Purdie is recognized as one of the preeminent session drummers of his generation, but certainly not considered an improviser worthy of note: session playing and improvising usually being considered an oppositional binary.

Anyway, me in San Sebastian, mesmerized by Purdie laying down the beat, I began to get a sense of the way in which the solidity of his playing was only made possible by an underlying rhythmic flow that can only be described as a kind of floating, one that, literally, had to be held down and grounded by a "tightness" that was neither rigid nor leaden but both tense and intense to the point of explosiveness. The sheer energy of his playing, the almost inhuman control of this subterranean molten core was overwhelming.

Given the awkwardness of the situation, the band were *forced* to improvise, whether they felt like it or not, whether they were (mentally at least) prepared for it or not; although I have since learned from Lincoln Goines, the bass player that night, that, regardless of Barbieri's mental or physical state, the band members were used to jamming before he joined them on stage.[8] All credit to them anyway for doing such a great job, even if they couldn't really placate the increasingly ominous crowd. I remember some nice piano re-sounding across the intervening years, but that's all. Bill Washer is a lovely guitarist, he was there, but I have no recollection at all of his playing (and I'm a guitarist, shame on me). Goines reports that he did an extended fretless bass solo using an MXR Chorus pedal, which had a "mixed reception" from the crowd, many of whom had not heard anything quite like it before, but I have no recollection of that whatsoever. All I remember is Purdie: his frame, static and powerful, yet brimming with some barely controllable force; his feet (I was very close to them, he had two), yes, it was his feet more than anything that were the central loci of his improvisatory invention. It was here that you witnessed the production of rhythmic space—"*espacement*"—a space within which Purdie the improviser constantly moves, without needing the category of "improvisation" to identify and ratify what it is he does. Of course, as mentioned, he is a great self-publicist, and any quick surf of the Internet will offer up a multitude of videos with him explaining in great detail how he arrived at the famous "Purdie Shuffle" and how it works; but this simply reduces it to a formula that any half-proficient drummer can imitate with a bit of practise. But the difference between learning the Purdie Shuffle and *arriving at it* over "many, many, many, many . . . years" (as he always says) of improvising, and then affirming this multitude of chance events in a necessity that retrospectively obliterates chance, is absolute. *Watching* Purdie do his shuffle in San Sebastian (and I had heard of it at the time) was indeed a revelation. Never mind Steely Dan's *Babylon Sisters* or *Home at Last* (admittedly both masterpieces of their type), *watching* him subtly and endlessly move in and out of his multiplicitous grooves, was a reminder that even the most legislative of bands (Steely Dan for sure) have a (perhaps secret) place for improvisation, outside of the obvious solos that pepper their work. Actually, to be fair to them, when discussing Bernard Purdie in the 1999 documentary *Classic Albums: Steely Dan—Aja*, Donald Fagan and Walter Becker do agree that Purdie could always be expected to do the unexpected.

> BECKER: Listen to that beat [as they isolate Purdie's drum track in *Home at Last*]; . . . he always had some unique stylistic thing that he did, that you would never have imagined, that nobody else would do, . . . [brings up the hi hat in the mix] . . . real driving![9]

And this does raise again the issue of where the improvisatory act is located, something that we have already encountered with Lol Coxhill and will return to again, especially in what might be called the situational improvisations of Derek Bailey. Fagan and Becker flying in guitarists from all over to improvise a solo on the track *Peg* demonstrates (to me at least) that the apparent perfection of such an exemplary "studio" album as *Aja* is, in truth, more about an ongoing improvisation of possible situations until one "works": then you have a work, the "Work," and the improvisatory is then buried. Watching Purdie was a reminder of the infinite possibility that, once situated, is forgotten. Improvisation vanishes.

Why do people remember Gato Barbieri's drunken, shambolic, and ultimately insulting performance in San Sebastian and yet forget (there is absolutely no record of the improvisation) the glorious preamble to this disaster offered by his backing band? Proof, if proof were needed, that improvisation is essentially a vanishing form/form of vanishing: forgetfulness is its element—and its curse.

8   Case Study: Bernard "Pretty" Purdie

For old time's sake, we might start by reuniting Purdie with his San Sebastian co-improviser, the guitarist Bill Washer. "Grooving" has long since become a rather corny, unhip word, but, be that as it may, there simply is no other word to describe what Purdie, Bill Washer, and Craig Kastelnick (organ) put down at the Falcon Club in April 2011. It would be nice to imagine that this was the kind of groove that was laid down back in 1980 in the absence of the star saxophonist, but, as we know, all of that is long forgotten. Thanks to YouTube, we now live in a memorial culture *par excellence*, where any and every insignificance can be rendered significant, every forgettable experience can become a memory to be cherished and experienced over and over again: just touch the screen. But in addition to its infinite archiving potential, YouTube has also come to have something of a monopoly on the promotion of "liveness" as an event that we can all experience through the singular eyes and ears (or camera lens and microphone) of the other; usually someone like us who likes what we like but who we will never meet: familiarity and estrangement, the YouTube relation. The well-known and now rather tired dispute between Peggy Phelan[1] and Philip Auslander[2] over the unreproducibility (Phelan) or reproducibility (Auslander) of the live experience is not really the main issue here, concerned as they are with the experiential rather than the evental. Of course we cannot directly experience a live gig through the eyes and ears of another—YouTube is inevitably of the order of simulacra—but then, as all the philosophers of the event agree (Heidegger, Deleuze, Badiou), the event is itself *not* of the order of experience. Unlike experience or experiences, there is no mine or yours; there is only *the* event. Also what they all agree on is that the event is, temporally, not of the order of the present or of presence. Deleuze puts it in a nutshell:

> The event [. . .] in its impassibility and its impenetrability has no present. It rather retreats and advances in two directions at once, being the perpetual object of a double question: What is going to happen? What has just happened? The agonizing aspect of the pure event is that it is always and at the same time something which has just happened and something about to happen; never something which is happening.[3]

For Heidegger, the task is to "remember" the event; for Deleuze it is a question of sensation, the sensing of the event; and for Badiou it is the "procedure" of showing fidelity to the event. In every case the event is absent and yet in different ways witnessed: something is happening but we don't know what it is. Long story short: the event *can* be witnessed and/or sensed on YouTube, so we'll stick with it, and return to the video of Purdie and "Friends" grooving at the Falcon Club.

A telling moment: just before Purdie kicks off *Mr. Magic/Cissy Strut Jam*,[4] he interjects: "OK, where were we now?" Time and time again, in the multitude of videos on YouTube featuring Purdie, he advises drummers to "never forget where you are," and "always remember where one is."[5] In the company of our philosophers of the event, such an apparently simple statement resonates in a number of different ways: who, what, or where is the "one?" Is Purdie referring to himself, the drummer behind the kit in front of an audience, or does he mean the "1," the first beat of the bar. In actuality it is difficult to separate the two, because, for Purdie, where one is, is (as he repeatedly states) "in time," which, in turn, means within rhythm and the eternal recurrence of the "1." But, in addition, the "1" is within the oneness of time or, more philosophically, the *event* of time: the "One." There is no space here, nor is it the place to rehearse the dispute between Badiou and Deleuze on the presence or not of the One in the latter's account of the "virtuality" of the event; suffice it to say that we find Deleuze's promotion of a multiplicitous "global" vertical virtuality, actualized "locally" in the moment as difference/repetition to be utterly compelling and, more importantly, a perfect way into Purdie's groove.

We proposed a distinction at the very start of this book (and previously) between the start and the beginning, where the emphasis was primarily on the claim that something must start before it can begin. Non-simultaneous, the beginning "happens," is a "happening," only *after* an improvisation has already started. Indeed, such a temporal order is assumed where, to recall Lincoln Moines's point, a backing band jams for a while to get things *started*, preparing for the moment when, let us say, Gato walks onstage, and things *begin*. In actual fact, such a model of performance would be very familiar, albeit in a condensed and less improvised form, to Purdie, who did exactly this, year in and year out, for performers such as Aretha Franklin, King Curtis, and James Brown (just as Hendrix would have done the same for The Isley Brothers and Little Richard). That is why such "stars" are seen as the "main *event*," the event being when the performance truly *begins*.

With Purdie, regardless of whether he is a sideman or the main event, the beginning always seems to come before the start. For him it is not a question of starting something so much as *restarting* what has already happened, is happening, and is about to happen: pure Deleuze! Purdie says somewhere that drummers should never use a click track; that the drummer *is* the click track; and one gets a strong sense with him that, existentially, he is a ticking clock in human form, a kind of time-bomb of rhythm, continuously exploding on the horizontal plane of the actual. One sees him in a multitude of locations, endlessly restarting his demonstrations or master classes with the tick tick tick of some obscure ontological rhythm that he reconnects with the moment he starts playing. This tick tick tick is what he describes as "simplicity," and, as he adds, "the simplicity of it is that I can go anywhere I want," reminding us that, in essence, and overlooked by most of those who celebrate him, he is an improviser. It is overlooked because improvisation is almost always understood as the production of difference, experienced as a surprising diversity; whereas, for him: "no matter where I go with it [his "locomotion"] it's always the same."

So, back to the Falcon Club: Purdie starts *Mr. Magic* with his hallmark tick tick tick, and the band starts—he (or it) began eons ago—this start is, for him, just one of an infinite number of resumptions. Yes, it's always the same, but, to return to our earlier considerations, it is a different sameness, the rhythmic sameness of difference in itself. Washer contributes the necessary descending chord progression, thoughtfully, almost ponderously, but with impeccable "feel" and timing; knowing, one senses, that moments of thought, reflection, choice, action, and reaction can all take place within the space created by Purdie's "locomotion." The band is extraordinarily tight but in a strange way, a severe tightness (to be returned to below) that, through rigorous discipline, always remains well within its limits, albeit limits that seem to be constantly, if subtly changing. Needless to say, the first indication of this is in Purdie's first serious drum fill, which characteristically overruns its snap point, thereby rolling one rhythmic phrase over into another, thus reminding us of the "1" precisely by defying it. "Always remember where one is" does not mean that the "1" is always in the same place.

Counterintuitively, Purdie often speaks of "melody rhythm:" for him individual beats are the equivalent of notes in a melody, rhythm is a form of song, and drumming is a vocal art (as his own completely unselfconscious "singing" testifies). He loves the sound of his own voice; he never stops talking, even when he's not talking; this helps explain why his grooves, like his mouth, "doth runneth over," a form of excess that both pushes beyond, while remaining within the rhythm of the one voice, the voice of the multiplicitous one. We have frequently referred to *sotto voce*, the voice beneath/within the voice, an otherness that, contra Levinas, is contained *within* the same. Maybe that is what makes what we are calling a different sameness different. In this regard, a peculiarity of Purdie's playing is that, once a groove is established, he "intensifies himself," to use his own expression, by playing a virtual rather than his actual kit. It is noticeable when things get intense that he begins playing, and sometimes theatrically refrains from playing, nonexistent drums and cymbals, a kind of kit in-between the kit, and it is this that opens up the interior spaces of his improvisation and thus opens up a space for others to occupy: he is, in spite of his famed egotism, a totally altruistic, other-orientated drummer; remembering, of course, that the other is not only the other player.

As Deleuze says, the otherness of the virtual should not be confused with mere possibility or potentiality; the virtual is *real* and thus always actualizable in the moment, from one moment to the next, from one "locality" to the next. The reality of this otherness, the other space that eternally opens up the improvisation, is not imagined but *sensed*; just as the voice beneath the voice is sensed: heard but not heard. In typical fashion, Purdie does not mystify this peculiar alterity of his playing; he *explains* it and then *demonstrates* how it is achieved. An example: whether or not (as he claims) he invented the "ghost notes" that are a fundamental feature of his drumming, his account of their origin is both illuminating and yet, at the same time, deceptive. He describes how he arrived at such ghosting through an obsessive tapping out of rhythms with the fingers of both hands on the snare drum. Recognizing the complex rhythms produced by such a seemingly lowly form of play, the challenge for him was to translate this into drumming proper using sticks (sometimes in combination with his fingers when playing at low volume). Once achieved, the ghost notes create a sense of another complimentary rhythm running beneath the primary pulse: *sotto voce* again. The result both enriches the rhythmic texture and multiplies (at least by two, with a "backbeat") the propulsive force of the primary beat: "locomotion." Rooting this in the fingers and hands of the player, while accurate, is also a deception, in that it fails to account for the *sensation* of other rhythms when they are not actually there: the presence of absence, a Derridian might say. In describing the "invention" of "his" ghost notes,[6] there is a wonderful moment where he recalls the "accidental" moment when he "discovered that I got some air in my hi hat,"[*sic*], a telling remark that reveals the way in which Purdie is always thinking and working with the *space between* the drums and the space between the beats—the "air"—to evoke a virtual, multiplicitous rhythm that is heard but not physically played: not the fingers, hands, drums, or hi hat but the *senses* of those (including Purdie) who listen. As Purdie often suggests, the less he plays, the more he is able to invite others (and otherness) in: the essence of improvisation.

Yes, but what do we mean, what does *he* mean by "in?" Groove drummers like Purdie are often described as "in the pocket," which conjures notions of stability, precision, tightness, and, as the word suggests, *containment*. To be "in the groove" is to enter *into* the rhythm while also allowing it *into* one's body: usually as dance or some form of quasi-dance. However, this emphasis on tightness and containment, while completely legitimate, might inadvertently be responsible for the paucity of material (is there any?) on "in the pocket" improvisation, which, thinking about it, is probably what is being attempted here. On reflection, it might be illuminating to propose a link between the "severe style," the dialectic of precision and indecision, and the dialectic of unfixing and fixing considered elsewhere in this book. Without rehearsing the detail of those discussions now, we might briefly consider the following proposition: It is precisely because, as Purdie announces, he can "go anywhere he wants," that he has to be absolutely (or severely) precise about where he *will* go within this or that situation. Using Deleuze and Guattari's terms: because the space Purdie describes is a "smooth space," it is, in actuality, necessary for him to "striate" it in order gain the purchase necessary to originate, initiate, or (better) get back *into* the "locomotion" required for something to happen or begin. As an affirmation of chance, within the contingency of the performative moment, getting "*in* the pocket," while a form of containment, is not strict but severe— severity being the renunciation of what Hegel describes as all "accessories" and an absolute concentration on "the topic alone." Point is: the "topic" in an improvisatory situation is an inherently mobile series of local actualizations that require, at any moment, the making of precise but, at the same time, utterly contingent choices. If the precision conceals the contingency, then the improvisational dimension of the situation will remain concealed, unidentified, and unacknowledged, and this, one presumes, is the case with most "groove" music. If, on the other hand, the contingency conceals the precision, then we're back with "free improvisation," and the consequent celebration of freedom and improvisation respectively.

The wonderful thing about YouTube is not the vicarious experience of a now-dead liveness that it allows but the direct *sensation* of an event which, while absent (in the performance/video/everything), is nonetheless *present*; just as the ghost notes are present for those willing or able to enter the space created by this presence/absence.

The wonderful thing about Bernard Purdie is that his incessant actualization of the multiplicitous virtuality that pulses through his very being, manages to be both severe and joyous at the same time; metronomic, yet fluid, but in a strange way that obeys the tick tick tick while secretly setting, resetting, and unsettling the virtual clock: always to one o'clock, or (better) the clock of the multiplicitous "One."

9 Fixing and Unfixing Idioms and Non-Idioms: Developing Derek Bailey's Concept of Improvisation

As a prelude to the chapter on Derek Bailey later on in this book, here we will expand upon his well-known distinction between idiomatic and non-idiomatic improvisation.

From a Deleuzian perspective, it would seem that idiomatic improvisation closely approximates the repetition of the same, while free improvisation is essentially engaged with the repetition of difference. However, this doesn't work for one obvious reason: in Deleuze's view (and this, above all else, is an idea that this book is striving to comprehend), the repetition of difference is not successive but "coexistent." In light of this, both idiomatic *and* free improvisation, assuming that free improvisation hasn't *itself* become a recognizable idiom, would fall within the domain of the same rather than of difference. Indeed, we can refine this further; idiomatic improvisation can itself be subdivided into performances that improvise around or from a *fixed* originary point (score, script, standard, map, charts, instructions, etc.) and those that more freely explore a fixed but open idiomatic domain. And then there is free improvisation, which works without or outside of both the above. Viewed along a continuum, these different variants of improvised practice might be more accurately positioned as follows: fixed idiomatic; semifixed idiomatic; unfixed idiomatic; unfixed cross-idiomatic; fixed non-idiomatic; unfixed non-idiomatic.

Fixed Idiomatic Improvisation

Fixed idiomatic improvisation is attached to and firmly contained within the given idiom and structure of its occurrence. Here improvisation is more a sign of commitment to the idiom and the given work than it is an agenda of exploration or originality. Within this context, improvisation is closer to variation and extemporization, where the goal is not innovation but renovation, the refreshing and reaffirmation of an individual work or, indeed, a whole tradition as a mark of love and respect. Often understood as largely decorative in nature, such improvisation does nevertheless inject "life" into what might otherwise be moribund forms.

To give a precise illustrative example of this is actually quite difficult, given the continuity of overlapping forms being discussed here. What, on the face of it, might appear to be fixed forms reveal, on closer inspection, degrees of unfixity that resist the precision being sought—if only as a kind of semi-ironic thought experiment. It would also be tempting to cast considerable doubt on the authenticity of such improvisation, where the apparent invention of the improviser conceals the sterile repetition of stock formulas and pre-pared/"pre-digested" gestures of "subjectivity:" something resembling Adorno's dreaded "pseudo-individualism."

> Even though jazz musicians still improvise in practice, their improvisations have become so "normalized" as to enable a whole terminology to be developed to express the standard devices of individualization. . . . This pseudo-individualization is prescribed by the standardization of the framework. The latter is so rigid that the freedom that it allows for any sort of improvisation is severely delimited. Improvisations—passages where a spontaneous action of individuals is permitted ("swing it boys")—are confined within the walls of the harmonic and metric scheme.[1]

But the truth is, such pseudo-individualism can only result in pseudo-improvisation, and, thus, should not concern us any further. However, instead of using such revelations to castigate improvisers and their so-called improvisation we might, unlike Adorno, think again about both the actual location of such improvisation and its function within a truly fixed idiomatic structure or scheme. As can be seen, Adorno, as is customary, identifies improvisation with the moments of spontaneity "permitted" within the breaks and solos of jazz performance. What is more, he also identifies these moments with a show of "freedom" that he wastes no time in revealing as a standardized sham. This is familiar stuff, provoking different responses from different writers on, and defenders of, improvisation: pro and contra. But such debates, played out year on year, are always staged on the terrain already marked-out by Adorno (pseudo/real; free/unfree): so, whatever the outcome, he always wins, even when he "loses."

The suggestion being made here is that we might try and mark out a different space altogether, one where the improvisatory dimension of a performance is *not* located in the solos and breaks; and the function of the improvisation has nothing whatever to do with the expression of individual freedom, pseudo or otherwise. As an appetizer for the Miles Davis memoir (chapter 22) and the Cyndi Lauper case study (chapter 23) still to come, let us give a moment's thought to the latter's classic pop song *Time After Time*. Like the equally brilliant and transcendentally beautiful *True Colors*, the continuing impact and resonance of this song—undiminished by time—has much (almost everything?) to do with the essential moment of improvisation that, to be clear, is not played out *within* it as expressive, gestural, rhetorical content; rather, it is responsible for bringing the song *into being*, time after time, always for the first time. This is a song where the start and the beginning *are* simultaneous, every time: that's quite rare. Indeed, Lauper is a very rare breed of improviser that (until now) has existed completely undetected, secreted within the fixed idiomatic "walls" of the popular song so detested by Adorno. This, perhaps, is where our "different sameness" lurks, and so I will return to it in much greater detail in our case study. In the interim, think of Dolly Parton and *Jolene*: there's another one. And another: Kate Bush, *Running Up That Hill*. But the list, just for a change, is a very short one, although we would have to add Glenn Gould, the master of repetition and difference.

Semi-fixed Idiomatic Improvisation

Semi-fixed idiomatic improvisation remains attached to both an originary work/piece/composition and its idiom but is not firmly contained within or constrained by a fixed method or mode of occurrence. What this means in practice is that the moment of, or the space for, improvisation is not strictly delimited at the outset but is, rather, something determined by the dynamic and scope of the improvisation *itself*, in such a way that the originary work is unworked and thus successively distorted, disguised, or diversified. Here the presence of improvisation ensures that the wider potential, possibility, and, one might say, plurality of the selfsame is revealed as a moment of its originary identity. In other words, the improviser does not import otherness into the same in the form of external material that interrupts and disrupts the source, but makes manifest the difference that is *already there* as a moment of inception itself. Where the fixed idiomatic form of improvisation sketched above is seen to disguise or secrete its improvisational moment within the apparent fixity of a "finished" and polished work, like Brecht (who claimed that some performances of his plays "showed much, but failed to show the showing"),[2] we were primarily concerned above with the *fixing* of the fixed rather than the fixed itself, because that is where the presence of such secret or "clothed" improvisation can be detected.

With semi-fixed idiomatic improvisation, however, the opposite is the case. Here the emphasis is on the unfixing of the fixed: perhaps the archetypical form of improvisation in many cultures and in many idioms, from Scottish Ballads to DJ-ing. But in addition to this, there is also a more significant opposition: instead of valorizing the very unsecret process of unfixing (the showing rather than the shown), categorized as creativity, invention, playfulness, transgression, and so on, here we are grasping for what is perhaps an equally concealed improvisation within the unfixed itself. Or, to repeat the above, the difference (or unfixity) that is *already there* at the moment of inception.

There are endless examples of improvisation as a process of unfixing; indeed, that is how most improvisers learn to improvise in the first place. Such a common experience allows all of us to marvel at the ingenious, often outrageous "liberties" taken by improvisers, who appear to be able to float carelessly above and beyond the fixed parameters of a given piece while at the same time always knowing exactly where they are within the structural space/time that, beneath the surface movement and transformation, remains ever-present as an unmoving and untransformed source. Charlie Parker at his peak probably remains unequaled in this form of improvisation; and, as an aside, his mastery, while undisputed, has very little to do with the dialogical approach already mentioned. On the contrary, his primary attention was never on his fellow improvisers but on the fixed, originary source (standard, song, composition, work) and the performative process of unfixing (himself, his instrument, his sound/voice, licks, his knowledge and virtuosity): a form of solitude, or what Miles Davis tellingly describes as "isolation:"

> Bird didn't teach me much as far as music goes. I loved playing with him, but you couldn't copy the shit he did because it was so original . . . See, Bird was a soloist. He had his own thing. He was, like isolated.[3]

The consequences of this isolation on his band members are noted by Miles later in his autobiography; a welcome reminder that nondialogical improvisation has its own "terrifying" beauty:

> Bird often used to play in short, hard bursts of breath; . . . so then,
> sometimes Max Roach would find himself between the beat. And
> I wouldn't know what the fuck Bird was doing because I wouldn't
> have never heard it before. Poor Duke Jordan and Tommy Potter,
> they'd just be there lost as motherfuckers—like everybody else, only
> more lost. When Bird played like that, it was like hearing music for
> the first time.[4]

Clearly, in Miles's view, Parker had "attitude" (the essence of jazz for Miles),
one that resulted in a headlong approach to improvisation that left everyone
to their own devices, literally "on their own," with only the fixed source as
a guide, if only they could find or re-find it. If and when they did, it was
as if transformed, not the given origin that has always already started, but
"another beginning" that, as Miles confirms, was like hearing music for the
first time. Elsewhere Miles describes Parker's improvisations as turning the
music "inside out," which captures well the process of unfixing that concerns us here—but only partially.

We will now return to a consideration of a form of semi-fixed idiomatic
improvisation that does not unfix the fixed through a processual unfurling
that reveals endless possibilities *a la* Parker, Sonny Rollins, Dizzy Gillespie,
Bud Powell, and so on, but makes manifest instead the "virtual" unfixity
or difference that pre-exists the work's "actualization" as a "work" or *this*
work, song, piece. And here we are drawing on Deleuze's vocabulary, to
which we will return in much greater detail later. Instead of turning the
piece "inside out," it would be better to describe this alternative or, more
accurately, other improvisatory form as turning the piece "back to front."
"Back to front" meaning that instead of being propelled out of an existing
and fixed work into a kaleidoscope of possibilities awaiting realization, such
improvisation creates, instead, a sense of an existing work as a work *yet
to come*; a virtual work that could have been actualized in any number of
ways; a fact that such a mode of improvisation allows us to sense again, as
if witnessing the uncertain becoming or beginning of the work—the uncertain certitude of an artwork's origin. Think Thelonious Monk. Especially
think of *Thelonious Monk Plays Duke Ellington* (1955) where, rather than
using the Ellington songs as source material or as a resource, Monk (as
with Parker, but differently) allows us to hear such familiar material as if
for the first time; not through novel or "outrageous" (as Miles describes
Parker) extemporizations but something closer to an act of reconstruction. Indeed, without wishing to slip into a facile quasi-poststructuralism,
Monk genuinely does represent something approximating a "deconstruc-
tive" improviser, especially if it is recalled that Derrida's central project was

not destructive at all but the affirmation of the buried difference(s), con-
tingencies, and arbitrariness secreted within the false binaries of Western
thought. Following Heidegger, Derrida often returns to the motif of listening, of developing an "ear" for the space that is both outside and within
the closed structures;[5] similarly Monk's legendary use of "space," is not,
as is common, simply a dialogical/empathetic laying-out to allow others
to participate; rather, it is the construction of a space through a series of
improvisatory acts that progressively demarcate the terrain as if in the dark
or half-light: feeling one's way around as if for the first time. It is ironic (and
slightly ridiculous) that one critic remarks negatively on the "hesitancy" of
Monk's playing on the *Duke Ellington* album. That is precisely the point:
a return to the beginning, the inceptual moment, the coming into being of
the work, with all of the hesitancy that accompanies the creative act—both
Ellington's and now Monk's—is how and why his improvisation turns the
music back to front.

Unfixed Idiomatic Improvisation

Unfixed idiomatic improvisation is not rooted in an originary work/tem-
plate but adheres only to the more general parameters of an idiom. An
idiom that, for whatever reason(s)—history, culture, aesthetic taste, age,
peer pressure, pure accident, force, conformism, lack of imagination, or
whatever—places a limit, whether self-imposed or not, on what is likely
to happen, not only within this or that improvisation but, more often than
not, for the whole lifetime of an individual improviser—think about it. In a
sense, here the periphery and center become indistinguishable, or perhaps
the periphery *becomes* the center. What this means in practice is that it is
now the idiom as a whole, rather than individual works within the idiom,
that is subject to repetition. Remaining within idiomatic limits, such improvisation wanders and drifts, but is not nomadic; meaning that although
the center is decentered, the periphery remains intact and un-displaced. In
other words, the idiom provides the improviser with a home and dwelling
place. Unlike semi-unfixed idiomatic improvisation, where we witness the
repetition of the same difference (diversity), here instead it is the *already
diversified* idiomatic field that is *diversely* repeated, which, contrary to what
might be claimed for such improvisation, results in the repetition of what
might be described as a same sameness. This might help explain why such
improvisation is often characterized by a noticeable homogeneity, albeit at
the level of idiom rather than work, as with fixed idiomatic improvisation:
all jazz standards, blues, bluegrass, funk, country, rap pieces sound (as individual works) much the same as any other, just as all unfixed drifting within

an idiom quickly attains a plateau of sameness that, to be clear, can none-theless produce improvisation of great beauty and intensity.

Obviously, and as before, there are significant overlaps that, admittedly, threaten the precision and, indeed, the usefulness of the improvisational forms being considered here. For example, while bands such as The Grate-ful Dead or Cream fall into the category of the semi-fixed idiomatic form above, given that their improvisations always take place within the param-eters of particular songs, no matter how extended; nevertheless, for vast tracts of time during, for example, a Dead concert (which can last any-where up to six hours), it is the idiom rather than the song that supports and guides the improvisation. And this fact is made even clearer by the fact that throughout a performance, the Dead shift through idioms, embarking on often quite subtle journeys of "deterritorialization" that, among other things, demonstrate how freedom-from or a freeing-from the work remains nevertheless bound to the idiom, thereby mixing autonomy and heteronomy in a strange brew of unfree freedom.

The reference work here, and precursor of much to follow, is undoubt-edly Ornette Coleman's *Free Jazz* (1961), which, apart from some brief, composed interjections or "fanfares" by the horns, is completely impro-vised over a forty-minute stretch that is particularly noteworthy in its radi-cal disruption of the subjective expressionist (Adorno would say "pseudo-individualist") jazz soloing tradition. Although Ornette describes this recording as a "collective improvisation," a tag that overdetermines much of the critical response to the album, it would be more accurate to think of it as a *multiplicitous* improvisation, an "assemblage" or "body without organs," to think with Deleuze and Guattari, rather than a communicative community. This can be witnessed not only horizontally at the point of actualization, but also vertically, as a virtual event. To explain, although revolutionary in its eschewing of a fixed idiomatic structure, the individual improvisations on *Free Jazz* still resemble typical jazz solos, only extended and radicalized. These lengthy solos are responsible for what might be called the searching quality of the music, something brought to its pinnacle in Col-trane's late work. Unlike Coltrane's though, Ornette's approach encourages constant interruptions of such singular striving by other singularities, clus-ters, or indeed the totality. Such interruptions, although sometimes dialogi-cal and collective in the familiar sense, are also frequently *disruptive*; they remind us that, at the point of actualization, the idiom itself (in this case jazz) is characterized by an infinite difference that such temporal, horizontal strands of improvisation bring to our attention as linear exploration and/or expression. While it is true that such a multiplicitous approach is evident in other bands (think of Mingus, Cecil Taylor, or even of Jon Zorn's *Cobra*),

Ornette's use of a double quartet, one performing in the left and one in the right stereo channel, is much more than an augmentation of the personnel, but represents, rather, a profound augmentation of the very concept of improvisation. This can be identified in two main areas: first, as the creation of a very specific, improvised *situation* (a recurring theme in this book), the improvisation begins long before the performance/recording itself. *Prior* to the improvisation, Ornette is already involved in a vertical journey of imagination up and down the register of the event of the jazz idiom itself, prior to its actualization on the horizontal plane of performance. The infinite multiplicity of the event of jazz can only be glimpsed locally as, to use Badiou's terminology, that which is "named" within the situation:

> Beyond the proper names retained as significant illustrations of the configuration or as the "dazzling" subjective points of its generic trajectory, there is always a virtually infinite quantity of subject points—minor, ignored, redundant, and so on—that are no less part of the immanent truth whose being is provided by the artistic configuration.[6]

Eric Dolphy, Charlie Haden, Don Cherry, Ed Blackwell . . . *ad infinitum* . . . these are the "proper names," "the 'dazzling' subjective points" that, on this occasion and in this situation, Ornette *chooses*, remembering that, following Heidegger, all choice takes place within the prior *decisiveness* of the event of Being, or truth (Badiou), or difference (Deleuze).

In addition, and second: the doubling of the quartet creates two parallel, albeit overlapping, planes of improvisation that, quite apart from what might be achieved in terms of "consistency," to use Deleuze's term, or "purposiveness," to use Kant's, also function as what might be described as a form of mutual othering that, ultimately, is less concerned with the differences between one quartet and the other, and more concerned with the other of this localized otherness figured as duality, dialectic, or dialogue—the in-between that points back to the infinite multiplicity of the event that is always present virtually, albeit as an absence: *sotto voce* (again).

Unfixed Cross-Idiomatic Improvisation

In unfixed cross-idiomatic improvisation, improvisers attempt to wander from one idiom to another, recognizing, perhaps, the futility of trying to mark and unmark space—all spaces are always already marked. Jazz-rock represents one classic example, although there are of course much more complex crossings, involving a multiplicity of idioms: think of Bill Frisell's

Intercontinentals (jazz, country, African, blues . . .); or one could go back to the sixties and listen to Carla Bley's monumental *Escalator Over the Hill* which mixes free jazz, raga, cabaret, show music, rock, and synthesized music, and includes beautiful playing from Gato Barbieri (just to salvage his reputation after our memoir). But even here there is little to suggest that the borders between one idiom and another are ever radically displaced in such exercises; on the contrary, if anything, they are reaffirmed. As Bataille observes, transgression always depends on the transgressed law remaining *in place*.[7] In truth, jazz-rock has rarely transcended the binary of jazzers trying (usually unsuccessfully) to be rockers (e.g., Miles Davis) or rockers trying (usually unsuccessfully) to be jazzers (e.g., Jeff Beck): the examples have been chosen for the true magnificence of their "failure." Miles, using a wah-wah pedal and desperately trying to look like Hendrix, or John McLaughlin playing a twin-necked Gibson SG (and also heavy on the wah-wah), donning cheesecloth and hanging out with Carlos Santana does not change the fact that their dwelling place is and always will be jazz. As Robert Quine says of Miles's playing on one of his great, ground-breaking jazz-rock projects *Jack Johnson*: "Miles is basically playing just Miles. He's not playing rock 'n roll solos on that record, he's playing really great trumpet on a jazz level . . . everybody's playing well on a jazz level. But it's still blatantly a rock 'n roll album." As Bill Milkowski continues, "Historically, *Jack Johnson* was the first album where Miles stepped over the line that separated the rock and the jazz camps."[8] Yes, he crossed the line, but he crossed the line as a jazzer, and the line remained and still remains firmly in place. And at the level of repetition, the result is the same as above: the repetition of a same sameness that, in music at least, has a tendency to deliver this sameness as modal or monotonic "grooves" . . . and grooves, as we all know, are what you get stuck in.[9] But there is certainly a lot to be said for being groovy, so this is in no way intended as a critique. There is no critique in this book (although Carlos Santana is a temptation): critique is for the critics.

Fixed Non-idiomatic Improvisation

Now this is a tricky one, not least because, as George Lewis has argued so cogently, the act of liberating oneself from the constraints of specific idioms, jazz in particular, might also (albeit often unwittingly) result in what Lewis describes as the "erasure" of, in this case, an alternative black aesthetic that might challenge the often unspoken Eurocentrism of much non-idiomatic improvisation.[10] Interestingly, he does not accuse Derek Bailey of this.[11] At the risk of being part of this self-same culture of erasure, that discussion cannot be taken up here: George Lewis's work remains the best reference point for this.

When suggesting "non-idiomatic improvisation" as an alternative to "free improvisation," Derek Bailey clearly still has the actual practices of free improvisation in mind. So to suggest that non-idiomatic improvisation might be fixed would be to suggest that freedom itself could be fixed, which certainly seems like a contradiction in terms. So does this make any sense? One approach might be a return to the idea that so-called free improvisation has *itself* become an idiom that, as such, contradicts the autonomy claims of its perpetrators. If this is indeed the case (questionable), does that render the notion of non-idiomatic improvisation redundant? Not really, all it would do is add one more category to the list of idioms to be avoided. But if we accept for the sake of argument that free improvisation *has* freed itself from all recognized idioms without thereby creating an idiom of its own, how is it possible to introduce fixity into this emancipatory moment? Following Isaiah Berlin,[12] one might make a distinction between negative and positive freedom: freedom-from and freedom-to, respectively. Clearly, to be free from all given idioms is the liberatory moment here, and this is certainly something non-idiomatic improvisation can claim for itself without too much risk of contradiction. But more problematical, as always, is the enactment of positive freedom: freedom to do what exactly? As with the celebrated "emancipation of dissonance" in twentieth-century composition,[13] dissonance itself, or in this case the non-idiomatic, become charged and laden with the task of *avoiding* at all cost consonance or idioms, respectively. Arnold Schoenberg describes the situation as being a search for an alternative form of "comprehensibility," one that does not rely on tonality, any more than non-idiomatic improvisation can rely on given idioms to render it comprehensible:

> The term *emancipation of dissonance* refers to comprehensibility, which is considered equivalent to the consonance's comprehensibility. . . . By *avoiding* the establishment of a key modulation is excluded, since modulation means leaving an established tonality and establishing *another* tonality.[14]

It is in this analogous sense that both free atonality and free improvisation are fixed and curtailed: they are only free to do what is not prohibited, and thus neither is absolutely autonomous. Indeed, as is well known, in the case of Schoenberg at least, the radicalism of his atonal and twelve-tone compositions is accompanied by an inherent conservatism that retained much of the classical/romantic idiom: hence the frustration of some of his students when confronted with him as teacher and with his equally conservative *Harmonielehre*.[15] Given the above aporia of freedom, perhaps Bailey was right to spurn the beauty of the "free" for the inelegance of the "non-idiomatic"; needless to say, not many appear to have followed him in this direction. This is a pity because, in fact, a shift into this clunky terminology, and our additions to it, does help to explain some peculiarities of free improvisation, particularly as contrasted with the *laissez-faire* grooving of so much unfixed idiomatic improvisation, often quite erroneously considered to be a close relative. The *avoidance* of the idiomatic, like the avoidance of tonality in atonal music, requires great agility, discipline, and massive powers of renunciation: the gravitational pull of the idiomatic being almost insanely irresistible. As Nietzsche proclaims, the strongest will of all is the will *not* to will, and not to will the idiomatic certainly does require such strength, coupled with vigilance and supreme concentration. The fact that this might not be in evidence to the audience or the performers in no way changes the situation: this is the way it is. And this explains why the joyousness, exploration, and grooviness of the other forms of improvisation here give way and return us to *severity*. And, to reiterate, for Hegel, the severe style wastes no time with "accessories" but concentrates all attention on "the topic alone."[16] In other words, improvisations, rather than being the means and medium by which an idiom is perpetuated and engaged with, now become *the* topic—exclusive and excluding ends in themselves. And as with all Hegelian severity, it is precisely the *absence* of clearly determined belief systems, in this case idioms, that requires determinacy to be transposed into the formal articulation of any given topic. Without such severity, improvisation will either be unsustainable or return to the complacency and comfort of one or more of the awaiting idioms. And just to say, in conclusion, severity does not have to appear or sound severe in the colloquial sense; the issue is rather the choice of topic, the consistency of its realization, and the rigor and discipline necessary for this to determine the outcome on a case-by-case basis. The most luscious work imaginable can still be a product of the severe style.

Unfixed Non-idiomatic Improvisation

We here confront the most speculative or, perhaps, the most imaginary and misguided aspect of this book. Only a few more uncertain steps can be made at this point, as a continuation of the ground-testing necessary to see if anything sensible or believable emerges. To begin though, one thing is clear: the unfixing of the non-idiomatic improviser cannot be equivalent to simply removing or relaxing the boundaries between the non-idiomatic and the idiomatic. All that would do is return us and the improviser to one or another of the forms of improvisation discussed above. So what other form of unfixing might there be? To start drawing on Deleuze again here, perhaps it is possible to conceive of unfixing not in terms of an untethering, which would allow improvisers to roam freely from the non-idiomatic into one idiomatic territory or another—a mode of autonomous succession that we are still only partway through considering—but as a *vertical* movement that, as he says of nomadic thought, can take place "on the spot." Where Deleuze describes this as a moment of intensity, suggesting a burrowing down into the displaced center, one might also identify a move to the displaced periphery that is *ironic* rather than intense, closer to Derrida's "mental reservation," inside but looking out. In this view, unfixed and fixed non-idiomatic improvisation would be identical, although absolutely different—the different sameness that keeps returning in our discussion, but which remains a "secret." Perhaps at the heart of this is the difference between irony and commitment within the non-idiomatic realm: irony unfixes, commitment fixes. But, to be clear, irony unfixes through an infinite series of fixes: *that* is the "secret."

> The repetition of dissymmetry is hidden within symmetrical ensembles of effects . . . everywhere the Other in the repetition of the same. This is the secret, the most profound repetition . . . forms itself by disguising itself.[17]

Deleuze, like many continental philosophers, is fond of referencing Borges, so it is no surprise that he mentions the short story "Pierre Menard, Author of the Quixote," where one can read the following (this is Borges's text):

> It is a revelation to compare Menard's *Don Quixote* with Cervantes's The latter, for example, wrote (part one, chapter nine):
>
> > . . . truth, whose mother is history, rival of time, depositary of deeds, witness of the past, exemplar and adviser to the present, and the future's counsellor.
>
> Written in the seventeenth century, written by the "lay genius" Cervantes, this enumeration is a mere rhetorical praise of history. Menard, on the other, writes:
>
> > . . . truth, whose mother is history, rival of time, depositary of deeds, witness of the past, exemplar and adviser to the present, and the future's counsellor.

History, the *mother* of truth: the idea is astounding. Menard, a contemporary of William James, does not define history as an enquiry into reality but as its origin. Historical truth, for him, is not what has happened; it is what we judged to have happened. The final phrases—*exemplar and adviser to the present, and the future's counsellor*—are brazenly pragmatic.

The contrast in style is also vivid. The archaic style of Menard— quite foreign, after all—suffers from a certain affectation. Not so that of his forerunner, who handles with ease the current Spanish of his time.[18]

After Cervantes, after "Menard," after Borges, after Deleuze, now our own repetition; each one the same, each one absolutely different. Where Deleuze speaks of repetition, we speak of improvisation, but like him, we suspect that secreted here might be the most profound improvisation of all. Indeed, typing out, yet again, Borges's words might be first moment of improvisation in this book so far.

10   A Different Sameness: Borges and Deleuze on Repetition

As a reminder, the task Borges has his fictional character Pierre Menard set himself is the writing of *Don Quixote*, but a writing *not* conceived as a rewriting. This is how Borges introduces the idea:

> He did not want to compose another *Quixote*—which is easy—but the *Quixote itself*. Needless to say, he never contemplated a mechanical transcription of the original; he did not propose to copy it. His admirable intention was to produce a few pages which would coincide—word for word and line for line—with those of Miguel de Cervantes.[1]

Echoing Nietzsche and prefiguring Deleuze, Borges in this story recognizes that repetition (or the recurrence) of the same is in essence a movement whereby that which returns contains difference, in fact difference of the two distinct types encountered above: first, the *same difference*, whereby the same inceptual moment (in this case, of writing *Don Quixote*) returns along with all the contingency and thus openness and possibility that such a moment contains as its essential futurity—"a book *not yet* written." It is this that allows Menard to consider the task: "The *Quixote* is a contingent book; the *Quixote* is unnecessary. I can premeditate writing it, I can write it, without falling into a tautology."[2] In other words, the task is not to copy, imitate, or reproduce the work but to reaffirm the contingent moment of the work's *inception* and the spontaneity that accompanies it, which returns as an essential moment of the recurrence of the same. To "*be* Miguel de Cervantes," as Menard describes it, is to inhabit and reanimate this spontaneity and all of the difference that it implies: "I have taken on the mysterious duty of reconstructing literally his spontaneous work."[3]

The second type of difference that we might associate with the *Pierre Menard* story concerns not the *same difference* noted above but, conversely, the *different sameness* that we have been struggling with throughout. As suggested, Borges is prefiguring Deleuze here in suggesting both a horizontal and a vertical concept of improvisation, the first associated, as we have seen, with "actualization"; the second, with "virtuality." We need to repeat this passage yet again so as to make the necessary links between *Pierre Menard* and our earlier discussion of Lol Coxhill:

> One [form of repetition] is bare, the other clothed: one is repetition of parts, the other of the whole; one involves succession, the other coexistence; one is actual, the other virtual; one is horizontal, the other vertical.[4]

If, in addition to his fictional role as an author of repetition, we recast *Pierre Menard* as an improviser, then it is possible to imagine two modes of improvisation related to two modes of repetition and two forms of forgetting. To "forget difference"[5] as Borges suggests, in order to think, create, improvise, in the first instance requires a forgetting of the reiterative moment of rewriting in order to remember the iterative moment of actualization, whereby the inceptual spontaneity returns as the same difference inhabiting the original virtuality of the work: its beginning. As Deleuze observes, this takes place at the "bare" level of a succession of parts. In other words, as a becoming but, crucially, one shielded from the horrors of memoriousness by the originary sameness of the virtual idea that, as *Pierre Menard* demonstrates, must be both remembered *and* forgotten, just as Menard must simultaneously remember Cervantes in order to forget him and be Menard:

> To be, in some way, Cervantes and reach the *Quixote* seemed less arduous to him—and, consequently, less interesting—than to go on being Pierre Menard and reach the *Quixote* through the experiences of Pierre Menard.[6]

To "reach" the same sameness through, respectively, remembering and forgetting an originary work is, Menard suggests, essentially not a difficult task except for one small detail: "I should only have to be immortal to carry it out." But conceived as an improvisation, where it is the working rather than the "work" that is the issue, and where the repetition of the same *difference* is the goal, the question of immortality becomes redundant: this task *can* be and *is* actualized "in the moment." And such forward repetition, understood here in Deleuzian terms as the actualization of the virtual, completely removes from repetition the burden of resemblance, replacing it instead with a performative principle that describes perfectly the particular becoming of our imaginary Borgesian improviser.

> Actualization breaks with resemblance as a process no less than it does with identity as a principle. Actual terms never resemble the singularities they incarnate. In this sense, actualization or differenciation is always a *genuine creation* . . . . For a . . . virtual object, to be actualized is to create divergent lines which correspond to— without resembling—a virtual multiplicity. The virtual possesses the reality *of a task to be performed.*[7]

In this instance then, it is *Don Quixote* that is the "task to be performed," the repetition not of a work but of a work yet to become a work, "a book not yet written," and thus the repetition of a decision to make a work, an improvisation of premeditation that also recalls the Nietzschean "threshold" of the moment where the "it was" is willed again—"thus I willed it."

Returning now to Deleuze's idea of the virtual with a view to imagining Menard not only as an improviser but as a "vertical" improviser, it will be necessary to try and grasp more firmly the notion of a *different sameness*. This shift again takes us away from the more familiar terrain of what Deleuze describes as *diversity* (same difference) into the heart of difference and repetition itself, a place where one would not expect to find an improvisatory dimension. As before, Borges appears to prefigure Deleuze in his recognition of the fact that, prior to the actualization of the virtual as a "task to be performed," the virtual is *already* multiplicitous and thus *already* the embodiment of difference and repetition, albeit secreted within the "clothes" of co-existence and the holistic illusions of the whole. We have been culturally conditioned to think of improvisation as a successive performative event at the level of the part, as that which takes place *within* the whole. But Borges, ostensibly through Menard but really through his own singular writing, suggests a manner of improvising that, in operating at the level of the whole, is in danger of going unrecognized and thus unremarked.

So, where the above has concentrated on the becoming of the work made possible by the forgetting of difference and a reaching out for the same, understood as (to use Blanchot's terminology) the book "to come," we now need to consider what Borges has to say about the coexistent differences within the work itself, understood as a multiplicitous whole. Observing that Menard's text is "more subtle" than Cervantes's, he continues by remarking on the richness of the former's *Quixote*:

> Cervantes's text and Menard's are verbally identical, but the second is almost infinitely richer. (More ambiguous, his detractors will say, but ambiguity is richness).[8]

A transition is in evidence here; now it is the reading rather than the writing of the work that becomes the focus for Borges. Unlike the writer, the reader is denied direct access to the endless improvisations that, as a succession of parts, must be erased and forgotten for the sake of the whole.

> He multiplied draft upon draft, revised tenaciously and tore up thousands of manuscript pages. He did not let anyone examine these drafts and took care they should not survive him. In vain have I tried to reconstruct them.[9]

In this vain attempt to reconstruct the secret actualizations that are "actively forgotten" by the improviser in the drafting, redrafting, and then erasure necessary for the creation of a work, we witness the center of gravity shifting from the writer to the reader, and improvisation shifting from the part to the whole. We begin to see this the moment the narrator begins to engage with Menard's *Quixote* as a work rather than as a "futile" and "impossible" task. At this point it becomes evident that the rich ambiguity/ambiguous richness of the work is not a function of the improvisations secreted within it but an essential difference actualized by the reader, not through the successiveness of reading but, to borrow an idea from Paul Ricoeur, through the "appropriation" of the text as a "world."[10] But, to be clear, the appropriation of a text is not, for Ricoeur, an act of possession; on the contrary, to enter the world of the text through an act of reading is to become dispossessed:

> Thus appropriation ceases to appear as a kind of possession, as a way of taking hold of. . . . It implies instead a moment of dispossession of the narcissistic *ego*.[11]

Instead of the crazed possessiveness experienced by Funes as the retention of everything and anything, the meaningful interpretation of a text and appropriation of its "world" are only achieved through a creative/interpretive process of forgetting that Ricoeur describes, following Gadamer, in terms of "play," a very familiar term for improvisers. But here it is used differently. It is not the writer or the reader who play in the active sense; rather, they are both *in play* within the "world" opened by the text—they are *played*. This is a useful model of reading, not least because it suggests a way of approaching the improvisatory nature of reading without having to fully invest in the dialogical "world" of improvisation.

> Appropriation does not imply any direct congeniality of one soul with another. Nothing is less intersubjective or dialogical than the encounter with a text.[12]

To enter the "world" opened by a text is, then, to forget oneself and the other; it is to put aside the distinction between writer and reader (and their different modes of play) and to recognize or remember that the play of the text is precisely the vertical movement of the differences "coexisting" within it. To imagine a Borgesian form of improvisation requires the recognition not only of the becoming, but also of the *being* of the work or text. While it is easy to see considerable improvisatory potential in the repetition of the same difference, understood as infinite becoming, a more radical and certainly more fugitive form of improvisation is again all-too-faintly illuminated here.

But first let us try and make it clear what Borges is actually doing—in particular, what he is doing as an improviser. In fact he tells us himself in the last paragraph of "Pierre Menard," and it is indeed an improvisational form of reading rather than writing, although as Borges's own work testifies, one can follow the other—but in that order.

> Menard . . . has enriched, by means of a new technique, the halting and rudimentary art of reading; this technique is that of the deliberate anachronism and the erroneous attribution. This technique, whose applications are infinite, prompts us to go through the *Odyssey* as if it were posterior to the *Aeneid* and the book *Le Jardin du Centaure* of Madame Henri Bachelier as if it were by Madame Henri Bachelier. This technique fills the most placid works with adventure.[13]

The key is in the last word—"adventure"—whereby what is "to come" is separated from the becoming of the not-yet and the non-being of the unknown, and installed in the very *being* of the work as the already-there. This, as we have seen, is how Menard himself works. He does not copy the *Quixote*; he *improvises* it through an act of false self-attribution that demands the forgetting rather than the remembrance of Cervantes and his text. Borges does the same; he falsely attributes Cervantes's text (or sections of it) to Menard in order to have his own adventures within the vertical difference of the virtual as a demonstration of how the same text can open an infinity of "worlds." But are we to read Menard's *Quixote* as Menard's text or *as if* it were by Menard, as Borges suggests we might read Madame Henri Bachelier? Well, of course we should, given that Menard is a fictional character, but what about Borges's *own* text, should we read this *as if* it were by Jorge Luis Borges? Indeed, could we go further than this? Could we read this text *as if* it was us reading the text? What kind of world would open before us if we did? Probably one not unlike the one Borges tirelessly describes, and one that is usually described as "imaginary";[14] but the truth is, such a proliferation of "as ifs" creates an *ironic* rather than an imaginary world, and to use irony as a method of improvisation would seem, once again, to be the conclusion to be drawn from this.

For all of the richness and subtlety of his thought, Paul Ricoeur lacks one thing: irony. In common with Heidegger and Gadamer, from whom he draws heavily, Ricoeur offers us an account of textual appropriation and hermeneutic interpretation that seems largely oblivious to the ruses of reading suggested and encouraged by Borges, who, like Barthes, is primarily interested in the *pleasure* rather than the meaning of the text. While there is, no doubt, room for improvisation in the hermeneutical appropriation of a text, this very much takes place *within* the "world" or "worlds" opened by the text at the level of a particularly *receptive* mode of reading: something close to Heidegger's "hearkening." As Ricoeur writes,

> To understand is not to project oneself into the text; it is to receive an enlarged self from the apprehension of proposed worlds which are the genuine object of interpretation.[15]

Refreshing though this is in its break with the naïve dialogics of some hermeneutics and, in addition, its break with highly suspect philosophies of the subject, this approach to reading might itself be considered naïve to the extent that it assumes that the reader is simply (Heidegger-fashion) "thrown" into the "world" of the text. *How* we got into the text, *why* and *where from* are ignored by the non-ironic hermeneutist. Indeed, the very idea that a self might enter the "world" of the text in search of something *other* than understanding would almost certainly be considered absurd by the whole Heideggerian tradition of which Ricoeur is a part. But let us imagine a mode of reading that is specifically *about* the projection of the self into the text, a reading intent on adventure rather than understanding, the latter being consistently over-hyped and overrated. Would it not be possible to consider an act of projection that functioned completely outside of the "oneself"–"enlarged-self" dialectic that governs Ricoeur's thought? What is being suggested is an adventure of reading, and a form of writing could follow, that improvises the very self that is projected into the text, thus opening a world that neither reflects narcissistically nor enlarges hermeneutically a *given* self, but *creates* a "self" as an ironic gesture that transform the "as if" into a "task to be performed."

11 Memoir: Bluegrass in Cheltenham

I have only seen the Del McCoury band play live once, but I remember it well. They were on tour in the UK backing Steve Earle, and it was Earle I had gone to see. As with Lol Coxhill, I hadn't heard of them—another happy accident. It was at the Cheltenham Town Hall, May 23, 1999. Given the ostentation of so many performers, and particularly within the context of Cheltenham's Regency gentility, I was amused to overhear the backstage manager taking the band's post-gig "dinner" order from a very hairy roadie: KFC all round! I didn't feel the urge to encourage Steve Earle to adopt a healthier diet; he has a menacing edge.

Anyway, as I remember it, the band were playing warm-up for the great menacing man before he came on and initially played solo, being joined again later by the McCourys. As with most warm-up bands, they really only provided background music for the alcohol-distracted pre-gig bar crowd, of which I was one (although I was driving, so only drank one bottle of vodka). It was only two-thirds through their set (and the bottle) that I drifted into the concert hall and began to take notice. I very quickly discovered there was a great deal to watch.

Why is it I say "I remember when I first *saw* them?" Why "*watch*?" Why do we *hear* recordings but *see* performances? Perhaps this is just an insignificant form of words, but if forms of words are "forms of life," as Wittgenstein suggests, maybe there is something in this difference—something lived. I hope so, be-cause, as I've already claimed, improvisation should be *seen* as well as *heard*, something which I'm sure many musicians and improvisers would dispute: they can be a menacing bunch too. But that's too bad, not least because it removes from any discussion what I believe to be one essential dimension of all improvisation: the act of *showing*.

So what did I see, what was shown?

Picture this: at the center of the stage is one solitary microphone. It is set at an optimum height, one that is not perfect for any of the players (of which there are five), but allows each of them to find sufficient amplification when they need it to improvise. Note that, apart from the main vocal, only improvisation is deemed worthy of close-mic-ing, for the rest, each musi-cian remains in the background. In fact, the microphone is itself an essen-tial component of the improvisations. Del (the father and leader, full name Delano) is of above-average height but not a giant (which is just as well, as this wouldn't work, and I would have to rewrite this memoir); thus he has to lean forward and stoop slightly to sing but raise his guitar up to play solo, which he rarely does, or interject a fill, which he frequently does. Thus, even in Del's singular case, I witnessed, visually, a very particular use of or, I would say, creation of space—"*espacement*"—that was and is an essential dimension not only of his performative strategy, but also of his style and manner of improvising. Stoop down low, stand up tall; forward, back, and then to one side, all movement designed or developed to initiate and facili-tate what might be called a "visual ethics of the microphone" that underpins the unfurling spectacle: a musicality of space. So, Del stood and sang; he has a high tenor voice that only really works in Bluegrass; in just about any other context it would sound weedy and weak, but here it sounded plaintive; fragile, yes, but a strong, intense fragility that seemed to draw from a well with a depth that is all the more powerful for being absent from the voice itself: a deleted but not erased profundity that remains beneath the voice (*sotto voce*)—yes, that again.

But the real fascination for me, standing in the slowly swelling audience in Cheltenham, was not so much the sound of the music (it sounded like bluegrass) but the visual choreography of the performance, the deft utiliza-tion of space that literally, physically, performatively revealed the under-lying structure of whichever song was being played. It was almost as if each piece of music had its own unique floor plan within and around which the composed and the improvised elements were staged. Interestingly, by enact-ing the music in this way, the performance began to *show* me something I had been unaware of: that every piece of music, whether, as in this case, traditional or not, idiomatic or not, fixed or not, is a fluid, expanding and contracting space; one that breathes in and out, one that sees itself and can be seen, but which Del himself does not have to see: his eyes were closed much of the time, no doubt imagining the space he was both creating and occupying simultaneously. He didn't need to see what was going on; he was inside it, he *was* it—he just had to show. And it was a great show, not least because it brought me to an understanding of why we call such a performance a "show."

Even before I talk of the music then, of the players and the brilliance of their playing, and the ways in which such fixed idiomatic improvisation is played out, it became evident to me on that night back in 1999 that, strangely, the visual experience of improvisation was far from being a secondary, decorative issue alone. On the contrary, without this semi-somnambulant *spatial* choreography, I don't think I would have recognized the analogous differential and differencing duration within the successive *temporality* governing the repetitive unfolding of a work and a tradition so deeply known. Indeed, perhaps it is this knowingness that produces that temporal equivalent of *"espacement"* necessary to produce improvisation within such apparently tight and inflexible parameters.

12   Case Study: The Del McCoury Band

For Heidegger and Benjamin, . . . tradition was not the smooth and uninter-
rupted transmission of the past to the present but a handing over of tradition
fraught with danger and risk.

Howard Caygill[1]

What is *heard* at a Del McCoury Band gig is the "handing
down" or "handing over" of a musical tradition, the transmission of the past into the present and the future: the repetition
of the same. There is no question of that and no doubt that
this is the accepted perception of both the band and its obsessive "Del-Head" and non-"Del-Head" fans alike. So where is
the "danger and risk" in all of this? Certainly not in what we
hear, which, if one listens to any of their many CDs, only affirms and confirms a tradition and a mastery of that tradition,
respectively. This could hardly be described as "treacherous"
or "destructive." And yet, watching their live performances,
one witnesses the very performativity of tradition itself, the
fact that, unlike mere traditionalism, such tradition-ality is
not simply "handed down" willy-nilly without further ado,
but "*handed over*" in the moment, not as something pre-given
and pre-set but as that which must be forged and re-forged
again and again. Of course, once this is witnessed and understood, it *can* be heard, albeit with the necessary ontological
attunement of the ear, which reading the current book will
help to facilitate—but it needs to be *seen* too.

Old Settlers Musical Festival, Austin Texas, 2006[2]

Nowadays the Del McCoury Band often uses two microphones, sometimes even three (the accoutrements of fame? Do they still eat KFC?), but their on-stage choreography remains very much the same, and it is this that needs further comment.

What is the space of tradition? A collective, communal, shared space, no doubt, but it is not a space that is simply there to be occupied (the "there is"/ *il y a*): it must be *given* (*Es Gibt*). The giving of the gift that sustains a tradition is both a collective and an individual phenomenon, signifying both universality and singularity. So, with this in mind, it is significant that the Old Settlers show starts with a beginning, something very unusual. Of course, the tradition has already started, but the fact that the set begins with the Father handing over, or should we say handing down to the Son (Del McCoury to Ronnie McCoury, who begins the first number) presents the audience with an enactment of a beginning that is symbolically rich and performatively constitutive.

So, Ronnie begins alone, he literally *steps up*, not only to the microphone but into the role of one responsible for not just the perpetuation of a traditional idiom, but its re-origination in the "now." Center stage, before the microphone, at the heart of an illuminated space (*Lichtung*), he is the first band member of the evening to be exposed in this way, and they all are in turn, or *successively*, as technically we should be saying. He is literally ex-posed, made to stand outside and then reenter the given space/space to be given: extra-territoriality to intra-territoriality, to reverse a Deleuzian bias. Thus, the stepping up is also a stepping in, the crossing of a threshold, the inceptual marking of an unmarked space that, no matter how many times repeated, remains fraught with danger and risk, all smiles and banter notwithstanding. What danger, what risk? Well, certainly things could go horribly wrong: a string breaks, words are forgotten (actually, a specialty of Del's), notes are fluffed: disasters happen, but not often and especially not to seasoned professionals like Ronnie McCoury, who has been on stage since he was a kid. But then disasters take many forms, and perhaps a more serious risk is that things go just too *right*, the risk that there will be no risk, the danger that there will be no danger, just think how many performances start like that.

Ronnie begins the show with a self-penned instrumental, "Hillcrest Drive." It's a frantic piece that demands exceptional virtuosity from the outset and immediately places him at the upper limits of his considerable technique. No easing into the show or comfortable and comforting traditionalism here; he simply launches himself into the outer regions and hangs in there long enough to hand over to Jason Carter the fiddle player. Initially taking up the melody, Carter quickly starts stretching out (and his style of improvising is all about stretching and bending) and is soon in full flow. It is quite incredible how rapidly this band hits its stride—straight out of the traps, full tilt. But pace in itself is irrelevant; it is only at the moment that Carter begins to find and further create space within such pace that the band takes off. The impact is immediate; it is physical before it is musical: Ronnie begins to smile, Rob (his brother on banjo) briefly raises his eyebrows looking in Del's direction, and Alan Bartrum on bass is like a weather vane throughout the show, a physical read-out of performative ebb and flow, utterly engaging to watch. A risk has been taken, a danger has passed, their bodies relax as their accompaniment becomes tighter (a hallmark), and it is here that we can identify and situate the essence of their improvisational method: an embodied, breathing, collective space where degrees of tautness and slackness, tightening and loosening, are generated by the interpenetration of singularity and communality.

This is particularly evident in the second number of the set—"Hard on My Heart, Easy on My Eyes"—where it is Carter's turn to be ex-posed to the risk of a beginning. He does not merely step up; he literally rushes in, striding across the stage to the microphone with an urgency that is matched by the characteristic intensity of his playing. If anyone needed convincing that bluegrass is a "white-man's blues," then this would be a good place to start. The sheer audacity of Carter's playing throughout this piece (and so early in the set) is clearly the most obvious example of improvisation here, although it has to be said, he does always push the boundaries of "fixed" improvisation and on occasions comes close to straying into the realms of "semi-fixed idiomatic improvisation." But in many ways this obviously libertarian outlook on bluegrass, so enjoyed by his fellow band members, does obscure another dimension of improvisatory practice, one that is easy to overlook, secreted as it is within or behind the surface mayhem. In the case of Carter's fiddle playing, the risks and dangers of passing down a tradition are writ large as key moments of his improvisational strategy. As is so clearly evident in his approach to playing and performing, the act of handing on is rendered as a process of *unfixing*. But in order to do this without either destroying the tradition altogether or transforming into a generic, idiomatic zone of unfixed experimentation, such unfixing requires both an underpinning fixity, in this case provided by the band as indicated, as well as a mode of *re-fixing* that both protects but also *prolongs* the tradition as a living thing. It is here, within the constant and often indiscernible acts of re-fixing, that this other mode of improvisation takes place.

This is not to say of course that it is only Jason Carter who unfixes within the Del McCoury Band; they all do it, albeit to varying degrees, and all have the ability to repeat and diversify, as Deleuze describes it. But such looseness ultimately only produces the same difference, as already explained, which is fine of course. The necessary destruction or, better, de-struction of tradition considered by Heidegger and Benjamin can be better understood if we look at this process of re-fixing.

To begin with, it is not just a question of reaffirmation here. As sociologists know well, deviant behavior produces moral panics that are subsequently used to legitimate the reaffirmation of the very moral codes that were perceived to be under threat. The Del McCoury band do not reaffirm, they *affirm*. In this regard the process of re-fixing is not the reaffirmation of what is already there in the face of its possible destruction but the affirmation of what is there as a moment of that very de-struction. One cannot reaffirm what has never been; one can only affirm it, an act which re-fixes not just the given but, crucially, the giving too. With the Del McCoury band, this is happening all of the time—this is their improvisation—it is just that it is clearest when Jason Carter is soloing. At such moments, it is not just the limits of his technique that are tested but also the structural parameters of the song and, as a consequence, the wider limits and limitations of the idiom itself. This alone would be impressive, but in truth only for those impressed by empty technique, vacuous virtuosity, and/or cheap thrills. Actually, what really makes this impressive is the significant, indeed vital, role played by the band as a whole. Without the rest of the band, all of Carter's flights of fancy would amount to nothing, or at best to no more than that peculiar flatness attained by all of those one-man/woman would-be improvisers and their stagnant backing-tracks—a form of Karaoke Hell echoing through metros, shopping malls, and tourist traps throughout the world. It is not a question of call and response or of empathetic interplay, of which there is little or none, but of a constant process or adjustment and readjustment that, with great agility and collective precision, allows the band, the music, and the tradition to accommodate the de-structive interventions of the improvising soloist. In actuality then, we can identify two levels of de-struction: one that is largely (and non-derogatively) gestural, while the other is barely perceptible, minimal, and radically undemonstrative—a dialectic of overkill and understatement. While, no doubt, both are necessary, it is the fact that the former generally obscures the latter that has resulted in insufficient attention being paid to this largely subterranean improvisatory form. To repeat, the defining concept here is *agility*. If we really are going to consider tradition as treacherous, then of course it is not risk avoidance that is the issue but the avoidance of the dire consequences of risks taken. Agility is not risk-averse; rather, it is the skill necessary to manage the potential consequences of risk-taking: de-struction rather than destruction, re-fixing rather than unfixing, resulting in a process of re-structuration that is infinitely provisional and thus itself a different form of de-struction.

Of course all of this can be heard by those who would listen for such things, but it can also be sensed both physically and visually as a pulsation that contradicts the prescribed rhythmic structure, as a respiration that contradicts both pulse and rhythm—shallow/deep, light/heavy, rapid/relaxed—as an unconcealment/concealment that approaches and withdraws; . . . the list goes on and on. One can detect a sudden but subtle change in stance, a slight shift in position, a delay or acceleration in the collective choreography, an infinitesimal pause an infinitesimal anticipation; now just before, now just behind the beat, a moment of anxiety, a moment of relaxation, pleasure, joy, surprise, wonder; . . . the list goes on and on. Del opens his eyes briefly, raises his eyebrows, smiles, and closes them again; Rob, not of the ear-shattering dueling banjos school, flashes an eye at Jason, a hint of a smile, and then a sudden shift of register, ear closer to the banjo—listening—then back to work; Ronnie, a supreme player, hugging his mandolin close beneath his chin, microphone-ready, creates an improvisatory space between picking and strumming, between individual notes and chords, a micro-respiration that ebbs and flows with an independence that must be constantly accounted for by the other band members. All of this is going on all of the time, a relentless process of unfixing/re-fixing; there is something slightly unhinged about Del—a kind of hoe-down lunacy— which is not altogether surprising. But it is actually quite exhausting watching the Del McCoury Band for any length of time, as it is writing about them—so I'll stop.

13 Virtuality and Actualization: Deleuze and Bluegrass

Drawing together Deleuze, Heidegger, Benjamin, and the Del McCoury Band, we can perhaps now add something to the Deleuzian account of repetition as repetition of the same, producing the same difference: diversity. In particular, by concentrating on what is, on the face of it, the most fixed form of such repetition—fixed idiomatic improvisation—it is interesting to see that the successive nature of tradition and the traditional forms that articulate and perpetuate it are, when thought together, more complicated than might be assumed. Yes, such repetition *is* successive at a number of levels: global, local, and micro (with associated modes of precision)—from the tradition to individual works and to the individual performers and their individual techniques of performance, right down to individual phrasing, the bending of notes, and the idiosyncrasies of "feel" and "touch." But this temporal unwinding of the always already given has a spatial dimension that, in order to contain or retain the diverse (even perverse) giving of the given—the Jason Carter moment—provides a stable *but not static* reference by which diversification can be both measured and enjoyed—and then ignored. To ignore something is not to take no notice; to ignore something demands an extraordinary act of will, one that has a profound impact on the space within which the successive de-struction of tradition takes place. Put another way, the desire to endlessly diversify through a radically libertarian approach to improvisation, thought temporally as infinite variation, must, when a tradition is at stake, be countered by a performative resistance and subsequent re-fixing that, in ignoring the destruction at hand, nonetheless repeatedly de-structures the space within which such gestural destruction takes place. Thought in Deleuzian terms, this might challenge, or at least modify, his apparent separation or differentiation of succession and coexistence as regards repetition and (for us) improvisation.

What the Del McCoury Band reveals is perhaps a deeper notion of coexistence: the coexistence of coexistence and succession, the secret improvisatory structure of fixed idiomatic improvisation. Here coexistence and succession are no longer separate modes where the same difference (diversity) is counterposed to a different sameness (real difference for Deleuze). Instead, we are trying to grasp an intertwinement whereby that which coexists within the coexistential mode—its real differentiation—is incessantly produced as a response to, and re-fixing of the unfixing effected by successive improvisation. In fact this is probably putting it too dialogically, or certainly too interactively. It is easy to see the ways in which the singular successive unfixing of one improviser is the occasion for a collective response that repeatedly re-fixes a constantly de-structured structure, one that coexists with actual acts of destruction, and *actual* is the key term here, as will be shown in a moment. This has already been noted in the case study above, but there we were only describing, at the level of performance, the acts of five performers engaged in collective, interpersonal aesthetic acts, the norm for such discourses on improvisation. To try and get away from such an approach is difficult, not least because it requires a radical rethinking of exactly what improvisation enacts, a rethinking that is required to dispense with the familiar humanisms that, to be sure, make improvisation so attractive in the first place.

Actualization

Deleuze makes a crucial distinction between the realization of possibilities and the actualization of virtuality. If we can begin to understand this, then we will begin to understand the Del McCoury Band, and then we might begin to understand everything there is to understand about improvisation— perhaps.

> The only danger in all this is that the virtual could be confused with the possible. The possible is opposed to the real; the process undergone by the possible is therefore a "realization." By contrast, the virtual is not opposed to the real; it possesses a full reality by itself. The process it undergoes is that of actualization.[1]

If nothing else, this passage begins to clarify one thing: the set of binaries underpinning the discussion above—part/whole, succession/coexistence, actualization/virtual, horizontal/vertical—are in fact not binaries at all but different aspects of repetition (for Deleuze) and improvisation (for us). The fact that, as is revealed here, the real binary is not between virtuality and actualization but between virtuality/actualization and possibility/realization helps explain why the discussion of the Del McCoury Band ended up having problems with a perceived succession/coexistence binary that, as it turns out, doesn't exist, either for Deleuze or for them—or for us anymore. Before leaving the McCourys, then, let us quickly reconsider their improvisatory strategy, not in terms of an erroneously perceived binary of succession and coexistence but as the actualization of the virtual. Hopefully, this will then better reveal the successiveness of coexistence: thank goodness for bluegrass!

We need to start by thinking along a double axis: the vertical and the horizontal (coexistential and successive). Vertically and virtually, bluegrass, like any tradition or traditional form, is always already complete—the necessary past-ness or historicity of tradition: complete but not finished. But, for Deleuze, the completeness of a virtual *idea* (the idea of bluegrass in this instance) is inherently and infinitely differentiated, which explains why the idea must be considered coexistentially rather than existentially. At any point, the idea is complete but not a whole; it is always *to be* integrated but is never integrated as such, and it is the successiveness of these endless "local integrations" that Deleuze describes as *actualization*.[2] It is here that one witnesses horizontal differen*c*iation at the level of the actual as distinct from vertical differen*t*iation at the level of the virtual, and the difference between these differences is rooted in a prior differentiation of the multiplicity of the *idea* and the identity of the *concept*. To which we might add a thought: the live traditions of what we have called traditionality are ideational, the dead traditions of traditionalism are conceptual; so here we inhabit a quasi-Kantian world of aesthetic ideas rather than determinant concepts which are, of course, excluded from any form of Kantian aesthetics. Thus, not surprisingly, Deleuze speaks of actualization/differenciation in terms of creativity and performance, which fits nicely with our current concerns. To repeat:

> Actualization breaks with resemblance as a process no less than it does with identity as a principle. Actual terms never resemble the singularities they incarnate. In this sense, actualization or differenciation is always a *genuine creation* . . . . For a . . . virtual object, to be actualized is to create divergent lines which correspond to—

without resembling—a virtual multiplicity. The virtual possesses the reality *of a task to be performed.*[3]

Just as Brecht complained that he was not sufficiently shown *the act of showing* in some performances of his work, so here Deleuze offers up a model of actualization that is concerned with precisely that: the creative act of semblance (showing) rather than the passive transmission of re-semblance (re-showing). And it is here that the McCourys are exemplary. What we have described in some detail above, both musically and choreographically is, in essence, a performative actualization of a virtual idea of tradition. Deleuze considers this to be, of necessity, an example of "genuine creation," which on the face of it would seem to be ill-suited to a musical form such as bluegrass, which, unlike unfixed non-idiomatic improvisation, appears to have no ambition to create from degree zero—quite the opposite. But that is why the improvisational dimension of the McCoury's performances is so crucial; indeed, the "task to be performed," the task that *is* performed is the joint revelation of the coexistent idea and the successive actualization of that idea. One might even go further and suggest that it is improvisation and improvisation alone that *shows* how, in order to survive its own traditionalism, a traditional form must repeatedly enact or perform its own non-resemblance to itself. And this is not just the familiar dialectic of flamboyant unfixing and the collective responsibility of re-fixing already described, but a more essential self-differentiation that inhabits both of these procedures, but differently. Perhaps then, improvisation is only really possible within the infinitely differentiated space of the idea, no matter how proscriptive or fixed the idea might appear to be; while the concept, no matter how open, can only instigate a regime of resemblance that completely short-circuits the improvisatory current before this space can be illuminated. But if it is the idea that makes improvisation possible, could it be that it is improvisation and the spaces (no matter how vestigial) that it creates and inhabits that brings the idea into view and thus makes it possible in turn?

14 Deleuzian Improvisation

> One launches forth, hazards an improvisation.
> But to improvise is to join with the world, or meld
> with it. One ventures from home on the thread
> of a tune. Along sonorous, gestural, motor lines
> that mark the customary path of a child and graft
> themselves onto or begin to bud "lines of drift"
> with different loops, knots, speeds, movements,
> gestures, sonorities.[1]

"One launches forth . . ."

This beginning is, of course, about the nature of a beginning.
To launch oneself into an improvisation has a familiar ring
to it—this, after all, is the way improvisers themselves often speak of improvisation. Whether thought in the negative
terms of what has been called "idiomatic" improvisation (the
unfixing of the fixed) or the positive terms of "free" improvisation (the fixing of the unfixed), the discourses of freedom
used to conceptualize so much improvisatory practice continually propose a model of improvisation that is understood
as a liberatory practice often closely aligned to other forms
of liberatory practice. Such a view takes it for granted that,
whether fixing or unfixing, beginnings can be made—spaces
within or spaces beyond spaces. In this regard, the "space"

so often discussed by improvisers is conceived as the territorial equivalent of a beginning: virgin soil, upon which to destroy or construct a dwelling. Deleuze, in spite of the apparent familiarity of his language, is actually talking about something much more radical and very different. For him, to launch forth, if it is to be a genuine liberatory act, is precisely to break with the existing conception or philosophy of beginnings, all of which, he believes, assume an "image of thought" anterior to the so-called and oft-celebrated beginning, something shared by philosophers and improvisers alike.

> . . . there is no true beginning in philosophy, or rather that the true philosophical beginning, Difference, is in-itself Repetition.)[2] . . . [Philosophy] would discover its authentic repetition in a thought without image . . . as though thought could begin to think, and continually begin again, only when liberated from the Image and its postulates.[3]

Given that the essence of improvisation is commonly considered to be the avoidance of repetition, it should already be clear that Deleuzian improvisation, whatever it might turn out to be, is something very different from the prevalent conceptions.

". . . hazards an improvisation . . ."

Once again, the language is familiar: the language of risk and chance that forms such an important part of the improviser's self-image and which contributes to the fear instilled in those non-improvisers who feel the need to rely on all of those "how to" manuals designed to manage such fear. But what is there to be afraid of? What exactly is the risk? Well, certainly for the least experienced improviser—the novice—the risk might be the complete inability to choose a way of beginning and then a way of effectively continuing in the absence of a pre-given structure and the guidance available to negotiate this structure. Conversely, for the most experienced improviser, the danger might be an altogether too-developed talent for choosing the most effective or creative response. And this is a very real but often unacknowledged risk in all improvisation, from the most "idiomatic" to the "free-est": predictability. But, and this is the issue for Deleuze, such a concept of risk, and the uncertainty and arbitrariness associated with it, are situated, as with Heidegger, at the level of choice rather than decision—"the power of decision at the heart of problems."[4]

Using the language of *One Thousand Plateaus*, the improviser territorializes by moving from an unmarked to a marked space, indeed by making the mark that creates the territory:

> The territory is not primary in relation to the qualitative mark; it is the mark that makes the territory. Functions in a territory are not primary; they presuppose a territory-producing expressiveness. In this sense, the territory, and the functions performed within it, are products of territorialisation.[5]

While, no doubt, many improvisers are aware of the territory-forming nature of their practice, the contingency of the "being-in-the-moment" moment, and the subsequent arbitrariness of choice as regards which mark to make, result in a conception of improvisation that is dominated by aesthetic judgments of taste and moral judgments of value. In other words, confronted by chance, the task of the improviser is to make the "best" choices in an effort to fend off the evil of arbitrariness. Thus we see a peculiarity of improvisation, a paradox: improvisers are keen to celebrate risk-taking, chancy-ness with all of the surprises and wonderment that (it is hoped) follows, but at the same time, they do everything in their power to dispel the accusation or suspicion of arbitrariness by means of what Deleuze calls a moralization of territory-formation intended to displace chance and install "good" judgment. In fact, this fear of the arbitrary does not merely describe the particular attitude of improvisers; it also, more importantly, explains the very spatiotemporal structure of improvisation understood as the attempted abolition of chance. And if there is any doubt about this conception of improvisation, the following words from Martin Davidson (proprietor of free-improvisation record label Emanem) should be considered:

> CHANCE MUSIC: Often lumped together with improvisation even though the two methods are diametrically opposed. One has humans completely in charge, whilst the other makes humans totally subservient to random outside events.[6]

So, to repeat, the structural effect of this "diametrical opposition" helps explain what gives much improvisation its particular form. Deleuze describes this precisely:

> To abolish chance is to fragment it according to the laws of probability over several throws, in such a way that the problem is already dismembered into hypotheses of win and loss, while the impera-

tive is moralised into the principle of choosing the best hypothesis
which determines a win.[7]

This statement could, without much difficulty, be translated into the language of improvisation, where it might function as an effective articulation
of the underlying aesthetic and moral processes that—mediated by the art
of judgment—give form to the predominant forms of improvisation.

Needless to say, Deleuze's relation to chance and the subsequent improvisation that his work hazards, chances, or risks, is radically different
from any of the above. To "hazard an improvisation" is not, for him, the
instigation of a series that, through trial and error (the motor of judgment)
and the testing of hypotheses produces a work capable of throwing off the
yoke of chance and the stigma of arbitrariness—this could hardly describe
Deleuze's own *modus operandum*! Following Nietzsche and Mallarmé, Deleuze does not attempt to avert the arbitrary through an aesthetics or ethics
of judgment; it is not a question of choosing the best moves within an unfolding game of, and against, chance but of having the "power of decision"
to affirm chance and thus abolish arbitrariness.

> The most difficult thing is to make chance an object of affirma-
> tion. . . . Chance is arbitrary only in so far as it is not affirmed or
> sufficiently affirmed, in so far as it is distributed within a space . . .
> under rules destined to avert it. When chance is sufficiently affirmed
> the player can no longer lose. . . . Once chance is affirmed, all arbi-
> trariness is abolished every time.[8]

Why is so it difficult to affirm chance? More to the point, why do improvisers find it so difficult to affirm chance, the ideology of chancy improvisation notwithstanding? Martin Davidson puts his finger on an essential issue
when he identifies chance as that which "makes humans totally subservi-
ent to random outside events" as opposed to "humans being completely in
charge"—(at least humanism is still alive and well in the world of improvisation). But, of course, as Deleuze is only too well aware, to affirm chance in
the manner he suggests is precisely to overthrow the sovereign self in favor
of the world, the "chaosmos"—improvisation as a melding with world.

> The power of decision, . . . this creation or throw which makes us
> descendants from the gods, is nevertheless not our own. The gods
> themselves are subject to . . . sky-chance. The imperatives and ques-
> tions with which we are infused do not emanate from the I: it is not

even there to hear them. The imperatives are those of being, while every question is ontological. . . . Ontology is the dice throw, the chaosmos from which the cosmos emerges.[9]

". . . to improvise is to join the world, or meld with it."

Once again we start with a thought expressed in words that could be uttered by any improviser. Within the improvising fraternity, fraternity itself figures large. The suspicion of singularity and solitude, the valorization of dialogue, the collective, the communicative community, and the performative vaporization of hierarchies, boundaries and exclusion—all speak of a desire to meld with the world or for the creation of a "world" that can be joined. The ecstasy of improvisation has attendant dangers then: the submergence of the singular in the collective will, the reduction of the Other to the Same; and, thus, to "hazard an improvisation" is also to confront this risk, one that is doubly dangerous in being both the flip-side of arbitrariness while also posing as its solution. Obviously, there are strategies available to resist the much-celebrated melding process, and many astute improvisers use them effectively. For now, following Deleuze, we will consider a different manner of joining the world, one intended to avoid the organicism often favored by improvisers but anathema to Deleuze.

To begin with, and just as an initial contrast, a great deal of collective improvisation is dialectical and teleological in nature. The goal is often to mark the unmarked space in such a way that differences can be resolved, separation can be dissolved, and a world or space can be created and joined. Deleuze's "world" idea is very different. As can be seen above, the world is not a goal but an originary emergence from chaos to cosmos. It is not a question of joining this world as if from the outside—there is no outside—but of acknowledging the nature of the chaosmos and affirming it: this returns us to the encounter with chance. To affirm chance is to meld with the world, a gesture that seeks to fuse improvisation and fate—improvisation as *amor fati*. But how can we confront and affirm our fate? By confronting and affirming our habits, to which we now turn.

15 Improvisation and Habit

The best we can do is to confront our inherited . . . nature with our knowledge of it, and . . . inplant in ourselves a new habit, a new instinct, a second nature, so that our first nature withers away. It is an attempt to give oneself, as it were *a posteriori*, a past in which one would like to originate in opposition to that in which one did originate.

Friedrich Nietzsche[1]

Mediating instinct and habit in the above epigraph is knowledge, always a dubious term in Nietzsche's vocabulary, the significance and function of which will be crucial in the framing of the following three chapters. Nietzsche is of course famously critical of the will-to-knowledge, preferring instead the will-to-power, but what is often forgotten is that, as is clear above, the latter depends upon the former. Knowledge is Janus-faced: it is the will-to-knowledge that brings a recognition of the need to confront our inherited nature (instinct); it is, conversely, the knowledge-to-will that acknowledges the need to transform what is known into new habits of willing, thus allowing such preliminary knowledge acquisition itself to be "forgotten." The ultimate goal then is to supplant both instinct and knowledge with habit. And unlike instinct and knowledge, both of which are value-neutral, habits can be good or bad, happy or sad, sane or mad, and most of all, they can be broken and changed again and again. And we certainly need to get into the habit of understanding habit as a form of transformation rather than, as is usually the case, mechanization, determination, and stagnation. It is this that will allow us to consider an essential congruence between habit and improvisation.

But first we need to get to the end of the Nietzsche epigraph above, not least because it is here that we witness one of the most radical dimensions of his thought and, for us, the most radical challenge to the ideals of much improvisation. That is to say, we ultimately want to be talking about things that happen in the moment, in the now of the improvised event. This "in-the-moment" moment, which, as we aim to show, is by no means contrary to habituation, is nevertheless almost universally conceived as a moment of origination that through extraordinary feats of improvisatory agility is able to outwit and outrun the leaden weight of habit. And this itself does sound very Nietzschean. But, returning to the epigraph, it is evident that Nietzsche's primary focus is not on origination understood in the familiar and prevailing terms of originality, innovation, and the new, but on the exigency to originate an *origin* out of which, and by or through which, origination can take place. First, this immediately challenges two common assumptions, or perhaps they are aspirations: the (or desire for the) unadulterated now-ness of the "in-the-moment" moment and the (or desire for the) unadulterated newness of the "in-the-moment" moment. What is also evident is that this thought, while situated in the moment, is essentially concerned not with the present now but with the future and the past, a willed future-past, to be precise, that, as we shall see, is crucial to an understanding of the temporality of the improvised event: always past or to come. Aping the form of Kant's categorical imperative, we could say, with Nietzsche, that it is necessary to acquire the habit of: *willing the next moment as if it would return eternally*. This does not deny the nowness of the moment, but it does radically alter the nature and significance of the event.

Second, the above dislocation (for want of a temporal rather than spatial term) of now-ness in the momentous moment of the eternal recurrence also problematizes the newness of the live event by—and here we return to the epigraph—proposing a model of creative willing that subsumes novelty under the more essential origination of origins, while, we would argue, accepting that the desired forgetting of this more originary origination (as habit) allows the novelty of mere "originality" to remain as an inspiring but inessential epiphenomenon. Again, this does not in itself deny the newness of the moment, but it is the ontological significance of the new as an aspect of the event that will need to be reevaluated. And to do so will require us to go "beyond" the current and predominant improvisatory *doxa*, which is predominantly pro-novelty and contra-habit.

The allergy to habit might be seen against the backdrop of modernity's and modernism's increasing suspicion of naïve self-consciousness and the subsequent aversion to the unmediated "I," understood respectively as the locus of falsity, *ressentiment*, and illusion (to follow Paul Ricoeur in his identification of a "school of suspicion," with the "masters of suspicion" being Marx, Nietzsche, and Freud).[2] As Ricoeur describes it, suspicion is a necessary response to the "threefold guile"[3] identified by these three "masters" as the latent motivation of what we might call the lied-to/lying self. But, as he hints and we would further emphasize, suspicion alone is barely distinguishable from skepticism, a predominantly destructive force far removed from the creative thrust of these three thinkers. As a result, suspicion itself has to be transformed into a secondary guile in order to confront the primary guile of the self-same self. This is the agonistic drama of the mediate "I."

> What all three attempted, in different ways, was to make their "conscious" methods of deciphering coincide with the "unconscious" *work* of ciphering which they attributed to the will to power, to social being, to the unconscious psychism. *Guile will be met by double guile.*[4]

If we limit ourselves to Nietzsche and keep in mind the substance of our initial epigraph, then we can see that Ricoeur here captures one (but only one) aspect of the former's thought: the confrontation of our "inherited nature" (instincts and habits) and knowledge. In this regard, knowledge, understood as the result of a "conscious method of deciphering," does indeed require the necessary guile to outsmart the trickery of the unconscious situated or secreted within the mind and the body. But, in itself, such a hermeneutical reduction of Nietzsche's thought ultimately fails to account for the subsequent displacement of knowledge and understanding by new habits and the necessary overcoming of suspicion and guile. But before trying to follow Nietzsche's thought through to the end, let us pause here and acknowledge that such a guileful auto-hermeneutic does undoubtedly offer considerable insight into the nature of much improvisation, particularly where the outwitting of habit is a central issue, as it so often is. In this respect, John Cage's well-known negative association of improvisation and habit casts a long shadow:

> KOSTELANETZ: You've frequently spoken out against improvisation, because it relies so heavily on habit and personal taste.

> CAGE: I'm finding ways to free the act of improvisation from taste and memory and likes and dislikes. If I can do that, then I will be very pleased.[5]

While this suggests that Cage's so-called opposition to improvisation is more nuanced than is often claimed, the Jurij Konjar/Steve Paxton case study below (chapter 16) will not attempt to free improvisation from habit but to free habit from our own habitual thinking in order, thus, to reassess it and relocate it *within* improvisation itself.

16 Case Study: Jurij Konjar and Steve Paxton: The Goldberg Variations

We can begin by reintroducing the concept of novelty here as we see it embedded in Slovenian dancer Jurij Konjar's 2007-to-the-present re-improvisations of Steve Paxton's (the "inventor" of "contact improvisation") original improvisations on the Goldberg Variations performed in the early 1990s. We might also note the provocation (whether intended or not) of Konjar's initial gesture: the attempted repetition of an existing improvisation, not even his own, but one performed by another improviser and already very well known. On the face of it, this alone would seem to challenge the predominance of novelty (albeit in quite a novel way). But then, perhaps inevitably, in Konjar's subsequent correspondence with Steve Paxton in *Contact Quarterly*,[1] it is clear that his intention is not mere copying. As Konjar writes of *Fake It!*—the name of the production in which he participated, and the initial context for "his" Goldberg Variations: "It could be that *Fake It!* shows that each copy of an art work becomes a *new* original," and he continues in an e-mail to Steve Paxton:

> After I got over copying your way of moving, which happened pretty fast, I started focusing more on what I could see you were busy with, beyond the form. . . . I found it was to address your work, addressing these themes was much more im-

portant than simply putting on black trousers and copying some
movements. (7)

In the sense or origination as re-origination, something already encountered
above, such "copying" allows him to create a "new original" that is "real"
and "sincere," and, to repeat: *new*: re-*novation* rather than innovation.

If, as Konjar states, his focus is more on the repetition of what Paxton
was "busy with, beyond the form," then we need to try and make it clearer
what this is. Obviously a performer is busy with many things when performing, but the important issue here is how both improvisers deploy a highly
self-reflexive, auto-hermeneutic governed by a powerful desire to avoid being
sucked or seduced into the determining idiosyncrasies or habits of the immediate "I." As a consequence, improvisation is, for both of them, required
to become extraordinarily agile and guileful, committed to dancing *around*
rather than from out of the self; a form of negation and trickery, as Paxton
describes it:

> The score for the *Goldberg Variations* was to *not* do what I have
> done before . . . finding ways to trick myself. In '91, when I couldn't
> find ways to trick myself anymore, . . . I stopped. [He continues] . . .
> having worked on contact improvisation to see if I could figure out
> why this thing called improvisation has a reputation for not having
> a structure, I kept finding structure. At a certain point I decided that
> the structure was *me*. That I couldn't get outside of that. I couldn't
> continue the process because I kept running into myself, and my
> habit. (16–17)

The degree to which Konjar, as he claims, is concerned not with the copying
of form but the repetition of the thinking ("busying") "beyond the form"
is evident in his own statements, where Paxton's original concerns and language here resonate—re-sound—as if in an improvisatory echo chamber.
Here are some fragments from Konjar's "Chapbook:"

> "I" is not part of the landscape of the moment. . . . The moment
> "I" comes into focus stop and while stopping continue immedi-
> ately . . . (11)
>
> I start planning and I fall back into my habits. . . . But it's a
> choice . . . that I'm trying to avoid having habits . . . (13)
>
> The NO Score . . . is based on "no-ing" many impulses. . . . This
> is like tricking myself. . . . I ask myself what is the "me"? . . . The
> "me" is the dancer of "I do," the self-conscious being of "I want,"

the private life person of "I am," and they all manifest through the body. . . . I . . . exclude all of the above "me's" from the process (20).

On the face of it, Paxton and Konjar appear to be engaged in a very similar process, a shared commitment to the exposure and obliteration of habit as embedded in the very structure of the I, me, mine; but is this really the case? Quite apart from the obvious fact that these two dancers are from different generations (Paxton in his 70s, Konjar in his 30s), it is a deeper cultural reorientation—crudely figured as the shift from the modern to the postmodern—that is also in evidence in their exchanges in *Contact Quarterly*. This should not be misunderstood: the fact that the original performance of Konjar's *Goldberg Variations* was part of the production *Fake It!* is not to suggest that this was in any way an archetypical postmodern gesture reveling in inauthenticity and parody. On the contrary, the production was conceived as a serious political response to the cultural marginalization (and cultural starvation) of Slovenia, a response made possible no doubt by the celebration of simulacra typical of both postmodernism and certain poststructuralisms, but also, as Natasa Zavolovsek states, not without humor: "The project directly reflects one of the prevailing interpretations of the Slovene national culture, i.e., the theory of lagging behind" (2). This consciousness of *coming-after* is, interestingly, something that can also be felt throughout Konjar's "observations" and, indeed, his repeated reference to *observation* as an integral part of his performative strategy marks a significant difference between himself and his precursor, Steve Paxton. If ever a work exemplified the will to create *a posteriori* a past in which one would have liked to have originated, then this re-improvisation of an improvisation would be a contender.

So, for example, on first hearing of *Fake It!* Paxton's response to Zavolovsek raises the issue of influence:

> It is an amusing, serious and political proposal. I think you are doing formally what dancers have always done, to be influenced by other dancers. Usually the influence *slips into the body without public notice*, so this event brings to the front of the mind how dance, seeming to have a life of its own, transfers from one studio to another. (2)

Needless to say, while acknowledging the inevitability of influence, there can be no doubt that, for Paxton, the manner in which the determining power of the other "slips into the body" has a lot to do with the unconscious accumulation of habits which are ultimately responsible for the contamination of the "pure," utterly autonomous, improvising gesture. For him, the event of improvised dance is, to repeat, for it to have a "life of its own" and for the improviser to take ownership of the improvised event by wresting it from the other and the otherness of the self-same as sedimented in habit. The extent to which an event can be owned *at all* is a question that will be returned to, but for the moment, Paxton's "suspicious" auto-hermeneutic can, in spite of their shared language of self-trickery, be contrasted with the greater transparency of Konjar's more detached method of observing the very process by which the other slips into the body of the "I." It is perhaps no coincidence (and here we note again a generational divide) that Paxton uses the vocabulary of encounter and discovery so typical of his formative years in the sixties. His is an intensive and intense language of an interiority that ultimately cannot be escaped—"I couldn't get outside"—but which is endlessly stumbled upon or "run into" as a habitual structure that emerges from the pre-given coordinates of the improvised performance itself. By contrast, Konjar, whether "lagging behind" or not, is inevitably the product of a spectacular culture, where it is the exteriority of surfaces, signifying chains and the sense of sight, that predominate, and where observation displaces participation as the primary performative mode: "It seems to me that the creator, performer, and analyst all start with—**observing**" (9; original text in bold).

> I'm looking at a recording of Paxton
> . . . looking at the form and copying
> and looking further . . .
> in order to be here . . .
> I need to find answers
> so I observe and embody beyond form. (5)

Paxton's *Goldberg Variations* start with a negative act: the desire to guilefully trick the habitual self through the performance of pure, nonhabitual movement—"It's about movement that I haven't done before" (16). Konjar's *Goldberg Variations* start with an affirmative act: the desire to observe and then preserve both the habitual and nonhabitual movements of the other, through a performative reserve or "restraint" that makes possible the creation of new habits of thought and movement. And it should be noted here that, following Heidegger, the word *preserve* is not conceived as the fixing of the given but, precisely its *unfixing*.[2] In a sense then, Konjar unfixes rather than fixes Paxton with a gaze, and not only Paxton, but, as a consequence, himself too.

To explain: as Konjar observes, when dancing, "Steve goes fully for it"

(13), and, as Lisa Nelson adds, "Steve's attention and yours are very different, Steve's is more internal, and yours is more in the space" (16) What both are suggesting in their different ways is that, for Paxton, the improvised act or movement has an immediacy that momentarily integrates (or strives to integrate) the inside and the outside in a pure space without history or habits. To "fully go for it" is to commit absolutely to this moment of fixity. To *see* the space rather than *be* the space—to, as Konjar says, "have time to observe the inside *and* the outside"—is different in that, as indicated, it introduces time into this space as a moment of unfixing. *Seeing* the space introduces a moment of delay into the improvised movement whereby the observation of an other and/or the observation of oneself is indeed an enactment of "lagging-behind" that is not only historical but existential and ontological.

Addressed in turn, the historical delay returns us to Paxton's earlier remark concerning the ubiquity of "influence" and the inevitability of repetition, whether secreted in the body or openly acknowledged in the re-improvisation of a prior improvisation. Here the question of habit largely revolves around the witting or unwitting inheritance of given models or patterns of practice, whereby that which is essentially un-owned is, over time, transformed into that which is thought and *felt* to be owned, and it is the latter which, following Nietzsche, is in danger of becoming "instinctual" in a bad sense—a "first nature." Perhaps the first step in the creation of a "second nature" and better habits, then, is precisely to openly confront the historical dimension of both creation and preservation, and out the moment of repetition, and acknowledge that coming-into-being is also and always, as Cole Porter refrained, a coming-back.

Getting into the habit of recognizing and responding to the habitual acquires existential significance—and here Konjar is exemplary—as a heightened self-reflexiveness (what Susan Leigh Foster calls "hyperawareness")[3] that introduces a delay into the moment of performance itself.

> I've never tried doing things without seeing what they are before they happen. I realize I've always imagined what I will do a moment before doing. . . . And you're almost not involved; . . . you're observing. (14)

Here we see the imagining "I" and the doing "I" as mediated by this splitting of the "in-the-moment" moment into two: the "moment before" the moment. This intra-improvisatory delay is articulated by Konjar as "patience" (7–10), and described by his friend, the dancer Martin Kilvady, as "held-back . . . observant . . . thoughtful . . . kind of marking . . . or testing. Looking at yourself" (11).⁴ Thought existentially, such reflexivity does, through this doubling of the self, undoubtedly complicate the subjective experience of the performance both for the dancer and the audience, not least because such restraint does or can point us back to the guileful (Paxtonian) self, engaged in a tussle with its own habitual proclivities and predilections. This is certainly how Badiou sees things in his reading of Nietzsche on dance:

> The movement of dance can certainly manifest an extreme quickness, but only to the extent that it is inhabited by its latent slowness, by the affirmative power of restraint. Nietzsche proclaims that "the will must learn to be slow and mistrustful." Dance could then be defined as the expansion of slowness and the mistrust of the thought-body.⁵

Such suspicious and mistrustful thinking maps well onto the existential and performative predicament Paxton describes when explaining the eventual termination of his *Goldberg Variations*, but does it capture the restraint that Konjar describes as patience; indeed, *is* Konjar guileful and mistrustful at all? One way of answering this is to return to Badiou for a moment and consider the dialectic he proposes between restraint and vulgarity:

> Nietzsche writes that all vulgarity derives from the incapacity to resist an entreaty. . . . Accordingly, dance is defined as the movement of a body subtracted from all vulgarity. . . . Dance offers a metaphor for a light and subtle thought precisely because it shows the restraint immanent to movement and thereby opposes itself to the spontaneous vulgarity of the body.⁶

Badiou is quite right to remind us that, in spite of his reputation as an essentially Dionysian philosopher, Nietzsche from his earliest writings onward is a severe proponent of discipline and a staunch opponent of laissez-faire liberalism and, indeed, of any associated romantic models of creativity and improvisation. That said, there is a confusion in Badiou's reading that is in danger of obscuring the ontological dimension of restraint and, as a consequence, blocking access to a fuller understanding of the place and essential significance of habit as a moment of improvisation. The heart of the problem is that Badiou understands dance as a "metaphor for *thought*," which immediately puts him at odds with Nietzsche, who, as we saw at the outset, places thought and knowledge between, as a vanishing moment, first and second nature, as that which allows us to "confront" our bad habits and will new habits that originate a future past, as, and this is the point, *willing* not thinking. At the moment before the moment of willing—that split second Konjar refers to—thought and knowledge must be *forgotten*. Nietzsche is explicit—and note especially the promotion of doing above knowing here.

> He who cannot sink down *on the threshold of the moment* and forget all the past . . . will never know what happiness is—worse, he will never do anything to make others happy. . . . Forgetting is essential to action of any kind.[7]

Metaphor is a means or form of *remembering* correspondences and differences, and has nothing whatever to do with dance or the will to dance. The only thing that thought can learn from dance is not to become more "light and subtle," as Badiou believes, but to forget itself. Indeed, a good definition of habit would be a doing that has forgotten thought. So, the issue for Konjar is not vulgarity; there is no question of him resisting the entreaties of the spontaneous body, a body that Badiou believes is (outside of dance) "constrained by itself,"[8] another way of saying habitual. There is no question of Konjar working inside of a dialectic of constraint/unconstraint such as that described by Badiou,[9] any more than there is a requirement that the dancing body enter into a "state of disobedience vis-à-vis its own impulses,"[10] something which, as will become clearer now, distinguishes Paxton's improvisations from Konjar's re-improvisations. There is certainly no "disobedience" in Nietzsche's thought, largely because he does not see it as thought but as *will*. Where is the disobedience in this famous passage from *Ecce Homo* on the writing of *Zarathustra*?

> Suddenly, with indescribable certainty and subtlety, something becomes *visible*, audible; . . . one hears, one does not seek; one accepts, one does not ask who gives; like lightening, a thought flashes up, with necessity, without hesitation regarding its form—I never had any choice.[11]

The emphasis is Nietzsche's: something becomes *visible*. It is not a question of obeying or disobeying; it is about observing and accepting. There is constraint in obedience but not in acceptance. Similarly, Konjar speaks of acceptance and, interestingly, such acceptance acknowledges the vulgarity of the obedient or habitual body, here described as "bad taste:"

> Include the obvious, the yours, the already done.
> Don't fall in love and don't criticize.
> Accept—that mistakes and things of bad taste will happen.

Most of all, don't panic.

When you realize you're panicking, don't panic. Observe.

Treat movement not as something you do, but as something that is
  there and does not need you in order to be happening.

Don't plan and don't reflect on what has happened.

"I" is not part of the landscape of the moment, neither is the view
  from the outside. (11)

Again, there is no disobedience in evidence here, and what is more, it would
be difficult to see how such a method of dancing-improvising could act as a
metaphor for thought in the sense Badiou intends. If there is thought here, it
is a thoughtless thought that forgets itself on the "threshold of the moment"
and *acts*, observes, and continues to act, accepting that the *will* to dance is
one that must inevitably include the habitual—the "obvious, the yours, the
already done"—and the vulgar: this is in fact a long way from both Paxton
and Badiou.

   The question that arises is: If Nietzsche is a thinker who wishes to *overcome* thought and knowledge through the formation of "new habits," and
if our Nietzsche-inspired reading of Konjar's re-improvisation of Paxton's
improvisation is also open to the habitual, then what impact will such a
perspective have on our understanding of the live improvised event? Clearly,
by placing a question mark above Badiou and his dancing metaphor, we are
in danger of stripping improvisation of the very eventfulness that it so often
claims for itself in the momentous moments of its much-heralded live-ness.
And, indeed, any anxiety about this can only be heightened by Badiou's
own promotion of dance not only as a metaphor for thought but also as the
very embodiment of the event. Given this, we will either have to abandon
the event in favor of habit, or abandon Badiou's philosophy of the event in
favor of an alternative conception that recognizes the habitual dimension
of the event: that's the choice, and it is the latter that will be attempted. But
first Badiou:

Dance would provide the metaphor for the fact that every genuine
thought depends upon an event. An event is precisely what remains
undecided. . . . Dance would mimic a thought that had remained
undecided, something like a native (or unfixed) thought. Yes, in
dance we would find the metaphor of the unfixed.[12]

The language used here would be very familiar and very attractive to most
improvisers, where undecidability and unfixity are the existential norms of
their day-to-day performative lives. So, against this grain, a Nietzschean

form of improvisation, if we are to remain committed to some form of event-ness, would have to conceive of the performative moment as a *fixing* of that which has *already* been decided, the recurrence of a past that the will has already willed for itself as a "second" origin. If the return of the already-decided is another way of describing habit, and if we accept that it is precisely the *undecidability* of the event that is responsible for its essential surprising-ness,[13] then it is clearly going to be difficult to bring the habitual and the eventful together in a way that doesn't require the destruction or at least sublation of one pole of this apparently contradictory binary. But this remains the task.

Before trying to move forward though, a reminder of the hegemony of "surprise" within the discourses of the event. To begin with, some archetypical passages from Derrida's "A Certain Impossible Possibility of Saying the Event."[14]

> It is worth recalling that an event implies surprise, exposure, the unanticipatable . . .

> There can be an event only when it's not expected, when one can no longer wait for it, when the coming of what happens interrupts the waiting . . .

> One of the characteristics of the event is that not only does it come about as something unforeseeable, not only does it disrupt the ordinary course of history, but is also absolutely singular.

> The event as event, as absolute surprise, must fall on me. . . . A predicted event is not an event. The event falls on me because I don't see it coming.

> [And here linking the event to improvisation] What is happening here, to the extent that it was unforeseeable, that it was unanticipated for me—since we improvised to a large extent—is that an event will have taken place.[15]

This all sounds familiar, and such familiarity has the effect of rendering any contradiction wantonly perverse; be that as it may, the following will try to imagine a notion of the event and a form of improvisation that has managed to emancipate itself from the hegemonic structures and strictures of the absolutely surprising.

To begin with, there is nothing inherently surprising about improvisation; we do it all the time, usually with perfectly unsurprising results. The ability to cobble things together and concoct makeshift solutions on the hoof is an ability shared by many of us as we stumble through our under-resourced and ill-equipped lives. Indeed, that *is* life, as played out in its own unremarkable and largely unremarked live-ness.

Returning to Steve Paxton and habit, the reason for the eventual cessation of his *Goldberg Variations* was that—never mind the audience—*he* could no longer surprise *himself*, on account of his evil twin, the "habitual Steve Paxton," who constantly imposed the structures of the deeply known on the surprising otherness of the unknown. But, interestingly, it is precisely this subjectivization of habit that is responsible for the subjectivized yearning for infinite surprise, one that, in turn, is all too easily translated into the similarly subjectivized experience of the expectant audience. These aspects of improvisation are held together by what Paxton describes as a "contract":

> So part of my work in developing the *Goldberg* was to work on lines of thought. My lines of thought did not include how to relate to the public. I thought the public and I had an unspoken contract. . . . So instead of being concerned with the public, I was concerned with what I was making, . . . what my body was making. In each moment, I felt like there was some place to go, some place to change from. To listen for a place I can change from is what I choose to choose.
>
> So there's a choosing going on in this improvisation. Not that I know where I'm going, but I am very aware of what I'm not doing. (17)

There is a lot of "I," "me," "mine" here, and it is this that ultimately gets in the way of a more essential understanding of both the nature of habit and, indeed, the surprise of the event, which, as it turns out, is not necessarily all that surprising at all.

This is where the slowly emerging differences between Paxton and Konjar are quite telling: the former here speaks of *listening* for ways to change from one place to another, while the latter, as we have already seen, *observes* that which is unfolding within the *given* space of the performance. One is an intensely engaged form of negative self-discovery (of the habitual "I"); the other is a more neutral acceptance of the event as independent of subjective design. Konjar himself captures this well, but ironically, in describing Paxton performing: "But I love this selflessness, because that is what I see" (14) But it is precisely the fact that Paxton is fundamentally concerned with the *transformation* rather than the *neutralization* of the self that actually stands in the way of the desire to find some way of conjoining habit and the live event.

On the face of it, and in common with his friend Derrida, Jean-Luc Nancy also conceives of the event as being governed by the experience of surprise, as his essay "The Surprise of the Event" would seem to confirm,[16] but what is particularly interesting is the way Nancy begins his essay:

> The "surprise" is not only an attribute, quality, or property of the event, but the event itself, its being or its essence. What eventuates in the event is not only that which happens, but that which surprises— perhaps even that which surprises itself (turning it, in short, away from its own "happening," not allowing itself *to be* event . . .).[17]

Straight away we can see that Nancy is at pains to separate the surprisingness of the event from the subjective experience of surprise in the face of what "happens," understood as mere epiphenomena of the event itself. Thought in this way, it is perfectly possible to imagine an improvised event that is utterly unsurprising at the level of "attribute, quality, or property" but is absolutely surprising as an event. The point to be made here is that, far from denying or belittling the surprising quality of much improvised performance, the recognition and acceptance, indeed, *affirmation* of the fact that such improvisation is very often *performatively* unsurprising actually requires us to look again at what constitutes a surprise.

Steve Paxton would no doubt say that what is unsurprising is the product of accumulated habits—hence his desire to emancipate himself from them, whatever they might be and whenever they might emerge as the determining force of the performative choice he speaks of. And it is precisely this, the culturally dominant conception of a "*force of habit*" that is perceived as a threat by all subjectivized aesthetics of individual choice and freedom.

Thanks to the work of Catherine Malabou on both Hegel and Ravaisson, this "mechanism" model of habit can now be challenged by a more affirmative perspective, one that recognizes both the "plasticity" of habituation and one that embraces the idea that, following Ravaisson, habit is a "disposition" rather than a brute determining force, and that it is *responsible for* rather than *resistant to* the transformation of human action and the creativity associated with that. This is how Ravaisson himself begins his *Of Habit*, and it is the emphasis on *change* that we would like to draw particular attention to:

> Once acquired, habit is a general, *permanent way of being*, and if change is transitory, habit subsists beyond the change which brought it about. Moreover, if it is related . . . only to the change that engendered it, then habit remains for a change which is either no longer or *not yet*; it remains for a possible change. This is its defining characteristic. Habit is not, therefore, merely a state, but

a disposition, a virtue. . . . Habit is thus a disposition relative to change, which is engendered in a being by the continuity or *the repetition of this very same change* . . . . Nothing, then, is capable of habit that is not capable of change.[18]

Malabou's gloss on this passage recalls our Nietzschean starting point: the possibility of creating a different past that will inaugurate a future rooted in "new habits" of the will. For her, following Ravaisson, habit is a "resource of possibilities" rather than a "set of deactivated traces," and it is precisely habit that "makes possible a future."[19] She continues in a more Deleuzian vein:

> If being was able to change once, in the manner of contracting a habit, it can change again. It is available for a change to come. Certainly, change generates habit, but in return *habit is actualized as a habit of changing.*[20]

What is interesting about Malabou's work is that, while here her writing is in a recognizably Nietzschean/Deleuzian register, her key foundational work on "plasticity" is a prolonged and very affirmative (re)-reading of Hegel, who is, to say the least, at some distance from the former pair.[21] But in order to better grasp what we are suggesting might be the inherent unsurprisingness of the live event, it is essential that we pay some attention to the role of habit within Hegel's phenomenological trajectory.

The originality of Malabou's work is in her identification of habit as a crucial moment in the dialectic of universal substance and individuality that is proposed by Hegel as the processual manifestation of Absolute Spirit. In brief, her claim is that, rather than being either a *universal* mechanical determining force that completely absorbs singularity in an undifferentiated totality (closer to instinct, or what Hegel and Nietzsche call "first nature") or, conversely, the *singular* mannerisms and idiosyncrasies of the self-obsessed self (*á la* Paxton), habit both mediates these binaries and thus *liberates* the self: a fascinating reversal of the spoken and unspoken improviser's charter, where the demand is to liberate oneself *from* habits.

> Habit emerges as a liberating process, saving the soul from the two forms of dissolution—either lost in the emptiness of ideality or absorbed in a determinate part isolated from the whole.[22]

If we resist taking up, as Malabou does here, the Hegelian language of the "soul" and speak instead of what we might call the essence of habit, then the task of "saving" or more fully understanding this essence is central to our subsequent view of the surprisingness, or not, of the improvised event. But before moving on, one thing should be emphasized: as Hegel and Malabou recognize, the word *habit* derives from the Latin *habere*: "Habit is a way of 'having,' and a kind of possession or property."[23] While this is true, there is a duality here; possession signifies both the ownership of something (*having* property) as well as being possessed *by* something—the very opposite of ownership. The mediating role of habit described by Hegel and Malabou is one that frees the habitual self from both having and being-had; neither possessed nor dispossessed, one might say that the habitual self is precisely the one most attuned to the nature of the event, which in one of its most profound iterations—Heidegger's—is characterized by just such an in-between-ness. This is clearly evident in Heidegger's shifting attempt to arrive at an appropriate vocabulary to translate the notoriously allusive and elusive German term *Ereignis*, which is most commonly rendered as "event" or "appropriation" or "the event of appropriation." That these latter fall short of the etymological richness of *Ereignis* is made evident in Heidegger's *The Event*,[24] where, in the section entitled "The Event: The Vocabulary of Its Essence" one finds, as well as *appropriation*, both *expropriation* and *dispropriation*.[25]

Although, strangely, there is no place where Heidegger offers an extended discussion of habit, throughout his work, he repeatedly remarks on the habitual nature of metaphysical-representational thinking, thus recognizing that the event of being "delivered over" to Being is not primarily about the transformation of thinking through academic-philosophical debate,[26] but the much more difficult task of breaking ingrained habits. Indeed, the "forgetting of Being" bemoaned by Heidegger throughout his work can be understood as a forgetting that is proper to habit, which, as Bergson observes, "*acts*" rather than remembers the past.[27] So it is not just a question of thinking differently, but of *acting* differently too. Essentially, Heidegger is not concerned with the intentional act of the transcendental ego in pursuit of knowledge of the life-world, but with a de-subjectivized *comportment* toward existence, which is not a thinking-about but more of an act of orientation that, through a certain "releasement" (*Gelassenheit*) of the self, opens beings to the event of Being. If this can be described as an act, and a "new habit," it is more an act of "waiting" rather than doing:

> SCHOLAR: In fact (supposing that it is waiting which is essential, that is, all decisive), waiting upon something is based on our belonging in that upon which we wait.
> TEACHER: Out of the experience of and relation to just such wait-

ing upon the opening of that-which-regions, waiting came to be spoken of a releasement.[28]

Waiting is not thinking but a willing *not* to will, a reminder of Nietzsche's "strongest will" (the will *not* to will): "When we let ourselves into releasement to that-which-regions, we will non willing."[29] But what are we waiting for here? Waiting to be surprised? Is this what Konjar is waiting for when he writes,

> You are monitoring "patience," not movement.
>
> You don't know what is coming, . . . but you can sense what is not "it" yet, . . . so you wait, now. You don't remember ideas and you don't look for them (plan them), you just wait. (8)

Improvisers wait for something to "happen" or "occur"; but if we follow Heidegger and get into the habit of ignoring happenings and occurrences, just as Nancy ignores the attributes, qualities, and properties of the event, then perhaps Konjar's comportment might be understood as a waiting for something other than a surprise. Nancy certainly believes that the event has nothing to do with the subjective experience of surprise:

> But it is not a surprise for the subject. . . . The surprise—the event—does not belong to the order of representation. Surprise is the leap—or the "it," the "some*one*" who comes about in the leap and, indeed, as the leap "itself"—that surprises itself. . . . The leap surprises itself precisely inasmuch as it neither represents "itself" to itself, not its surprise. It coincides with this surprise; it is only this surprise that is not yet "its own."[30]

Once again, it is the question of belonging and ownership that comes to the fore as a reminder that it is not what we—as subjective I, me, mine—say, think, or do, but the "patient" *observation* of an opening of being that we appropriate through what we might describe as the re-habitualization of our comportment. And this is the crux: there *is* no beyond or outside, there is no escape from habit; as Ravaisson recognized, "Habit is a general and permanent way of being." This means we are now back where we started with Nietzsche and the exigency to use the knowledge of our instinctual (first nature) habits to instill in ourselves new habits of willing (second nature) that, as habits, must be "actively forgotten" in the sense that (and here again Bergson is illuminating) the forgetting of habit does not forget to the extent that it becomes an *act*—the act of forgetting, the habit of forgetting, the forgetting of habit. And if this act of forgetting is in service to a will-to-power intent upon willing an originary past *as if* it would eternally return, then it is not altogether surprising that the very concept of surprise is beginning to look questionable as the essential moment of improvisation.

Yes, it is true, habits, as Ravaisson emphasizes, are the product of past changes and always "open" for future changes, but in the moment—the performative present—they *enforce* themselves as forgetful habitual acts that one can either choose to combat (Paxton) or choose to observe and resign oneself to (Konjar); but as already seen, for Heidegger, choice in itself is not the decisive thing, it is *decision* that is decisive:

> What is decision at all? Not *choice*. Choosing always involves only what is pregiven and can be taken or rejected. *Decision* here means grounding and creating, disposing in advance and beyond oneself.[31]

In light of this, perhaps the locus of surprise changes. While the live-ness of the live improvised event has much to do with the choices made in the moment—some perceived as surprising, some not—the truth is that we (especially the audience) *expect* to be surprised in this way and, indeed, *anticipate* witnessing the unforeseeable consequences of unexpected choices. In short, at the epiphenomenal level of choice, surprise is often the most unsurprising thing imaginable, so much so that it is more of a surprise when we are *not* surprised. This brings us to the question of boredom and the consideration that it is precisely the boringness of the event that is most surprising of all.

As Heidegger reveals in his famous lectures on the subject,[32] boredom is not in essence the psychological experience of boring things, one that, as an antidote, endlessly craves surprising events as a means of fending off such tedium. On the contrary, he *affirms* boredom as a profound "attunement" to a particular "limbo" that reveals both the absence or ontological insignificance of lived clock time and the more essential temporality of being, one that encompasses all time—past, present, and future.

> What is boring is neither beings nor things as such, . . . nor human beings as people we find before us and can ascertain, neither objects nor subjects, but *temporality as such*. Yet this temporality does not stand alongside "objects" and "subjects," but constitutes the ground of the possibility of the subjectivity of subjects, and indeed in such a way that the *essence of subjects* consists precisely in *having Dasein*, i.e., in already enveloping beings as a whole *in advance*.[33]

Pulling a few threads together, we might suggest that improvisation, under-stood as a regime and enactment of choice, surprises us to the extent that it fends off boredom, something frequently associated with the accretion of habits. Keith Johnstone's *Theatresports* were unusually overt about this in their deployment of "judges" to identify and punish boringness:

> After much heart-searching, we decided that justice was less im-portant than getting dead scenes off the stage, and we said that any Judge could end any scene at any time (without consultation), but even then dreary scenes were sometimes allowed to continue while the bored Judges toyed with their rescue horns but were reluctant to "do the deed."
>
> These days the so-called Hell-Judges (improvisers who are sit-ting at the rear of the audience) can press a button when they're bored. This flashes a red "Hell-light" at the Judges' feet and in the lighting booth. The official Judges can ignore this, but it's likely to shake them out of their apathy.[34]

Amusing, but while this might keep the live event endlessly surprising, it distracts us from the essence of boringness which, as Heidegger claims, "en-velopes" our being "in advance." And the attunement to this is not a choice made in the moment before an audience of "judges" but an *a priori decision* that, to repeat Heidegger's phrase, "constitutes the ground of the possibil-ity of the subjectivity of subjects." This disjuncture between the time of the performance and what we might call the temporality of the event is captured in this brief remark by Konjar:

> One cannot be completely concentrated for 10 minutes a day while improvising, and be like a young goat for the rest of the time. It's a *decision* that improvisation becomes a life. (8)

And we must remember where our earlier epigraph comes from: Ni-etzsche's "The Uses and Disadvantages of History for *Life*," where life is understood as a creative and transformative process that requires the forget-fulness of will and habit as an antidote to the predominant remembrance of knowledge. Thus, *in essence*, the life of an improviser is not a life dedicated to the mastery of improvisation as a performative strategy, any more than it is an improvised life made up on the spot; nor is the decisive moment the moment when the improviser announces: "I have decided: improvisation will from this day onward be my life." No; for all of their importance, these remain *a posteriori* choices made as part of the actualization of decisions already made "*in advance*" of conscious self-knowledge and subjective commitment. So *who* makes the decision then?

In spite of their often profound differences, all of our thinkers—Hegel, Nietzsche, Heidegger, Derrida, Badiou, and Deleuze—arrive at some form of constructed or deconstructed singularity/subjectivity that is consequent to a confrontation with *chance* (contingency, *amor fati*, Mallarmé's "dice throw" . . .) and which, through either negation, reservation, or affirmation, ultimately makes possible some conception, no matter how fluid or discontinuous, of an individual life. In an interview with Lorenzo Fabbri shortly after Derrida's death, Jean-Luc Nancy acknowledges the idea being grasped for here:

> It is as if, with Derrida, it is not just a great or even a very great philosopher who has passed away but . . . an entire epoch, that is, an entire chance for philosophy. Indeed, the chance of philosophy or else philosophy as chance.[35]

And in a postscript to the interview, he adds,

> Beyond the personal chance that Derrida will have been for me, he was and he remains a chance for everyone, for all of philosophy.[36]

So, we become who we are by taking or not taking chances as they arise. The philosopher becomes a philosopher by taking different chances than those taken by the dancer (although not all that different, if Badiou is to be believed), but it remains chance that governs the decisive moment, or "the beginning." Indeed, and here we return to the possessive/de-possessive hybridity of the event, to *take* a chance is too voluntaristic, ignoring as it does the disappropriative moment of being *taken-by* chance or *taken-by* surprise. This helps explain why, in spite of the differences mentioned, all of our thinkers recognize the *a posteriori* nature of singular and/or universal identity. Like Hegel's "owl of Minerva" and Walter Benjamin's "angel of history" ("the storm irresistibly propels him into the future to which his back is turned"),[37] the decisive event is always, to use Badiou's term, "retroactive":

> Strictly speaking, a site is only "evental" insofar as it is retroactively qualified as such by the occurrence of an event. However, we do know one of its ontological characteristics, related to the form of presentation: it is always an abnormal multiple, on the edge of

the void. Therefore, there is no event save relative to a historical situation.[38]

But, and this is the crucial issue for us here, we *do* take possession of what we are possessed by to the extent that we embark upon a life that is formed and transformed by the repetition of this evental moment in habitual acts that, in a reversal of our prevailing improvisatory *doxa*, and to return to Catherine Malabou, "ends up canonizing being's improvisations."[39]

> "Plastic individuals" are those that synthesize in their very "style" the essence of the genus and the accident which has become habitual. What in the beginning was merely an accidental fact— Plato's commitment to philosophy, Pericles' to politics, Phidias to sculpture—is changed through the continual repetition of the same gestures, through practice, achieving the integrity of a "form." Effected by habit, the singularity of the "plastic individual" becomes an *essence a posteriori* . . . . The philosopher, the political man or sculptor, are determinations which could not have been anticipated just by the simple generic definition of man: they are destinies contained *virtually* in the genus "man," but remain there as something unpredictable. By forming themselves, by undergoing repetition and practice, these determinations ultimately construct a state which is habitual and accordingly *essential*. Habit is the process whereby the contingent becomes essential.[40]

Everything is here: improvisation, habit, the unanticipated, the unpredictable, retroaction, and the evental beginning; the remaining problem is to bring all of this to bear on the actuality of a live improvised event.

After repeated readings of his *Chapbook*, it becomes clear that Konjar's repetition of Paxton's *Goldberg Variations* itself reveals a significant difference not only in their approaches to improvisation but, underpinning that, to repetition itself. As Paxton explains to Konjar, his primary aim was "to not repeat myself" (16), to which the latter perceptively responds, "If the score was not to do what you know you have done before, wouldn't the shows be very similar to one another?" (17). This brilliant question brings back into play the boringness of improvisation, while also allowing us to call upon Deleuze to help us consider a crucial distinction.

Paxton's conviction is that it is the *avoidance* of repetition that creates *difference*, whereas for Deleuze such a strategy can only produce diversity, which for him is a form of sameness and which, for us, helps explain the boringness of so much improvisation that strives to be infinitely different but achieves only diversity: the same difference rather than a different sameness. This is how Deleuze articulates it in *Difference and Repetition*: "Difference is not diversity. Diversity is given, but difference is that by which the given is given, that by which the given is given as diverse."[41] Underpinning this is the already-encountered distinction Deleuze draws between two forms of repetition, which, in this context, will offer us a way into the differences between Konjar and Paxton. Here is the crucial passage:

> In one case, the difference is taken to be only external to the concept; it is a difference between objects represented by the same concept, falling into the indifference of space and time. In the other case, the difference is internal to the idea; it unfolds as pure movement, creative of a dynamic space and time which corresponds to the idea. The first repetition is repetition of the Same; . . . the second includes difference. . . . One is negative, occurring by default in the concept; the other affirmative, occurring by excess in the Idea. . . . One is horizontal, the other vertical.[42]

Setting up a very crude dichotomy here, it might be suggested that Paxton's improvisations exemplify the first of Deleuze's forms of repetition, while Konjar's exemplify the second. This, incidentally, is not a critical statement; it has no bearing on the quality of the dancing or improvising, but simply marks a difference.

The originary *concept* for Paxton is clearly the self; the deep structure of the habitual "me" that he constantly confronts and then tries to negate through the creation, on the horizontal plane, of non-habitual gestures, which, however, ultimately "fail" to recognize or sufficiently address the difference or "excess" of the idea of the originary self *itself*. The result is a repetitive, improvised gesture of difference that produces only a *diverse* perspective on an unchanging, undifferentiated, and ultimately static concept of the habitual "me." In other words, for all of his talk of choice and "choosing to choose" (17), Paxton leaves unacknowledged the *decisive* moment in his own life as a dancer/improviser, one that renders all subsequent habit-breaking action epiphenomenal and, in fact, testimony to and in service to the improvisatory essence of habit formation itself. What is beyond choice is fate, as Nietzsche (quoted with approval by Deleuze) is at pains to remind us:

> There is something irreducible in the depths of the spirit: a monolithic bloc of Fatum, of *decision already taken* on all problems in their measure and their relations to us; and also a right that we have

> to accede to certain problems, like a hot-iron brand imprinted on
> our names.[43]

In a sense, it was Paxton's inability to follow Nietzsche and Deleuze and develop a love of fate (*amor fati*)—an acceptance of his brand—that resulted
in his final choice to give up the task:

> So there is a choosing going on in this improvisation. Not that I
> know where I'm going, but I'm very aware of what I am not do-
> ing. And I am doing something. I'm really trying to do the dancing
> strategy that I have arrived at. Until it became too complex, until I
> had done everything. (17)

But the *decisive* issue is not about *doing* but about *having* (*habere*) and
of being-had-by. Looked at again, it is clear that Konjar's "NO score," although reverberating with Paxton's negativity is, in truth, much more affirmative than it seems. While he speaks of excluding "all the 'me's'" (I
do, I want, I am), the very plurality of the concept reveals a more decisive
multiplicity in the originary idea. But, more directly, having made this exclusive gesture (in the spirit of his mentor), he immediately considers the
circumstances by which they come back into play.

> If the flow itself becomes the focus, the other "me's" can become
> active elements in the process; elements that can play or not, enter
> or exit, be observed. . . . They can be looked upon from some dis-
> tance, and manipulated; instead of dogmatically limiting (through
> the "no" logic) what the movement can or cannot be. (20)

This reference to the dogmatism of a "no" logic is a sure sign that Konjar is increasingly aware of the space between himself and Paxton, and his
proposal of a new "YES dance" compounds this while, at the same time,
confirming his commitment to a *vertically* differentiated model of the self
that promises more than surface diversity.

> A new score for GV—a YES dance of one hour.
>   The movement does not need "me" in order to be happening,
> but the flow of movement can be played with by *all I am and [am]*
> *able to observe.* (20)

There is a subtle but real distinction here between the performative "me"
that takes ownership of the horizontal and successive improvisational space-

time and the "all I am," which is in excess of this performative moment and, through restraint, observation, and relinquishment brings into view the decisive vertical difference that *simultaneously* allows choice and habit to coexist—the choice of habit/the habit of choosing.

> Bottom line: There is more than just a moment, that's an illusion I've built for myself which was useful for a time. Now my mind tells me there are also habit, composition, and making choices. There is planning, assuming; and there are thoughts about an audience. (21)

Note the difference: where Paxton valorizes the moment of choice in a doomed effort to outrun the *a priori* presence of *decision*, Konjar recognizes that such choices can only be made within an improvisatory "flow" that is *already happening*. To be crudely dichotomous again, Paxton is primarily concerned with the improvisation of *beings*, whereas Konjar is more willing to "accept" what Malabou described as "being's improvisations," improvisations only revealed through the formation and transformation of habit. This explains Konjar's move away from the "NO" of his mentor to the "YES" of his own situation.

Near the end of the "Chapbook," Konjar begins enumerating his "own" habits (the habits that "own" him): "continuous turning . . . a movement initiative from the spine . . . the habit to use the hands in a sort of "stay away" of "I give up" gesture . . ." (32), and so on. The question he then asks again marks the distance he has traveled from Paxton since the *Fake It!* project began.

> My question to myself is not how to avoid these elements [habits], but what to do with them when they appear. I could take a different approach and try to do something completely different, but actually I've done that too, several times, until it became another pattern [habit]. (32)

Like Paxton, Konjar recognizes the futility of trying to outwit habit, which can only result in the habit of outwitting habit. But, as he says, his response is different; it is not a question of avoiding habits but of *doing something with them* when they appear: but what does he do? Almost Nietzschean, Konjar returns again to the theme of restraint and a recognition (with Nietzsche) that the strongest will is the will *not* to will. Indeed, the following passage could have been written by Nietzsche himself! Perhaps he was reading him at the time.

> It seems that the hardest thing to do in life sometimes is to let go, to fall in love, or to be patient, or not to say something. . . . So the hardest thing becomes to do less, or not to do. . . . I could say I'm *discovering the improvisation* through this process, not unlike the simple folk who, when Dionysus plays the flute, are unable to stop themselves from dancing and laughing. . . . And so again, it's a circle through time, and it's a game of question and answer where each calmly follows each other's tails, knowing they'll never catch them (though when they try too hard DO catch them, they quickly let them go again and keep playing the game). (30)

What does he do? He *affirms* both habit and the choices made available to the improviser by habit. In this way he *discovers* the improvisation that, in a sense, has *already* had to take place in order for him to develop the habits necessary for any performance to take place. But this affirmation is by no means a weak and sycophantic yea-saying (Nietzsche assigned this role to Zarathustra's donkey), one that merely accepts the given as given, the habitual as habitual; no, the will not to will is essentially different from not willing at all. Heidegger would say, in the same vein, it is precisely "letting be" (the *affirmative* act of renunciation) that reveals the work of truth, the opening-closing/approaching-withdrawing "sway" of Being, without which its ontological difference would be obscured, and the subsequent actualization of this difference through the eternal repetition of chance events (improvisations) would pass unnoticed. To repeat, if habits are nothing more than the repetition of chance events within the flux of an infinitely differentiated Being (Heidegger) or Idea (Deleuze), then it requires the *affirmation* of chance in order to reveal the decisive or evental character of such habits; otherwise, they will remain contingent, arbitrary, ontologically and performatively insignificant. Deleuze manages to distil these thoughts in one brilliant passage:

> The most difficult thing is to make chance an object of *affirmation*, but it is the sense of the imperative and the questions that it launches. Ideas emanate from it just as singularities emanate from that aleatory point which every time condenses the whole of chance into one time. It will be said that by assigning the imperative origin of Ideas to this point we invoke only the arbitrary, the simple arbitrariness of a child's game, the child-god. This, however, would be to misunderstand what it means to "affirm." Chance is only arbitrary in so far as it is not affirmed or not sufficiently affirmed; . . . when chance is sufficiently affirmed, the player can no longer lose,

> since every combination . . . is by nature adequate to the place and
> the mobile command of the aleatory point.[44]

Where Paxton "loses" his battle against his "own" habits, Konjar, like Deleuze, recognizes that it is not a question of winning or losing but of accepting and affirming: as Nietzsche says, "I never had any choice."

17 Habit and Event: Rehearsing, Practising, Improvising

> The event . . . in its impassibility and its impenetrability has no present. It rather retreats and advances in two directions at once, being the perpetual object of a double question: What is going to happen? What has just happened? The agonizing aspect of the pure event is that it is always and at the same time something which has just happened and something about to happen; never something which is happening.
>
> **Gilles Deleuze**[1]

So, does this mean that there *is* no live event? That the intensity of the improvised moment, where things really start to "happen," is nothing more than a sham, a self-deception or, worse still, a concoction cynically manufactured to satisfy an event-hungry audience only too eager to pay good money for a few *ersatz* surprises and some unpredictability? Once again we can here bemoan the fact that Deleuze rarely speaks of improvisation, probably because, like Derrida, he is deeply skeptical of the over-inflated, emancipatory claims too often made for it. However, when he does all-too-fleetingly touch upon the subject, he does offer some clues as to how we might begin to answer the above questions: what *is* happening? Inevitably, we have to return to the same passage in order to read it again, *differently*.

> One launches forth, hazards an improvisation. But to improvise is to join the world, or meld with it.

One ventures from home on the thread of a tune. Along sonorous, gestural, motor lines that mark the customary path of a child and graft themselves onto or begin to bud "lines of drift" with different loops, knots, movements, gestures and sonorities.[2]

"One launches forth, hazards an improvisation . . ."

Improvisation prides itself on being chancy, on *taking* chances, on being hazardous (*hazardeux*), but what does taking a chance actually mean anyway? It is commonly assumed that the unpredictability of the improvised event relates to the unanticipatable results of the improviser(s) leaping into the unknown, of "launching forth" into the uncharted waters of the new and what Peggy Phelan would see as the unreproduced and unreproducible.[3] Steve Paxton attempted this and "failed"; much of what passes for improvisation doesn't even make the attempt, partly because the results are too boring. If audiences want improvisations to be eventful, which seems likely, then they have to be surprising, but the fact is that what counts as a surprise has become closely associated with the ability of the improviser to "play" with the very well-known either collectively or individually: the improviser's own past remembered as an accumulation of trademark mannerisms, idiosyncrasies, and familiar stylizations, the unfixing of the fixed, the breaking of external or self-imposed rules—improvisation as transgression. The latter is all about habits, of course, but in the bad sense intended by Nietzsche at the outset: bad habits are not transformed by being played around with; they remain bad until they are "sufficiently affirmed." This brings us back to Deleuze, who is suggesting something very different. For him, improvisation is hazardous to the extent that it neither leaps into the unknown nor falls back into the all-too-well-known; it has nothing to do with ignorance or knowledge, except to the degree that, as we have seen, knowledge is the vanishing moment between our first and second nature. To take a chance is to *affirm* chance, an act of *will* that in willing *not* to will, not to leap in and take possession of the moment, allows "being's improvisations" to emerge and be "discovered" as the swarming of universal habitual gestures around the singularity of the momentary act. The discovery of an improvisation through the revelation of habitual behavior is not to confront the deeply known but the radically unknown, that which, as will, is outside of all knowledge, neither mine nor yours, neither subjective nor objective, but *Neutral*. The word Blanchot always links with neutrality is "fascination," and perhaps this is one way of moving away from idea that the event is surprising: the *fascination* of the event.

"To improvise is to join the world, or meld with it . . ."

Another word for the neutral would be *world*. Following Heidegger, to whom he is closer than is often acknowledged, Deleuze is not referring to "our" world, the familiar surroundings that offer us a home. He is not suggesting for a moment that joining the world in any way resembles the collective consciousness of belonging to the "world of improvisation," a place of dialogue, interaction, sharing, and enabling, celebrated and affirmed for its own reasons. For Deleuze, joining the world is a hazardous enterprise; indeed, his use of the word *meld* is itself very telling, given that it means not only to blend or fuse different elements, but also refers to the initial laying down of one's cards in a card game: the affirmation of chance that inaugurates the game.[4] Here play is not playing around with what is there and available, but putting things *into* play. Thus to join the world is both to affirm chance and to accept that the self is only self to the extent that it is welded to the improvisatory becoming of being and its localized actualizations in habitual gestures.

"Motor lines that mark the customary path of a child . . ."

In its purest form—arguably, "free improvisation"—Niklas Luhmann's model of creativity as the "marking of an unmarked space" has some legitimacy, as long as we remember that the mark *itself* is already marked, as Konjar observes "the movement is marked"[5] when discovering that he anticipates what might seem to be an unanticipatable movement. Once again, this reminds us of the going forward facing backward model of improvisation, where it is the path *already trodden* that provides the improviser with the marks or lines to mark or striate the virgin space behind one's back so to speak. As Deleuze asserts, these marks are customary, the product of repetition and habit, produced as the very "foundation of time"[6] during what might be called, in quasi Hegel-fashion, the "infancy" of the self. Also, the child is "passive" and receptive to habit in a way that is anathema to the guileful self-consciousness we have witnessed above, but essentially the child is also a beginning, an exemplar of the dynamic transformative moment of habit formation that, thanks to the moment of *contemplation*, can literally make a difference.

> These thousands of habits of which we are composed—these contractions, *contemplations*, pretensions, presumptions, satisfactions, fatigues; these variable presents—thus form the basic domain of passive syntheses. The passive self is *not* defined simply

by receptivity—that is, by means of the capacity to experience sensations—but by virtue of the contractile *contemplation* which constitutes the organism itself before it constitutes the sensations . . . There is a self wherever a *furtive contemplation* has been established, whenever a contracting machine capable of *drawing a difference from repetition* functions somewhere.[7]

In the seven-hour *A–Z* video interview with Deleuze, there is no *H* for Habit but, interestingly, he does discuss habit briefly under *K* for Kant.[8] The subject arises in relation to Kant's famously habitual character, exemplified by his daily walks, by which "you could set your watch," . . . etc. But the point Deleuze is keen to make throughout this excursion is not the exterior form of the habit—the fastidiousness, the regime, the walk—but the *contemplation* that, Deleuze imagines, must have taken place on these habitual outings, something of which we know we have no knowledge—the essence of neutrality. This, of course, is what is so fascinating about Kant; that this most rule-bound of philosophers was responsible, through such "furtive contemplation," for the most radical transformation of Western thought. Indeed, a thorough reading of Kant reveals him to be an exemplary improviser: "Kantian Improvisation"—another book!

". . . begin to bud 'lines of drift' with different loops, knots, movements, gestures and sonorities."

In a world of "how to" guides to everything—not least improvisation— what advice can we give to the budding improviser? First off: actually *be* budding and begin to bud lines of drift. That would be an excellent starting point; the different loops, knots, movements, gestures, and sonorities will, if the budding is successful, follow as a matter of course. But seriously, to recognize that the "customary," habitual motor lines are, in fact, lines of *drift* and are thus the traces of repeated "erring" (as Heidegger would describe it), or "being's improvisations" (with Malabou), rather than the iron-clad teleological linearity of an irreversible destiny, is to recognize that we both contract, *but also contemplate* the habits that form and, through contemplation, also transform us. Deleuze again:

> One is only what one *has* [habit]: here, being is formed or the passive self *is*, by having. Every contraction [of habit] is a presumption, a claim—that is to say, it gives rise to an *expectation* or a right in regard to that which it contracts, and comes undone once its object escapes. . . . It is always a question of *drawing a small difference* . . . .

> In all its component fatigues, in all its mediocre auto-satisfactions, in all its derisory presumptions, in its misery and its poverty, the dissolved self [the melded self that has "joined the world"] still sings the glory of God—that is, of that which it *contemplates*, contracts and possesses.[9]

We can now go back to our question: If the event has always *already happened* or is *about to happen*, then what do we experience in the "now" of an improvised event? We obviously experience *something*, or else why bother showing up. Obviously, on one level, what might be described (post–Merleau Ponty) as the phenomenologically embodied level, we seek out the aliveness of the live in the presence of the other's body/bodies; we speak of seeing the performer "in the flesh," and it is this, the intense physicality of the live moment, that cannot be re-presented or re-produced. Just as obviously, we are also aware, thanks in part to Philip Auslander, that the experience of live-ness can be just as intense when witnessing a performance that is both disembodied and endlessly reproducible (such as visiting a multiplex screen). But do these different, and now somewhat entrenched, positions really grasp the essential issue? Instead of dwelling on what might or might not constitute the live-ness of the event, would it not make more sense to consider the event-ness of the live? This may not solve any problems or settle any disputes, but it at least has the potential to change the parameters of the discussion.

In a way, we are suggesting a new habit of thinking to break the apparent deadlock. As Malabou announces at the end of her preface to Ravaisson's *Of Habit*, in an effort to herself break out from under the rule of her own teacher and mentor Derrida,

> Because we are habituated to habit, we end up as seeing in it only something bad. . . . Perhaps this has happened to ourselves. Perhaps it has happened to deconstruction. But the rejection of habit . . . can become a tic, like anything else. . . . Prepare, then, before being overwhelmed by tics, to get out of the habit of rejecting habit, to habituate yourself to habit![10]

Can we do the same?

What both of the above positions on live-ness have in common is what Derrida describes as a "metaphysics of *presence*." While this is obvious in the case of Phelan, it is just as true of Auslander, given that whether what is experienced in the live moment is produced or re-produced, embodied or disembodied, it is nevertheless valorized as a presence, "now." Live-ness *is* presence, regardless of its immediacy or mediacy. It would be fairly straightforward to deconstruct these binaries and counter such presence with the inherent absence of *différance*, but that, as Malabou admits, would be to fall back into yet another habit of thought.

Maybe the way forward is to forget presence and absence and remind ourselves of the dualisms we have already been working with: having and doing, possession and dispossession, past (the already happened) and future (the about to happen), decision and choice, contraction and contemplation, surprisingness and boringness, . . . and so on.

We might begin with decision and choice. It is Konjar who describes improvisation as a life rather than just an event, the first being decisive, the second being the temporary enactment of choices in an improvisation. Indeed, not forgetting another dualism—Badiou's site-situation—we could even hazard the suggestion that the life of the improviser is the evental site, while the performative moment is a situation—a live situation rather than a live event. This might help Konjar's answer to his own question:

> The question that came up was: what am I rehearsing every day? If this is improvisation (which you can't do if you know what you're going to do), what am I doing every day in the studio, and why? [11]

Practising, Preparing, and Rehearsing

This is indeed a very good question. One way of answering it might be to consider such rehearsal as *preparation*, whereby the improvisation in a sense begins before the live event itself. Something similar to the (perhaps apocryphal) stories of John Coltrane beginning some of his extended improvised solos long before he actually walked out on stage, only for them to continue long after he had left the stage. What is certain is that he often did (with Eric Dolphy) practise not just between gigs but between sets! In an interview with Grayson Cooke, Mike Cooper makes a useful distinction between rehearsal and preparation.

> I don't rehearse as such unless I'm forced to. . . . I think preparing is a better word. . . . I often go weeks, if there are no public performance commitments, without touching a musical instrument, but I am always listening to and thinking about music. . . . Preparation for performance depends on the situation I am about to engage with. If it's a solo performance I don't do anything in particular immediately before a concert or event. *I have been preparing for that all my life.* It is an ongoing thing. I actually avoid even think-

ing about it if I can because the moment I start playing, the event takes over.[12]

In spite of the expressed desire to separate his preparation from the event, and indeed to conceive of his own life in these terms, there can be no escaping the preparatory teleological thrust of such thinking, which ultimately conceives of life's course as one punctuated with perpetually prepared-for performances. Detectable here perhaps, albeit prior to the event, is the familiar suspicion of practise as a process by which habits are formed and further ingrained: "preparation" seems so much more open to the future and its possibilities, so much more anticipatory.

Derek Bailey is sensitive to this suspicion of practising and preparation, acknowledging that many improvisers "subscribe to an approach which prefers an abrupt confrontation with whatever is offered by each performing situation. A self-contained unique experience undiluted by anything in the nature of preparatory musical press-ups. . . . "[13] Having said that, he is unapologetically "heretical" as regards his own regime of practising, which he divides into three different but interrelated categories:

> Firstly, the normal basic technical practise, the musical equivalent to running on the spot; . . . perhaps I do it because I actually like practising. . . . The second area of practise is centred on exercises worked out to deal with the manipulative demands of new material . . . The third area . . . is similar to something known in jazz circles as "woodshedding"; . . . it is the bridge between technical practise and improvisation. . . . The playing might be the same as when improvising but the focus of attention will be on the details of playing rather than the totality, and what is being exercised is *choice*.[14]

Looked at in reverse: practise as "woodshedding," whether situated within an idiom that provides the resources from which choices are made or outside such canonic parameters, opening onto the "freedom" of one's own invention, is essentially the preparation for a performance to come. Although concentrating on what is there and available, and thus backward-, or at least sideways-looking, the orientation is toward what Heidegger might call a certain but indefinite future: something will happen, but we don't know exactly what or when. The "woodshedder" attempts to make the best choices in preparation for, and *in advance of* the "in-the-moment" moment of an improvisation, which, as Bailey is only too well aware, is never absolutely unique or "undiluted." The second form or dimension of practising is also in essence the result of choice; the improviser chooses to put himself into situations that will demand a response to the demands of manipulating new material. And, in a sense, here we see a desire for the new or the other, which is, whether consciously or not, pitting choice against the habitual and the all-too-familiar. But, as Bailey's first form of practising should remind us, familiarity does not always breed contempt; on the contrary, the repetitive treadmill of practising what is so deeply known that it no longer functions as a form of knowledge brings a feeling of pleasure that has nothing to do with choice. Indeed, it has nothing to do with practise either: what Bailey is actually describing is rehearsing.

Unlike preparation, which may or may not have a repetitive dimension, rehearsal is inherently and thus inescapably repetitive, and for some, let's face it, "life *is* a rehearsal." What is more, rehearsal encompasses preparation in way that is not reversible: to prepare is not necessarily to rehearse, as Cooper confirms, but to rehearse is necessarily to prepare, if only in an abstract sense. But Konjar's question remains: What is he rehearsing? If there is not an existing work, score, script, screenplay, or whatever in place, then what exactly is being repeated? This is why the concept of preparation seems to fit the improviser's situation so well; its inherent futurity and focus on the *yet-to-happen* seem to remove it from the order of repetition, which in itself may be viewed as an emancipatory gesture. It should be remembered, however, that, for Deleuze at least, emancipation from repetition is also emancipation from difference, and thus enslavement to the order of the same.

So what *does* the improviser rehearse? At the most general and perhaps most essential level, it is rehearsing *itself* that must be rehearsed; the very act of rehearsing—as a life-long task—bespeaks a decisive commitment far more significant than the choices made while rehearsing or performing. Without "contracting" the habit of rehearsing, the "contemplation" necessary for the habitual to become transformative and "make a difference" in the way described above would never take place.

How is it possible to speak of the surprise of the event in the wake of such tedious repetition? How do we get from boredom to wonder? Or perhaps boredom itself is wonderful. One aspect of Heidegger's discussion of boredom is well worth considering here. He describes boredom as a form of "attunement" to Being, an idea that would surely resonate with many performers as they engage in the daily grind of rehearsing. This also brings us back to the contemplative moment of habit insisted on by Deleuze. Rehearsing could certainly be considered boring to the extent that it consists in the endless repetition of that which is already deeply known: the all-too-familiar battery of exercises, scales, gestures, clichés, and tics—from the most instructed to the most habitual—that drive this eternal recurrence of the same. And yet, something else is taking place: out of this rote (and here we are forced to use another battery of tired clichés) a certain "one-ness" with the "world" and with "ourselves" is sensed, a feeling of "balance," "well-being," of "harmony," coupled with a heightened "sureness of touch" and movement and a heightened "certitude" bringing a sense of "clarity" and "focus" rarely achieved outside of the rehearsal room. In short, attunement, an attunement that, to recall Deleuze, is "passive" to the extent that it is a product of the "thousands of habits of which we are composed" but also *active* in that it is *us* who are responsible for their activation and deployment. Put another way, we are all possessed by our habits, but we *take possession* of them to the extent that we rehearse them and then "contemplate" the results in the realm of the senses, and for Deleuze (contrary to Badiou), the event always takes place within the sphere of the sensible.

The problem with the above clichés of attunement is that, since being hijacked in the swinging sixties by assorted liberals and hippies, they have become overly subjectivized and enslaved to a touchy-feely, well-being agenda that would be enough to make Merleau-Ponty's flesh crawl. As Heidegger is at pains to emphasize, it is not the fact that you or I might be bored that is of interest, but that "*one* is bored." His concern is not the subjective experience of boredom but that "it" is boring. For him, the subjective experience of boredom relates to an existential un-event-fulness that is essentially different from the *event* of boredom as an ontological category. Perhaps this helps explain what Konjar means when he describes improvising as waiting for "it" to arrive. Of course, "it" is not itself boring; it is rather the presence of boredom that offers, through attunement, access to "it," which is the event.

Looking past the clichés then, but retaining some of their sense, there is clearly a concern with *discovery* that is important here—not the discovery of the new but the discovery of what is already there: the given. But, importantly, what is given is not just the self; there is much more to discovery than "self-discovery," which, to repeat, is a sixties thing, so it can be safely ignored. To be sure, the act of *re-hear-sing* allows performers to hear themselves sing again and again, perpetually rendering themselves audible/visible to themselves as performers, artists, improvisers, and thus enabling the "self-recognition" that Hegel saw as fundamental to the dialectical formation of subjective identity. But for Heidegger and Deleuze, there is much more to "hear" than the cacophony of the self; indeed, Heidegger's favorite sense is hearing, and his work is full of the demand that we learn to "listen" and "hearken," not to ourselves or even to each other, but to Being. This is why he is so keen to break with Western aesthetics, which, in spite of or, indeed, *because of* his increasing interest in art, he believes obscures the essence of art by placing the subject (artist) and the object (artwork) in the way, thus rendering art both inaudible and invisible. Here is a well-known passage from Heidegger's "The Origin of the Work of Art" as an example of his thinking:

> The artist is the origin of the work of art. The work is the origin of the artist. Neither is without the other. Nevertheless, neither is the sole support of the other. In themselves and in their interrelations, artist and work *are* each of them by virtue of a third thing which is prior to both, namely, that which also gives artist and work of art their names—art.[15]

The *a priori* nature of art in Heidegger's thought is often confused with an aesthetic conservatism, which has led to the prevalent view that he is only concerned with art of the past. In fact art history is of no interest to him; his primary concern is with the ontological *a priority* of art as that which supports and makes possible the subjective-objective actualization of artist-artwork in the *present*. In this respect, as with virtuality and actuality in Deleuze, to which this is related, artist, artwork, and art are all co-present as the vertical and horizontal dimensions of Being. Similarly, it would be quite wrong to understand Heidegger's concern with the origin of the work of art as having anything to do with an interest in the historical origins of art in any archaeological sense. On the contrary, in his view the origin (as source, *Ursprung*) is ontologically irrelevant, nothing more than an insignificant commencement or trivial beginning. No, the origin—to the extent that it relates to the temporal unconcealment of truth—is itself in need of preservation, which itself implies an ontologically prior moment of creativity. In other words, the inceptuality of the origin is not merely the start of something but its *beginning*, its *origination* in the on-going creation and preservation of art through the fixing and unfixing effected by artists and their artworks. Although rather laboring the Heidegger-style wordplay, to conceive of re-hear-sing as the site where the originary truth of art and, by implication, Being can be "hearkened-to" as it sings out repeatedly through the working of the work of art does offer some insight into real significance of rehearsal, not as the preparation for what is *to happen* but as the preservation of that which has always *already happened*, preserved in order that it might *happen again*, repeatedly.

For Heidegger, the importance of hearing as a means of opening the senses to the event of Being is that, unlike the "covetous vision of things" and the "work of the eyes,"[16] listening to song, as he conceives it, is more attuned to the disappropriative/dispossessive/un-enowned dimension of the event. In particular, it is the extent to which we can bring the re-sonance and re-sounding of song into tune with the possessed dispossessiveness of re-hearsing that will allow us to identify the ontological significance of the endless work in the studio, at home or, indeed, in one's head. Above all else, though, what we are trying to grasp here is the fact that the origination and re-origination of art does not take place as a consequence of the artists' increasing mastery of "our" aesthetic form and its associated gestures—rehearsal is not training—but through the daily ritual of witnessing our habitual second nature unfolding before our eyes/ears as that which is un-owned but which must nevertheless be preserved. This returns us to our earlier discussion of fixity and unfixity, improvisation as fixing or unfixing, where the emphasis usually falls upon the latter. Counterintuitively, Hei-degger, who acknowledges the necessity of both creation and preservation as essential to art, conceives of the latter rather than the former as being the moment of unfixing:

> Art is the fixing in place of a self-establishing truth in the figure. This happens in creation as the bringing forth of the unconcealed-ness of what is. Setting-into-work, however, also means: the bring-ing of work-being into movement and happening. This happens as preservation.[17]

Thought in this way, the relentless repetition of endless rehearsal—life as rehearsal—might be better understood as the necessary process whereby the creative fixing of Being in art production or the "canonization of being's im-provisations" in habitual aesthetic tropes, figures, and gestures are preserved not as tradition or "the canon" but as the happening or *event* that they were and, through such preservation, remain. This will help us answer Konjar's question for him: "What am I rehearsing every day?" his assumption be-ing that, as improvisation does not involve the knowledge and mastery of an existing work, then there is nothing *to* rehearse. But obviously there is, else what are he and other improvisers doing all day? So let us add another related term and make another distinction: we have already distinguished rehearsal and preparation, so we can add here the concept of *practise*.

As the well-known cliché "Practise makes perfect" makes clear, practis-ing is essentially linear, progressive, and teleological, whereas rehearsing is circular, regressive, and without an ultimate goal, whether utopian or not. Practising is inherently futural; rehearsal is inherently historical. Practising is a form of work, but it is one in service to either the mastery of a work or the mastery of a practice, understood as a body of work, where the verb becomes a noun, and acts become things or skills. Practising is intentional, the intention being to progress within the parameters of given performative benchmarks; rehearsing is retentional and protentional, to stretch somewhat the reach of Husserl's phenomenological terminology. Rehearsal is not concerned with self-improvement but with the retention, preservation, and the continued "happening" in the future (protention) of what is already given as a *working* rather than a work; that is to say, as ontologically evental rather than existentially eventful.

The event for Heidegger is above all else the remembering of Being understood as the revelation of the happening of truth; but it is the ontic, existential and "dissembling" forms of Being's being that problematize this task of remembrance, not least because such forms, figures, and gestures become what they are through the forgetfulness of habitual thinking and doing. But it is not just a question of forgetting the forgetfulness of habit and remembering Being, because, as Nietzsche recognizes, "new habits" are still habits, just as the habit of remembering is fundamentally habitual in spite of itself—*all* being is habitual, to recall Ravaisson. So it is not a question of getting "beyond" habits and the concealment and dissemblance associated with them, but of capturing or sensing again and again the moment when the liquidity of chance is solidified into the fixity of habit. Heidegger, like Benjamin, describes this revelation of what might be called the dissembling of dissembling as a form of illumination or en-light-enment (*Lichtung*), where "concealment . . . occurs within what is lighted." He continues:

> Concealment can be refusal or dissembling . . . Concealment conceals and dissembles itself. This means: the open place in the midst of beings, the clearing, is never a rigid stage with a permanently raised curtain on which the play of beings runs its course. Rather, the clearing only happens as this double concealment. The unconcealedness of beings—this is never a merely existent state, but a happening. . . . We believe we are at home in the immediate circle of beings. That which is familiar, reliable, ordinary. Nevertheless, the clearing is pervaded by a constant concealment in the double form of refusal and dissembling. At bottom, the ordinary is not ordinary; it is extraordinary, uncanny.[18]

In other words, the ordinariness, reliability, and familiarity of our habits—their habituality—is not something to be transcended or escaped (*à la* Paxton) but rendered unfamiliar and uncanny through what Deleuze would call sensation and Heidegger often describes as dwelling, which, as we shall see shortly, are closely related. In particular it is the manner in which, by distinguishing dwelling from the home and homeliness, Heidegger believes we are capable of dwelling *within* that which has been rendered un-homely and extraordinary.

> The real dwelling plight lies in this, that mortals ever search anew for the nature of dwelling, that they *must ever learn to dwell*. What if man's homelessness consisted in this, that man still does not even think of the *real* plight of dwelling as *the* plight? Yet as soon as man *gives thought* to his homelessness, it is a misery no longer.[19]

Obviously, and in spite of his "turn" to art, Heidegger's primary concern, as can be seen here, is always with the task of *thinking* and, implicitly, with habits of *thought*, whereas our concern with improvisers is more about habitual patterns of behavior rather than figures or structures of thought. Of course improvisers think, but they think in order to do. Having said that, though, it is clear that Heidegger's interest in *techne* is aimed at capturing a mode of thinking that is more essential and more decisive than this superficial binarity of theory and practice. What is particularly useful about the notion of *techne* is that it enables us to refine further our distinction between rehearsing and practising as each relates to the ordinariness and extraordinariness of habit, respectively.

Undeniably, the daily grind of rehearsing and/or practising has much to do with the origination, maintenance, and development of technical ability: technique, properly understood, is everything in the arts, and particularly, one might say, in the performing arts. The aforementioned intentionality of practising is focused primarily on the solidification of chance idiosyncrasies and tics to the point where they take on law-like characteristics and facilitate a law-like delivery at the point of performance. Technical facility, prowess, and virtuosity become, through practise, defining *properties* of the self that can and often do take on moral, spiritual, and even mystical qualities for audiences hungry for "special ones." By allowing the artist/performer to take ownership of "being's improvisations" and, in a sense, privatize the infinite resources of universal fate, personal technique becomes the paramount means of concealing the happening of truth's work of unconcealment. We all know there is something phony about virtuosity, but can't quite explain why; well now we have it: virtuosity is, in its misappropriation of *techne* as technicality, a fundamental form of dissembling, and practise makes perfect dissemblers, notwithstanding Kurt Cobain's views to the contrary.[20] This should not be misinterpreted; in this view we need virtuosos just as we need dissemblers. Indeed, it is the singular and subjectivized desire or will to seek the perfection of habitual figures and gestures that creates or produces the technical resources necessary to re-think and re-enact the more essential event of *techne*. The more profound the concealment, the more profound the unconcealment, and, for Heidegger, it is technicality that conceals and *techne* that unconceals; both are essential, and thus he is clearly *not* a "critic" of technology in any banal sense.

Having looked at practising in terms of technique, we can now turn to rehearsing and consider it alongside *techne*, which Heidegger describes as follows in his "Origin of the Work of Art":

> *Techne* signifies neither craft nor art, and not at all the technical in our present-day sense; it never means a kind of practical performance. . . . The word *techne* denotes rather a mode of knowing. To know means to have seen, in the widest sense of seeing, which means to apprehend what is present. . . . *Techne* . . . is a bringing forth of beings in that it *brings forth* present beings as such beings *out of* concealedness and specifically *into* the unconcealedness of their appearance.[21]

Or again in his famous essay, "The Question Concerning Technology":

> *Techne* is linked with the word *episteme*. Both words are names for knowing in the widest sense. They mean to be entirely at home in something, to understand and be expert in it. Such knowing provides an opening up. As an opening up, it is a revealing. Aristotle . . . distinguishes between *episteme* and *techne* . . . with respect to how and what they reveal. *Techne* . . . reveals whatever does *not* bring itself forth and does *not* yet lie before us.[22]

We might say, then, that practise relies upon a body of existing knowledge (*episteme*) that can be *put into* practice; it is the transference of what lies before us and is already known from one domain to another: theory to practice. Rehearsing, on the other hand, can be understood as an enactment of *techne* to the extent that it is a form of *knowing* rather than a knowledge of the already given. Such knowing, while "entirely at home" and thus profoundly habitual is, as we saw earlier, a form of dwelling that is at home in the very *un-homeliness* of the homely. *Techne*, unlike *episteme*, brings forth what does *not* lie before us: the unfamiliar and the extra-ordinary. So when Konjar remarks that, as an improviser, he is not supposed to know what he is going to do, we can interpret and respond to this in two ways. Clearly improvisers *do* know what they are going to do, they are going to improvise: that's their job. And while it is true that improvisers may not have knowledge of what is going to happen in any precise detail (although even this is debatable), they practise in order to acquire the necessary *know-how* (*episteme*), be it technical or experiential, to be able to function effectively within such an ignorance economy: they have to know how to not know. To recall again Benjamin's vision of Klee's *Angelus Novus*, rushing into the future gazing at the past, practising provides the improviser with that past and makes available the resources from out of which the improvised future is chosen "in the moment." Without practise there would be nothing to choose, nor would the improviser develop the ability, or "skillset," necessary to make such choices. But, having said all of that, it is nevertheless true that, *epistemologically*, the improviser does not know what is going to happen.

Practise *prepares* the improviser for this negotiation with the unknown; rehearsal does not. Rehearsal has absolutely nothing whatever to do with the love or fear of the unknown, any more than it does with the dramatic uncertainties of the improvised event. Interestingly, it is precisely this fact that makes rehearsal so vital for the event-ness of the event. This means that practise ensures that something *will* happen, in spite of all the uncertainty; a performance *will* take place, no matter what. But ultimately this is all quite trivial; it is not that *things* happen which is significant; rather, it is *that* things happen—the *happening* of what happens—that is what en-livens the live and "brings forth" the event-ness of the event.

So this would be our second response to Konjar's question: While it might be true that the improviser has no (or limited) knowledge (*episteme*) of what will happen in an improvisation, the improvisatory act—as *techne*—is, as Heidegger insists, *already* a form of knowing or knowingness that is ontologically prior to and essentially other than the technicalities of the knowledge economy. Such knowingness—as *techne*—is not concerned with the production of artworks, crafts, or performances—"*techne* never signifies the act of making"[23]—and yet it is a creative act. As Deleuze argues in "What Is a Creative Act?" what all disciplines or domains have in common (philosophy, science, painting, film-making, music, performance, etc.) is the creation of specific space-times,[24] meaning that it is not what happens within the space-time of, let us say, an improvised performance that is the essential creative act, but the creation *of* the space-time within which the performance happens: *that*—the happening that allows things to happen—is the event.

This links Deleuze with Heidegger, whose notion of *Lichtung* is essential as the illuminated space-time within which the knowingness of *techne* "brings forth" out of concealedness the unconcealedness of truth. Admittedly Deleuze would balk at the final word in the last sentence, but that would be to ignore the fact that, as Deleuze himself recognizes, Heideggerian truth is riven with difference, and, for Deleuze, it is precisely this vertical-virtual difference that is actualized horizontally through the repetition of multiple improvisations. But it is the *transition from* the virtual to the actual, or from concealment to unconcealment, that, in opening-up and bringing forth, marks the creative act for Deleuze and *techne* for Heidegger. The importance of Deleuze at this point in the discussion is that by focusing exclusively on the moment of repetition in the articulation of difference, he reminds us that the French word for rehearse is indeed *repeter*.

We have already encountered Deleuze's differentiation of difference and diversity, which he thinks in relation to the repetition of difference and the repetition of the same. To extend this thought, we might speak of the *same difference* (diversity) and a *different sameness* (difference). This in turn suggests the following: that in preparation for an improvised event, *practise* enables the improviser to manufacture in advance a diverse repertoire of "solutions" to imagined "problems" that might occur in the performative confrontation and negotiation with the unknown. But it is not just a question of know-how; the "in-the-moment" moment leaves no time for the careful consideration of the epistemological structure and available resources that allow a performer to perform; it is not what you know but what you *do* that counts. The ability to translate knowledge into action, in the blink of an eye, is something that needs practise. This should remind us that practising is not primarily about mastering what you know or what is available to be known; rather, it is about transforming knowledge into habit. It is only by doing this that a performer could ever be prepared for an improvised performance, and it is the endless repetition of what we know that allows us to forget it—as habit—when we are required to act *now*. Obviously, the best habits are those that have built into them the greatest degree of flexibility and diversity when faced with the unknown, and it is this skillset that promises the most when it comes to audience expectations of surprise and wonder. But, to be clear, what we are describing here is the same difference or, to be more negative, the same old difference—a difference that only *becomes* old by repeatedly creating an illusion of new-ness: the same old new.

It is rehearsing that creates a different sameness. Practise operates at the level of choice, in that endless repetition and the conscious formation of "good" habits, allow the performer to *choose* different improvised strategies within the performative moment. Rehearsal operates at the level of *decision*, where the decisive moment is, while enacted in the now, the a priori "canonization of being's improvisations," where chance is transformed into habit: not the habit of doing but the habit of being—"Plato's commitment to philosophy, Pericles' to politics, Phidias to sculpture"—to recall Malabou's examples. Here commitment is not being used as an existential category, where the subject commits to his or her art practice and the self-identity that this brings with it (the artwork and the artist), but ontologically as that which one is committed to (as one is committed to the asylum); there is no voluntarism intended here. Deleuze says much the same in his book on Hume:

> We start with atomic parts, but these atomic parts have transitions, passages, "tendencies," which circulate from one to another. These tendencies give rise to *habits*. Isn't this the answer to the question "what are we?" We are habits, nothing but habits—the habit of saying "I."[25]

Just as Heidegger sees the *working* of art, rather than the work of art or the artist at work, as decisive, so beneath or behind the necessary dissemblance of practise lies another form of repetition that, to repeat, creates a different sameness rather than the same difference produced by practise. In a sense then, practising and rehearsing take place simultaneously: one creating performative habits, the other repeating the decisive transition of chance into habit and the origination of one's singular fate and the burning of one's brand.

So, what is the relation between practise, rehearsal, and improvised events? They are different: practise allows the practitioner to develop a practice that is stable enough and recognizable enough—habitual enough—to allow an improvisation to take place; practise is, to say again, a form of preparation. As such, the practice is a given at the moment of any improvisation, but the practise necessary to produce and maintain this practice must cease before the commencement of the performance itself. Put simply, an audience would quite rightly feel conned if they discovered that a live improvised event was in fact merely a practise run for another event yet to come.

This is not at all the case with rehearsal, understood in the ontological or virtual sense being considered here. Indeed, it is as a work of *re-hearsing* that the live event attains to the very live-ness and event-ness that is so cherished by performers and audiences alike. In other words, rehearsing is not the preparation for, but the *preservation of* an event: the transition from Being to beings (Heidegger), or from the virtual to the actual (Deleuze), or from being's improvisations to habit (Malabou). All of those days, months, and years of practising are fixated on the fixing of the unfixed in order for a performance to take place; but the live-ness and the event-ness of a performance are directly related to the sense in which the fixity of creative practice is unfixed as a moment of repetition. Not the repetition of technical skills (*episteme*) as a public spectacle, but the repetition of an act of knowing (*techne*) that clears a space-time within which truth (Heidegger) or the sensible (Deleuze) are dis-closed.

Perhaps an improvised event can be best understood as the *re-enactment* of the decisive moment where art becomes artist and artwork, or performance becomes the performer and the performed work. Perhaps something close to what Kierkegaard describes as "contemporaneousness," where the time of an originary and decisive leap of faith is synchronized with the "now" of continuing faith. Understood in this way, the live-ness of the event is not primarily about the lived experience of the performer and the audience as live embodied creatures existing together in a unique *now*: that is just happenstance. No, the live-ness of the event relates to two times: an originary moment that is, over time and habitually, fixed in the creative act; and the performative time of preservation in which this act is re-enacted, unfixed, and thus *enlivened* and re-vivified. The rehearsal of this does not cease prior to the commencement of the live event; rather, it is the defining characteristic *of* the event: all events are rehearsals. When they are not, they are neither events in the eventual sense, nor are they properly "live": lived perhaps in the most banal sense, but not *alive*. Yes, of course, live-ness means that something must be happening *now*, but it is not the now-ness that is essential but *what* is happening now that needs to be grasped. Yes, of course, live-ness bespeaks a unique moment that is unreproducible, but this is trivial if we don't acknowledge the fact that each of these pristine, unreproducible moments is itself the actualization (or preservation) of a decisive moment-movement that can only be re-called, re-heard, and re-lived to the extent that it can be reproduced. Live events cannot be reproduced, but that does not change the fact that, ontologically, they are already and inescapably reproductive in nature, what Deleuze would describe as an order of simulacra, and Heidegger as dissembling, both without derogation. As such, live events are a mixed economy, containing both a productive and a reproductive moment, or a creative and preservative dimension. Needless to say, it is the productive/creative aspect that receives most attention in our celebration of liveness—something further exaggerated when an event is improvised and thus promoted as an encounter with the surprising and the unexpected. Such creativity is itself the product of practise, where, through the repetition of the same, performative habits are formed that, because they inevitably endanger the liberatory spirit of so much improvisation, demand the augmentary habit of avoiding habit, which, negatively, propels the improviser into an infinity of diversity without difference. And this is why practise has to cease before the improvisation begins, given that the performance is the moment where the "guileful" performer attempts to outwit the habits that practise has established.

Surprise

Something different happens, or *can* happen, or *must* happen if we are to speak of an event in the strict sense, rather than merely acknowledging the fact that something happens. This other thing—a thing that is other—is not in itself surprising in the usual sense; in fact it is always the same and, to that extent, and in the ontological sense already discussed, profoundly *boring*, just as rehearsing can be profoundly boring. So why, to return to Derrida and Nancy, is it such common practice to mobilize the language of surprise when trying to grasp the event-ness of the event? Certainly, such a language can be, and often is, misleading when describing the actuality of improvised live performance, where the habit of being endlessly surprising and the habit of allowing oneself to be surprised by such surprisingness has near hegemonic status. And it is true that Derrida himself sometimes falls into the trap of conceptualizing the event as that which attends the surprisingness of the unscripted, the impromptu, and the unpredictable nature of an improvised situation, as he does here.

> I must say, ultimately, what is happening here, to the extent that it was unforeseeable, that it was unanticipated for me—since we improvised to a large extent—is that an event will have taken place. It is happening and it wasn't arranged in advance; a lot was arranged but not everything. It's an event insofar as what's happening was not predicted.[26]

Here, as elsewhere, Derrida shows himself to have a peculiarly pure and un-deconstructed notion of improvisation, one that, in demanding absolute unpredictability, is bound to fall short and expose its own impossibility— hence the wariness Derrida often admits when finding himself (as he often did) in the midst of an improvised situation. This is captured perfectly in a famous clip from *Derrida*, the movie:

> It's not easy to improvise; it's the most difficult thing to do. Even when one improvises in front of a camera or microphone, one ventriloquizes or leaves another to speak in one's place. The schemas and languages that are already there, there are already a great number of prescriptions that are prescribed in our memory and our cul-

ture, . . . and so I believe in improvisation, and I fight for improvisation, but with the belief that it is impossible.[27]

As with the "impossible possibility of saying the event" then, Derrida here
plays a double game with improvisation, both fighting for it and denying
its possibility. In this regard, improvisations are always doomed to failure,
and the surprise of the event is always compromised by the possibility of its
inevitable impossibility. Here is another example from *Points* . . . :

> What is called improvisation . . . is never absolute, it never has the
> purity of what one thinks one can require of a forced improvisation:
> the surprise of the person interrogated, the absolutely spontaneous,
> instantaneous, almost simultaneous response. A network of appa-
> ratuses and relays . . . has to interrupt the impromptu. . . . So, one
> has to, one fails to improvise.[28]

In other words, improvisations often fail to surprise us, which, in Derrida's
view, denies us access to the radical, but also impossible, unpredictability
of the event:

> The event's eventfulness depends on [the] experience of the impos-
> sible. What comes to pass, as an event, can only come to pass if it's
> impossible. If it's possible, if it's foreseeable, then it doesn't come
> to pass.[29]

But perhaps Derrida is here becoming unnecessarily entangled in the aporia of possibility-impossibility and the investment of the subject (whether
performer or audience) in the *experience* of the event, rather than recognizing, with Nancy, that the surprise of the event "is not a surprise for the subject. No one is surprised."[30] Indeed, the real surprise of the event is *that* no
one is surprised, whether we call this boredom or not, which admittedly is
a loaded term; that the event can happen *without* surprises, that is the most
surprising thing, albeit overlooked in the desire for surprising experiences. It
is precisely rehearsal that preserves the decisive movement of the *it* happens.
In fact, whether improvising is possible or not, just as whether speaking the
event is possible or impossible, quickly becomes a matter of indifference
the moment we recognize that the peculiar alterity of the event is one that
is exterior to what is considered *humanly* possible or impossible—"*one* is
bored," "*it* happens." This is where Deleuze brings us closer to the essence
of the event than Derrida. By insisting on the redundancy of possibility as

a concept, and proposing virtuality and actualization as a binary that liberates thought from the task of representing *or not* the event as a horizontal becoming of surprising diversity, he allows us to develop a greater sense of the different sameness that eternally returns as the ontological verticality that, as we shall see later, remains unowned by the human. For the moment, however, here is a representative fragment from *Difference and Repetition* to set this thought in train:

> The only danger . . . is that the virtual could be confused with the possible. The possible is opposed to the real; the process undergone by the possible is "realization." By contrast, the virtual is not opposed to the real; it possesses a full reality by itself. The process it undergoes is actualization.[31]

What Deleuze describes as the "defect of the possible"[32] is that, contrary to the view that the realization of possibilities epitomizes the improvisatory production of endless difference, such realization is "produced after the fact, as retroactively fabricated in the image of what resembles it."[33] It is not so much, then, that practise makes perfect, but that practise makes possible, and the more we practise, the more we make possible, which, in Derrida's eyes, results in a saturation of the improvisatory field to the point where improvisation itself becomes impossible. Of course, improvisers, and perhaps even more their audiences, often speak of "impossible" feats of improvisatory brilliance, but this has more to do with expanding possibility than it does with transcending it: improvisers do not perform miracles. But to reiterate, Derrida has a strangely pure and un-deconstructed notion of improvisation, one which fails to grasp that improvisers function only too well within the ever-expanding realm of the possible, within the "network of apparatuses and relays" that facilitate rather than annihilate the creation of endless diversity. The fact remains however—and here we are with Derrida—that a live, improvised event, to the extent that it is indeed an *event*, cannot be reduced to the realization of possibilities alone. Where we differ is in the conception of this otherness or excess in Deleuzian rather than Derridean terms that will allow us to grasp the *reality* of the event, which is both prior to and infinitely different from its localized and, in our terms, improvised actualizations.

Improvisers practise in order to make improvised events possible. Year in, year out, all day, every day, they work on accumulating the habits of performance necessary for something (anything) to happen: but what happens? At one level, maybe the most familiar, these habits are put to work as the means by which nascent possibilities are realized, in the moment, before an audience, live. All improvisations have this element of realization, and its familiarity, although framed in terms of surprise, is no doubt what attracts audiences to improvisation in all of its different forms—acknowledging that audiences can be hard to come by in the world of improvisation.

In addition to this, something else is happening, something to do with live-ness, with the physicality of the performance, the proximity of bodies, the fallibility of the human, the phenomenological intensity of the "flesh," and the now-ness of the *now*. This perhaps is what lovers of live performance love above all else: the unmediated, unreproducible, and unwonted happening of improvisers improvising. We have already referenced this experience, or "feel," of the live event above, and, as with the realization of possibility, it is clearly an important dimension of any performance; however, and this is where Deleuze is an important guide, such phenomenological experience does not exhaust the richness of the event, nor does it ultimately reveal to us the essence of event-ness.

Something else is happening. For Deleuze, the relation between possibility and reality, through the becoming of realization, locks us into a regime of resemblance—of "like to like"—that produces only "pseudo-movement."[34] Instead, he proposes the non-dialectical, disjunctive binary of virtuality and actuality mediated by the becoming of actualizations that *do not* resemble that which they actualize. It is this non-resemblance that, for him, makes possible both creativity and performance.

> Actualization breaks with resemblance as a process no less than it does with identity as a principle. Actual terms never resemble the singularities they incarnate. In this sense, actualization . . . is always a genuine creation. . . . For a potential or virtual object, to be actualized is to create divergent lines which correspond to—without resembling—a virtual multiplicity. The virtual possesses the reality of a task to be performed.[35]

For our purposes this is not intended to displace or replace the possibility-reality model of improvisation outlined above, but to augment it. And, more importantly, it is not just a question of changing our terminology, but of giving some thought to *how* the actualization of the virtual can be distinguished from the realization of possibility and the phenomenology of the flesh, not conceptually but experientially.

Sensation

The key term for Deleuze, one that runs throughout his work, is *sensation*; and it is the degree to which we can *sense* the actualization of the virtual alongside or in addition to the experience of surprise and the proximity of the human body that we bear witness to the event-ness of the event. In particular, it is the inherent humanism of experience as the (post-Kantian) means of achieving knowledge of the world through the faculties of mind, that, for Deleuze, obstructs our access to the event understood by him in radically non-humanist terms. While implicitly acknowledging that phenomenology's (especially Merleau-Ponty's) valorization of art as the locus of affect appears to bring us close to the sensation of the event, it is precisely this proximity that most effectively *obscures* the event-ness of this very event: hence the following in *What Is Philosophy?*

> In short, the being of sensation is not the flesh but the compound of nonhuman forces of the cosmos, of man's nonhuman becomings, and of the ambiguous house that exchanges and adjusts them. . . . Flesh is only the developer which disappears in what it develops: the compound of sensation.[36]

As the reference to the "ambiguous house" testifies, prior to the affectivity of the human body is a compound space within which and from out of which the human becomes what it is. As does Heidegger, Deleuze and Guattari give priority to dwelling above the dweller, a perspective that, through an admittedly circuitous route, will bring us back at last to habit as an essential component of the event. This will be achieved by noting the importance of *habitus* not only as the originary dwelling place of the improviser, but as the pre-territorial and nonhuman swarming of habitual forms and functions that crystallize into the "expressive features" of the virtual: "the canonization of being's improvisations."

> Perhaps art begins with the animal . . . that carves out a territory and constructs a house (. . . in what is called habitat). The territory-house system transforms a number of organic functions—sexuality, procreation, aggression, feeding. But this transformation does not explain the appearance of the territory and the house; rather it is the other way around: the territory implies the emergence of pure sensory qualities, of sensibilia that cease to be merely functional and become expressive features, making possible a transformation of functions. (183)

"Art begins not with the flesh but with the house" (186). But a house—the *habitus*—is not a pre-given structure that houses the artist: it is not simply a home. On the contrary, the house is as *Unheimlich* as it is *Heimlich*, as universal as it is local, in that it is both the cosmic reservoir from which the "artist" draws the habitual patterns of behavior, as well as the territory *created* or *performed* by those habitual forms once transformed and liberated from their instinctive, "first nature" functions.

As with Nietzsche, Deleuze and Guattari are here trying to capture the decisive moment where the transformation of instinct into habit, and thus fate into will and the "love of fate"—the vanishing point of knowledge—produces art, understood as pure sensory quality. At the heart of this is repetition, which they articulate by using a common musical term—*ritournelle*—the refrain, also implying (Nietzsche-fashion) the return of the same, but a sameness that, in eternally creating territory, is always different: the different sameness we have been striving to bring into focus throughout.

> This is not synaesthesia of the flesh but blocs of sensation in the territory—colors, postures, and sounds that sketch out a total work of art. These sonorous blocs are refrains; but there are also refrains of posture and color, and postures and color are always being introduced into refrains: bowing low, straightening up, dancing in a circle and lines of color. The whole of the refrain is the being of sensation. (184)

Recalling Konjar's cataloguing of his own habitual postures—"continuous turning . . . a movement initiative from the spine . . . the habit to use the hands in a sort of 'stay away' or 'I give up' gesture"—the refrain not only returns, it is also *rehearsed*, and it is this rehearsal that both preserves and creates the territory from out of which art emerges as the infinite actualization of the virtual, here described (very revealingly) in Wagnerian terms as a "total work of art." We are also back with Heidegger, who, in helping us describe what is happening in a live performance, would remind us that it is "Art" which is decisive rather than, or at least in addition to, the localized actuality (or ontic being-at-hand-ness) of the artist and his or her artwork. But, other than describing Art as the "setting of Truth to work," there is little sense of exactly what the art-ness of Art is and how we might sense it, other than through an evocative but ultimately obscure process of ontological "listening." Given that Deleuze and Guattari's version of the total work of art is situated within the territorializing-deterritorializing flux of pure sensibilia, sensing its virtual presence in actual artworks/performances should be fairly straightforward, as long as one develops a sense of and for sensation, something which much of their work is itself committed to rehearsing. And in this regard Deleuze and Guattari, unlike Heidegger, do offer us something resembling a genuine aesthetics. Of course, Heidegger was rightly critical of post-romantic/modernist aesthetics in its valorization of the artist and the artwork (subject-object), but failed to adequately ground his own "turn" to "Art" in an ontology of sensation, which would have enabled him to re-ground rather than undermine the aesthetic: Deleuze's engagement with sensation gives us much more to work with.

So, returning one last time to our imaginary, improvised live event: the habits of practice and all of the spontaneous choices they allow are in full flow, which, in turn, excites a phenomenological experience of the other as human body and flesh that intensifies and thus enlivens the event as a unique moment of lived time. To be sure, all of this helps us to understand the celebrated live-ness of the live event, but the event-ness of the event remains obscure and will continue to do so unless we can find a way of further sensitizing ourselves to the sense that "something else" is happening. Not something "more"—this is not a quantitative statement—but something qualitatively different without being absolutely Other in the Levinasian sense. The difficulty is that, to follow Deleuze's lead, we are required to hone human sensitivity to enable ourselves to sense the nonhuman, both the animal— "art is continually haunted by the animal" (184)—and the cosmos—"from House to universe. From endosensation to exosensation" (185): "a world before man yet produced by man" (187). The difficulty is that what is "produced by man" obscures the "world before man," and thus desensitizes us to the pure force of sensibilia that courses through us all at the level of the habitual refrain (*ritournelle*).

Here we see the advantage of Deleuze over Heidegger: where, for the latter, the "singing" of Being can be "hearkened-to," but only in the obscure melody of the poet's dissembling intoning, Deleuze obsessively catalogues the infinite components of the "great Refrain" (189), tracing the "song's" territorializing-deterritorializing flight through the vertical multiplicity of the virtual "total work of art" that both precedes and succeeds the actualizations of "man." But, and this is the essential problem, the vertical difference of the virtual, understood as multiplicitous blocs of sensation, is profoundly resistant to a sensibility habituated to the aesthetic pleasures of surprising diversity played out across the horizontal plane of human interaction and dialogue, performers and audiences, and their mutual pleasures. For all of the dynamism of Deleuze's writing, the constant flight, becoming, nomadism, transformation—"launching itself on a mad vector as on a witch's broom" (185)—he is attempting to describe something that, *within human experience*, is always the same—the eternal return of the same— albeit a sameness that both produces and is the product of infinite transformation. This is not the same sameness where nothing happens. What we are trying to sense is a different sameness, where transformation is not measured from moment to moment in terms of *what* is happening, but outside of the "in-the-moment" moment, where *that* it happened and *that* it will happen are the issues.

If live-ness is all about what happens in the moment of performance—in the now—then this would seem to contradict the very concept of a live event. And yet perhaps the real essence of the live event is not the momentary occurrence of an habitual practice and/or its guileful and suspenseful avoidance, but the keeping alive—the preservation through rehearsal—of a *sensibility* capable of registering (re-hearing) the event of habituation outside of the social display and spectacle of human foibles and manners; and not just keeping alive the sensibility but, through sensation, the event *itself* in all of its infinite multiplicity.

> Art wants to create the finite that restores the infinite: it lays out a
> plane of composition that, in turn, through the action of aesthetic
> figures, bears monuments or composite sensations. (197)

For Deleuze and Guattari, all art, even (or especially) the most modest, is monumental. That is to say, vertical: a composite of habits that are contracted, contemplated, and inhabited long before and long after the action and actualization of singular, finite "aesthetic figures." As Ronald Bogue explains (ending with a passage from *What Is Philosophy?*):

> Sensation is fundamentally a conservation or retention of vibra-
> tions, a contraction of vibrations that takes place in a contemplative
> soul, not through an action, but a "pure passion, a contemplation
> that conserves the preceding in the following. . . . Sensation is pure
> contemplation, for it is through contemplating that one contracts,
> contemplating oneself to the extent that one contemplates the ele-
> ments from which one arises."[37]

The challenge then, particularly in the hyperactive world of improvised performance, is to sense that which "precedes" and "follows" the "action of aesthetic figures" rather than the figures themselves. Going against the empathic grain, this would require a certain dis-engagement from the action in order to contemplate a different order of passion, one quite distinct from the expressivity or intensity that has attained near regal status within the world of performance. Does this mean, then, that the sensation of the event-ness of the event is only possible for those outside of the action, for the (contemplative) audience? Is sensation merely the passive reception, conservation, and preservation of a creative act, rather than the act itself? Is it

possible for the performer, as creator, to sense the event-ness of the event
in the live moment of performance; or, following Badiou, is the event only
recognized and acknowledged *after* its occurrence, when all, including the
creator, have become an audience of preservers? In other words, does the
absence of the event from the experience of the "in-the-moment" moment,
necessarily preclude us—creator or audience—from sensing the evental as
a dimension of, indeed the essential dimension of, the live-ness of the live?

One avenue of response to these questions would be to consider making
a distinction between active and passive forms of creativity, with the former
mapping onto the familiar process of practise and the conscious formation
of performative habits discussed at length above, and the latter returning
us to the decisive contraction-contemplation of habit at the level of being/
cosmos/chaosmos prior to, and as a condition of, the very formation of a
creative identity: the subject, we have claimed, of rehearsal. It is the fact
that, as mentioned before, Deleuze always thinks of the contraction and the
contemplation of habits together that opens up the possibility of sensation/
contemplation, having a "mysterious" creative dimension:

> Contemplating is creating, the mystery of passive creation, sensa-
> tion. Sensation fills out the plane of composition and is filled with
> itself by filling itself with what it contemplates: it is "enjoyment"
> and "self-enjoyment." (212)

So, as Bogue observes, it is necessary to distinguish between two orders
of habit: "common" and, following Deleuze and Guattari, "primary," which
are active and passive respectively: "the sensori-motor habits we develop
as *active* creatures [which] presuppose 'the primary habits that we are, the
thousands of *passive* syntheses that organically compose us.'"[38] The question though, as regards the live-ness and event-ness of the live event, is this:
Can such active and passive enjoyment, as the contemplation of active and
passive creativity, be sensed together, simultaneously, in the moment? Deleuze, following Hume, believes they can, borrowing from the latter his conception of the imagination as a stand-in for sensation. The following long
passage is absolutely crucial to an understanding of our whole discussion
and any conclusions we might be able to draw from it:

> The contraction that preserves is always *in a state of detachment
> in relation to action or even to movement* and appears as a pure
> contemplation without knowledge. This can be seen even in the ce-
> rebral domain par excellence of apprenticeship or the formation
> of habits: although everything seems to take place by active con-

nections and progressive integrations, . . . the occurrences, must, as Hume showed, be contracted in a contemplating "imagination" while remaining distinct in relation to actions and knowledge. Even when one is a rat, it is through contemplation that one "contracts" a habit. It is still necessary to discover, *beneath the noise of actions*, those internal creative sensations or those *silent* contemplations. (213)

The discovery of this passive creativity beneath or within the active creativity of a performance introduces into the enjoyment of the moment another form of enjoyment that, while sensed in the "now," is necessarily detached from the present, as are the primary habits-contemplations that, as posture, lines of color, sonorous blocs, enjoy themselves as a condition of their own "nonhuman becoming." To bring these "silent contemplations" into the "noise of actions," to imagine/retain/preserve them as that which vibrates with self-enjoyment, is not only to experience the enjoyment of a performance but also to sense an enjoyment of enjoyment that *can*, to the extent that we can distinguish between the practicing of a practice and the re-hear-sing of rehearsal, in-habit the live event.

Such an enjoyment of enjoyment returns us to Nietzsche's desire to preserve, in imagination, an origin (a *fatum*) that we could love and will instead of the one we are given. One remains passive in the face of such a love of fate, but it is a fate that we have, nevertheless, created. "Being's improvisations" are, in this view, also *our* improvisations to the extent that we sense and contemplate what we contract as habit. The formation and deformation of habits witnessed in the singular psychodramas of the guileful improviser are secondary and epiphenomenal when considered in the light of this originary event of becoming, but as the localized actualization of this virtual monument of chaos, they remain essential. And it is for this reason that we should remain alert to the essential difference between action and actualization, the latter, as Andre Lepecki (following Arendt rather than Deleuze) reminds us, being characterized by an "anonymity" that diverts attention away from the "common" and toward the "primary."

> This is what Arendt called actualization—a process always involving three very important elements, two of which are deeply tied to dance's political and aesthetic ontology: "the unpredictability of its outcome" and "the irreversibility of its process." The third and last one, "the anonymity of its authors," offers the most complicated aspect of action, . . . [implying] a dance without choreographers (or without authors).[39]

This then leads Lepecki into a discussion of contact improvisation and Steve Paxton, something we have already done enough of, so we will conclude by merely reaffirming the importance of improvisation as that which, precisely through the removal of the figure of the author (and even, contrary to the view of Gavin Bryars, of the improviser)[40] brings a sense again of the aporia of *enowning*—the possession-by and dispossession-of the event— and the anonymity of primal habituation. But, to repeat, one has to create, if not a "work," then a becoming-work (or working), in order to preserve the anonymous virtuality of the event that, at the moment of actualization, will cast the creator aside. Maurice Blanchot names this moment the "essential solitude," and, like Heidegger and Deleuze, he believes that it is only to the extent that we can dwell within the unhomely/deterritorialized *habitus* of anonymous habit that we will be capable of creating anything at all.

18 Memoir: The Woburn Pop Festival, 1968

The following memoir was originally delivered as a short presentation, part of the 2013 "Black Heroes Month" at my university. The stipulation was that all presentations had to be five minutes in length. Being an unashamed hero-worshipper of (among others) Jimi Hendrix, I had, back in about 2008, recorded my own version of "Hey Joe" that I was quite pleased with (I'm easily pleased when it comes to my own work), and thus still had on file. I played it and, indeed, still found it to be very pleasing and, more importantly, almost exactly five minutes in length. So, on the evening of the presentation I delivered the text over this soundtrack in an attempt to suggest a doubling of the voice and/or perhaps a *sotto voce*, something that has always fascinated me. While, of course, this cannot be reproduced in the much-extended version of the presentation below, it should be borne in mind as an essential component of the underlying intention: the co-existence and co-erasure of the multiplicitous voice(s) of, in this case, both myself and Jimi Hendrix and, as will be seen, the event of improvisation as well—the point of the "memoir."

December 16, 1966: UK Release Date
of Jimi's First Single, "Hey Joe"

To be a hero (a derivation of *Eros*) is to be an object of love. From the moment I heard the ringing opening phrase of

"Hey Joe," and the mournful circling fourths/fifths—C G D A E—I loved Jimi Hendrix. But what I loved was something quite other than his flamboyant public persona; I loved, rather, a fascinating alterity (the essence of love?) that inhabited the sound within his sound, the voice beneath the voice: *sotto voce*.

But what is love?

Drawing on Badiou's thought, and particularly his often very touching *In Praise of Love*, we might suggest that his Lacanian view, where love fills the absence of the erotic (given that for the latter "there is no sexual relation"), might help us grasp the essential nature of hero worship: what Badiou would describe as the *event* of two-ness rather than the *experience* of one-ness—or, in other words, a liberation from the narcissistic solitude of sex, in the name of "difference" and the irreducible two-ness of love: the "two-scene."[1] For Badiou, this defines what he calls the "truth procedure" of love, which concerns above all else a "fidelity" to the event of this amorous "difference." For me, on this occasion, this relation and "procedure" will be considered outside of the more familiar parameters of coupledom and the intimacies therein. Instead of the loved one, I will be concerned instead with the hero—my hero: Jimi Hendrix. As such, my "two-scene" will not be the *experience* of listening to and seeing the Jimi Hendrix Experience (the experience of The Experience one might say), but the witnessing of an event of what might here be called (literally) *heroic* improvisation. What I want to describe below is something that, while it can be quite easily described, nevertheless remains different from this description, ontologically other, irreducible. Badiou himself describes this as an "encounter," and that is what this "memoir" (and no doubt all of the others) is ultimately about, an encounter.

> Love always starts with an encounter. And I would give this encounter the quasi-metaphysical status of an *event*, namely, of something that doesn't enter into the immediate order of things.[2]
>
> . . . a magical moment outside the world as it really is.[3]

July 6, 1968: The Woburn Pop Festival, with Jimi Hendrix Headlining.

OK, on the theme of love, it is true that 1967 was described as the "Summer of Love," and, indeed, in the previous year the first ever (I believe) rock festival was also held in August at Woburn Park—promoted as "The Festival of the Flower Children." But, to be clear, the encounter I am going to describe has nothing in common with this celebration of global and cosmic one-ness, nothing whatever to do with the collective love-in that erupted then and, to be sure, has left its mark on many improvisers and models of improvisation that continue to live that particular dream. And anyway, for old Marxists like me, it is the hopeless hope of "May '68" that still resonates as a genuine event (of love), one that effectively silences the kaftan-clad banality of "All You Need Is Love," released in July '67 (George Harrison's lovely little guitar solo notwithstanding).

Back to the 1968 Woburn festival.

Jimi Hendrix, headlining on the Saturday night, was running late, very late as it turned out. I distinctly remember announcements being made over the PA that he and the band (Mitch Mitchell and Noel Redding) were flying in from Holland and had been delayed on entry to the UK. Over what I remember as being a period of at least two hours, there were numerous further announcements assuring us that Jimi was on his way, which he was, in a separate car. Hence, when he did eventually arrive, he was without a band; they arrived some time later, I would say at least thirty minutes later, maybe more. In the interim, and to everyone's amazement, Jimi walked straight on stage and played solo. Neither I nor anyone else had ever *heard* anything like this before. And I emphasize the word *heard*.

Jimi was (and still is) renowned as a primarily visual event: the wild hair, the extravagant, dandified clothing, the chains, rings, and bling, all of the sumptuous hippy signifiers so different from the sharp suits and choreographed precision typical of his own past in the black soul and blues bands exemplified by Geno Washington, who (as a perfect contrast) preceded Hendrix on the Woburn Festival bill.

The Jimi Hendrix Experience obliterated all precision in an orgy of noise, feedback, viscerality and sheer violence. Long before philosopher Gilles Deleuze encouraged us to "become animal," Jimi was already devouring, bumping and grinding, humping and burning his guitar in a spectacle of sheer transgressive eroticism that would have made even George Bataille blanch.

But on July 6, 1968, in advance of the full band, we saw none of this. No, at this moment Jimi simply stood, solitary and stationary to one side of the stage in semi-shadow. He neither said nor did anything except play. In truth, he didn't even play; he simply allowed his guitar to resonate and emit a slowly increasing howl of such despairing intensity that the druggy love-in that had been so happily unfolding all day in the Bedfordshire sunshine suddenly became as trivial as its tinkling bells and faux Buddhist chanting.

My memory tells me this continued for at least thirty minutes, thirty minutes when (in philosophical retrospect) the Kantian concept of the sublime as the *experience* of the pleasure and pain associated with witnessing that which exceeds all experience, was *itself* experienced. Or, to use Badiou's terminology, witnessed as an *event* outside of all experience.

Yes, my memory tells me, but it is mine alone, increasingly fragile, increasingly questionable. Inexplicably, I can find no record of this improvised performance, absolutely nothing, silence, absence, an historical void, a momentous moment "blasted out of the continuum of history" to use Walter Benjamin's striking phrase. Yes, there is a recording of the Jimi Hendrix Experience at Woburn on CD, I have listened to it many times, but it is only of the set as played by the band. Actually, it is not even of the full set because the tape ran out at one point, but that point is precisely *the* point: it is the fact that what was not set by "the set" (Jimi's solo improvisation) was not considered worthy of recording or, as a consequence, remembering. There is a very informative Web site devoted to rock festivals which offers a detailed account of the whole Woburn Festival including Jimi's set,[4] but makes absolutely no mention of the event that I witnessed. Even more baffling, in trawling the Internet back in 2013, I eventually found a strange account of Noel Redding's activities and whereabouts on the day of the Woburn gig: he was not in Holland, he was in London, as was Mitch Mitchell and, I presume, Jimi Hendrix. I have been tempted to track down my long-lost friends who were with me on that night, but I know that, like everyone else, they will have forgotten everything; a collective amnesia, leaving me as the solitary witness. Bizarrely, it would seem that everyone around me saw but did not hear, or maybe they didn't even see: deaf and blind in the face of the event, maybe that's it, maybe such forgetting is an essential part of the event. When I discovered all of this, I was astonished. I experienced that strange momentary terror, the one where, standing at the checkout (always with ten impatient customers behind you, that's the rule) you can't remember your credit card pin number. And all the other desperate situations: you can't remember your own phone number, or your own house number. Suddenly you feel like a thief (are you sure it's your credit card sir?), a fraud, a fabricator, an inventor of your own identity, with your own imaginary past: did I ever actually see Jimi Hendrix live at all? Where are the photos? None. Where are all these friends who were there? Dead. Are they? Did I actually ever have any friends? No.

April 5, 1968: Newark Town Hall, New Jersey.

Almost exactly three months before, the very day after the assassination of Martin Luther King, The Jimi Hendrix Experience was scheduled to play a concert in Newark Town Hall, New Jersey. On taking the stage, and without warning, Jimi abandoned the planned set list and announced that instead he would be playing something "for a friend of mine." He then proceeded to play one long continuous improvised piece before quietly laying his guitar down and leaving the stage. This event has been described by one solitary witness, Mark Boyle, a light designer for the UK band Soft Machine, the support act for the tour. It is worth listening to what he says of this in full:

> He [Hendrix] abandoned his original, his normal set. The band played an improvisation which was absolutely, hauntingly beautiful. Immediately everyone knew what this was about. I mean, this was a lament for Martin Luther King, and within minutes the whole audience was weeping, and the much-maligned redneck stagehands came onto the side of the stage, they were standing there too with tears running down their faces. The music had a kind . . . I would describe it as having a kind of appalling beauty. It was harrowing music. And, of course, when you try and get a tape of it, for once nobody was making a pirate recording, there *is* no record of that gig. And when he came to the end of the music, there was no applause. He just put his guitar down and the whole audience was sobbing: he just walked quietly off stage.[5]

This account has since been doubted,[6] but, sadly, Boyle is no longer alive to defend himself or his memory. Such a waste of time anyway: what he heard, as I did three months later, is not something that *can* be shared; it is not something that *can* be communicated willy-nilly in our collective codes, not something I can speak of to you now or to anyone else for that matter. But, as Jimi Hendrix knew or intuited, in the face of the unspeakable, mere silence is not enough. As Nietzsche says, "My silence is too silent for your silence," and so it was with Jimi Hendrix: it was only through sound, pure unadulterated (or maybe adulterated) sound, that he could access that appalling void beneath the voice: *sotto voce*. It would seem though that only two people on earth remember this: one of them is dead, and the other one barely living. Living or dead, we both encountered the same "two-scene," the two-ness of our hero and ourselves, outside of the world of collective experience. The question of truth is central but misunderstood in the endless disputes between endless bloggers and their endless accounts of the "facts" of the Newark case. For Badiou, as with Heidegger, truth understood ontologically has nothing to do with the verification of facts—true or false—but is, rather a "procedure" (Badiou) or "task" (Heidegger). For both, it concerns a remembering, not of the facts, but of that which is forgotten, because erased by the facts. This remembering to remember (so to say) is described by Badiou as truth; not the truth-of the facts, but the truth-to an event: "fidelity." This is how he understands such a procedural truth:

> It [fidelity] means precisely that transition from random encounter
> to a construction that is resilient, as if it had been necessary. . . .
> In Love, fidelity signifies this extended victory: the randomness of
> an encounter defeated day after day through the invention of what
> will endure.[7]

What I and Mark Boyle are speaking of is not a past experience that can be verified by the collective wisdom of the blogosphere, but a random encounter as described by Badiou, one that requires endless "construction," reconstruction, and "invention" in order to free it from chance and the oblivion of the aleatoric. A strange truth indeed, dependent on a constant process or procedure of invention and re-invention, the necessary means by which we remain true to what and who we love. What Mark Boyle and I are speaking of is a random encounter with an improviser and an improvisation that, in order to be preserved, must itself be improvised "day after day," constantly rehearsed, in a cycle of repetition without which it will be forgotten. What am I saying? We have an obligation to improvise, as an act of fidelity to improvisation itself. Without this, improvisation, as an event worthy of such fidelity, would cease to exist, as it obviously has for many: the vanishing.

19   Case Study: Jimi Hendrix

What would a Hegelian make of Jimi Hendrix? Certainly, as a moment in the philosophical chronicling of the speculative history of phenomenological experience, The Jimi Hendrix Experience would have its place as, if nothing else, an exemplary case of what happens when the aesthetic hits its limit. It is here, at and beyond this limit, that (Hegelian) philosophy steps in to save us from the dangerous pleasures of the "pleasing" style and the related sophistry of the ironist: the dual dangers of pleasure and deception—the same old Platonic hang-up. An inversion of the "severe style" already discussed, where an ambiguous and arbitrary content or meaning is disguised by a rigid and severe form or configuration; the "pleasing" style is the "modern" (we might say "postmodern") manifestation of a decadent aesthetic form that is incapable of giving shape to an interiorized/subjectivized substance that transcends external/objective representation, thus rendering such a form fortuitous and arbitrary: ironic. Hegel considered such irony to be at the heart of what he describes (in a very expanded sense) as "romantic art."

> At the stage of romantic art the spirit knows that its truth does not consist in its immersion in corporeality; on the contrary, it only becomes sure of its truth by withdrawing from the external into its

own intimacy with itself and positing external reality as an existence inadequate to itself. . . .

We found romantic art from its beginning onwards afflicted
with the opposition that the inherently infinite subjective person-
ality is in itself irreconcilable with the external material and is to
remain unreconciled. This independent confrontation of the two
sides and the withdrawal of the inner into itself is what constitutes
the subject-matter of romantic art.[1]

To the extent, then, that the Jimi Hendrix Experience was the aesthetic
form by and through which the transcendental singularity or ego (in the
proper Kantian sense) of Jimi Hendrix could be represented and experienced (as that which is incapable of being represented or experienced), it
was a deeply romantic and a deeply ironic band. While this might seem like
an odd claim, it should be considered in the light of the fact that most forms
of irony do not appear to be in the slightest bit ironic: that is precisely the
irony. For example, while reading the current book, see if you can disentangle its apparent earnestness and its intended irony.

Leaving aside the question of irony for a moment, it is surely less controversial to associate the Jimi Hendrix Experience with Hegel's "pleasing"
style and the dubious pleasures of rampant aestheticism that he associated
with romanticism. Where his account certainly rings true is in his claim that
the arbitrariness of outward form constantly turns attention away from the
artwork to the individual mannerisms of the creative and destructive powers
of the artist or ego: "Well I'm standing next to a mountain, I knock it down
with the edge of my hand."[2]

This virtuosity of an ironical artistic life apprehends itself as a divine creative genius for which everything and anything is only an
insubstantial creature, to which the creator, knowing himself to be
disengaged and free from everything, is not bound, because he is
just as able to destroy it as to create it. . . . If the *ego* remains at this
standpoint, everything appears to it as null and vain, except its own
subjectivity, which therefore becomes hollow and empty and itself
mere vanity.[3]

Are the *hubris* and narcissism of romanticism so different from the excesses of the rock world so openly acknowledged by all members of The
Experience in countless interviews? Probably not; and certainly the undeniable charisma of Hendrix has a great deal to do with his being consistently
cast in the role of "divine creative genius" by a world keen to experience a

musical phenomenon that is "not of this world": he is a God, beside whom we are "null and vain." Such romanticism undoubtedly captures something of the Jimi Hendrix whose violent energy laid an endless supply of Fender Stratocasters and Marshall stacks to waste, as it offers a believable account of the infinite intensity and yearning that characterizes his inimitable playing. What is more, the failure on the part of cultural critics to convincingly politicize, ethicize, or spiritualize his transcendental (some would say transcendent) egotism, leaves us with the spectacle of a pure aestheticism that, as Hegel recognized, must explode all material forms. But this explosiveness, real though it is, only has any real impact within the dual constraints of The Jimi Hendrix Experience and the aesthetic experience of The Jimi Hendrix Experience: outside of constraints, everything changes—especially, for our purposes, the nature of his improvisation. Trying to trace these changes will be the task of the following reflections.

Given the profoundly improvisational nature of his *oeuvre*—and also of his performativity, his attitude, his very being—it is almost shocking to discover what little attention has been paid to Hendrix as an improviser worthy of serious study rather than a guitar hero worthy of adulation. For sure, many would see the two as inseparable: after all, what makes him a hero is above all else his incredible guitar solos, and what defines him as an improviser is, for many, precisely the same incredible guitar solos: soloing and improvising are, in this view, synonymous. This, as far as it goes, is true of course, but that is the question: how far does it go? Not far enough. And can we go further? Yes. Where would that take us? It would take us on a journey from the *experience* of The Experience to the *sense* of Jimi Hendrix; from the *situation* to the *event*, understood by Badiou as the "void" within the situation: the presence of a sensed absence: Hendrix as an *event* that has always already happened or is always about to happen. So, let us retrace some of these steps.

The Jimi Hendrix Experience was aptly named; its whole *raison d'etre* as a band was to offer the audience or the listener *an* experience, one that was unforgettable. In that they undoubtedly succeeded: who could forget the climax of the 1967 Monterey Pop Festival, where the band's rendition of Chip Taylor's humorous country ramble, "Wild Thing," descends into cacophony, mayhem, and a performative orgy of violence and incineration that even surpassed The Who's penchant for such onstage stunts. But that is the point: the creation of "experiences" through the intensification, exaggeration, and sexualization of performative tropes and figures has a long tradition of which Hendrix was a part—the latest and most extreme, but a part nonetheless. The outrageous antics of playing with his teeth, behind his back, and between his legs had all been done before by the likes of Buddy

Guy and Chuck Berry, with variations offered by Jerry Lee Lewis and even country-jazzers like Les Paul and the steel player Speedy West. As for sex: while copulating with inanimate objects takes things quite a way, one only has to think of Elvis, Little Richard, or James Brown to see where this was coming from, while Bessie Smith, Nina Simone, Etta James, and plenty of others were similarly responsible for degrees of raunchiness that predate Hendrix by some margin. The point is that such performances, while improvised to an extent, are memorable precisely because they inhabit what might be described as a performative culture of transgression; one that, alongside the particular idioms it might occupy—rock, jazz, blues, country, and so forth—imposes a set of parameters in order to test them. This recalls again Hegel's identification of the limits of the aesthetic and it's seductive/destructive potential.

But of course Hendrix's improvisations, while intensely embodied and performatively rich, are also musical explorations that, to return to our starting point, are predominantly staged as guitar solos within the parameters of a three-piece band, a given composition, and the finite, if flexible, time constraints of pop and rock music. Approached thus, and ignoring the hype, his solos are, to say the least, variable. Much of their content is semiautomatic noodling, familiar Hendrix-clichés and the occasional idiomatic twist to remind us of his versatility and his past. Even the more explorative adventures in feedback and general noise generation are too often domesticated by being, let us call it, programatized: that's a helicopter, that's a missile, that's a helpless Vietnamese child screaming "oh no!" that's an orgasm . . . yes, another one, that's a machine gun, . . . and so on. The moment "absolute music" becomes program music is the moment that the evental is reduced to the experiential and thus cherished as *an* experience. Just to be clear though, it is difficult to think of a single guitar solo of Hendrix's that does not have at least one moment, no matter how fleeting, that marks him out as a completely unique and, indeed, unequaled guitarist; but that is not the issue: even his "best," most inventive and convincing solos are still only solos, individualized vehicles of expression within a collective, shared situation that, as such, can never provide the material substance or form necessary to reveal what Hegel would call the "spirit" at work. Hegel is right.

What makes things worse, and again notwithstanding the hype, is that The Experience (Noel Redding and Mitch Mitchell) were a very poor band indeed, both as musicians and, worse still, as improvisers. Let's be frank: Noel Redding was not even a bass player; he was a very mediocre six-string guitarist who got the gig because Jimi liked his hair. Unlike his hair, there is nothing whatever to like about his bass playing: it is lightweight, fussy, directionless, ham-fisted, flashy, and deeply ignorant of the very rudiments of bass playing: plain wrong. Mitch Mitchell cannot be damned quite so comprehensively; he was a proficient drummer, albeit one rooted in the busy end of jazz and show bands rather than rock; but therein lay the problem. Like Redding, he is flashy, tippy-tappy lightweight, rhythmically unstable, insecure, unreliable, and incapable of listening to others, especially the bass player (but perhaps he can be forgiven for that).

If we turn to their abilities as improvisers, things get worser and worser. Above all else, what they had in common was that they were both obsessive and incurable space-invaders. Never once in all of their performances with Hendrix will you hear them create space; no, the one talent they share in mutual abundance is the ability to *fill* space; in this and this alone they remain without equals. What do they fill the space or potential space with? All of those attributes itemized above: in essence, surface trivia and insubstantial ornamentation. Not surprisingly then, the *"espacement"* effect of Hendrix's approach to improvising is constantly and brutally shut down, squeezed out, and suffocated by the invasive inanity of his co-improvisers, leaving him two options: doing something similar himself or ignoring them. It is noticeable that whenever a Hendrix guitar solo begins to transcend its limitations, both in length and in creative breadth, the backing band becomes increasingly and eventually almost completely irrelevant. It is not just that they are incapable of contributing anything meaningful to any improvisation that extends beyond the re-hashing of prefabricated tricks, but that the singularity and, one might say, the essential solitude of Hendrix's improvisation at its best has absolutely no need for such a contribution, whether from his hapless rhythm section or anyone else. Would his planned collaboration with Miles Davis have been any different? Who knows? Guess is, no.

As Maurice Blanchot understands it, the "essential solitude," has nothing to do with the human *experience* of loneliness but is, rather, a quality of the artwork itself, the *event* of art sensed but not possessed or "owned" by the artist. Indeed, for him, the "essential solitude" concerns dispossession, the moment of being "cast out" by the work.

> Every . . . artist is acquainted with the moment at which he is cast out and apparently excluded by the work in progress. The work holds him off, the circle in which he no longer has access to himself has closed, yet he is enclosed therein because, the work, unfinished, will not let him go.[4]

There are moments in Hendrix's performances that go beyond the loneliness and tragedy of the yearning romantic subject (a part he plays so well), moments where he seems to enter into the "essential solitude," a space that cannot be shared with others because it is precisely a space of dispossession: Blanchot calls it "the neutral," neither mine nor yours, positive nor negative and, significantly, a space of *ignorance* that, at the same time, is *known* as ignorance. This is how he describes it:

> Research—poetry, thought—relates to the unknown as unknown. This relation discloses the unknown, but an uncovering that leaves it under cover; through this relation there is a "presence" of the unknown; in this "presence" the unknown is rendered present, but always as unknown. . . . This relation will not consist in an unveiling. The unknown will not be revealed, but indicated.[5]

As should be clear, we are once again in the vicinity of the *event*; the present absence, the known unknown are all related to the same aporia: how to think outside of the domain of experience and enter in the sensation of the event—how indeed. Clearly, the artist, the musician, the improviser do not simply *express* the event through creative or improvisatory acts directed to and empathically shared with an assumed communicative community. Hegel is right; no aesthetic form would be capable of adequately representing the self, understood as spirit (spirit being his version of the event). But then does this mean that, in the desire for absolute knowledge, art has to give way to philosophy, as he insists? Yes, if the desire *is* for absolute knowledge, and if it is indeed an absolute desire: but is it? Even after the "death of art," as Hegel famously describes it, he still accepts that art lives on, albeit in a kind of afterlife that confronts its own death, not philosophically, as he thought, but aesthetically: a post-aesthetic aesthetic (think of Beckett).

Hendrix is renowned not only for his playing but also for his untimely death; however, the truth is he died long before he died; died by his own hand, a partial suicide that had nothing to do with drugs but was, rather, intended to eradicate the inscrutable, aestheticized romantic self in a perhaps hopeless attempt to escape the multiple ironies of performance associated with this predicament. As the "memoir" above is intended to reveal, there had from the start been moments when the "death" of his own art was confronted through a "neutral" improvisatory form that, in its impersonal and inhuman alterity, was, as Mark Boyle attests, "haunting," ghostlike, beyond the "death of the subject." Increasingly, Hendrix retreated from the performative histrionics required to satisfy his experience-hungry fans. He constantly spoke of a desire to change direction, to cut back, to simplify, to create a different space for his art; but the fact remains that the improvisations that allowed him to approach this other space, the "harrowing" sound sources that he plunged into, were no less ironic than before, only now in a "neutral" rather than a "romantic" way.

> Let us say that the one who does not enter into what he says is neutral; just as speech can be held to be neutral when it pronounces without taking into account either itself or the one who pronounces it, as though, in speaking, it did not speak but allowed that which cannot be said to speak.[6]

Not to enter into what one says is irony; not the playful irony of the "divine genius" but the cold neutrality of the ghost, speaking from beyond the grave of its own art. Only in his improvisations proper—not his famed solos—did Hendrix speak in this strange tongue: no wonder no one heard or comprehended them or him; no wonder that virtually all trace of these improvisations has been erased. But not all: there is a moment, late in the documentary film on Hendrix, when Eric Clapton and Chas Chandler are talking of Hendrix's death, a poignant moment when a tiny segment of an unidentifiable (is it?) performance of "Machine Gun" is intercut (there are numerous others, but this is the best). Hendrix is stationary, eyes closed, rapt; his guitar tone is crystal clear, and he is making very exaggerated use of the tremolo arm of his Strat. The guitar is "talking" in a strange tongue, a tremulous voice, fragile, almost pleading. Then a brutal but contained burst of machine gun from the guitar, silence, and then another, more silence. Forget program music, forget (if you can) the Vietnam war, forget aesthetics, but not in the name of a philosophy that thinks it can think beyond art, and try and get a sense of an appalling (because ironic) language that cannot be entered into, that casts not only the speaker but also the listener aside; thus allowing "what cannot be said to speak."

The only way we might even begin speaking of Jimi Hendrix as an improviser would be to attempt entry into this neutral language, outside of all aesthetics and aestheticism—but also outside of all philosophy. No wonder this chapter was so excruciatingly difficult to write. And, in truth, it has yet to really begin.

20 Composition, Improvisation, and Obligation: Schoenberg and Beckett on Duty

What I believe . . . is that if one has done one's duty with the utmost sincerity and has worked out everything as near to perfection as one is capable of doing, then the Almighty presents one with a gift, with additional features of beauty such as one could never have produced by one's talents alone.

Arnold Schoenberg[1]

Schoenberg, in characteristic style in the epigraph above, captures a moment of music production that is probably familiar to many: the felt obligation to work in order to produce a "work" that is irreducible to this working. Whether a gift from "the Almighty" or from the available musical resources, a gift from oneself, or pure chance, this revelatory excess is indeed often experienced as a "gift" nonetheless. For Schoenberg, with his self-image as a man of destiny, one has to be (like him) worthy of this gift: "A good theme is a gift of God," he announces (quoting Brahms); "Deserve it in order to possess it," he concludes (quoting Goethe).[2] The deserving are those who do their "duty with the utmost sincerity," a laudable Kantian ideal, no doubt; but who or what does the dutiful servant serve? Schoenberg's answer to this is unequivocal: the composer's duty is to serve the idea— the idea rather than the vagaries of mere style. Styles come and go, but *"an idea can never perish."*[3] Very much in the philosophical tradition of Hegel, Schoenberg's idealism, his fidelity to the immanent historical revelation of the Absolute, explains why he so ferociously denies that his music is revolutionary: the underlying identity of the Idea can only evolve as continuous variation.

For the moment let us concentrate on the word *duty*, and see if it can be traced as a persistent moment in the shift from the strict to the improvised style. The first thing to say is that, by embracing the concept of duty, Schoenberg casts himself in the double role of preserver of the past and creator of the future: a responsibility and obligation respectively. It is Kant who gives the classic statement on duty in his *Critique of Practical Reason*; here are some fragments from the famous passage:

> Duty! Thou sublime and mighty name that does embrace nothing charming or insinuating, but requires submission and . . . holdest forth a law which of itself finds entrance into the mind. . . . It can be nothing less than a power which elevates man above himself. . . . This power is nothing but personality, that is, freedom and independence from the mechanism of nature, yet, regarded as a faculty of a being which is subject to special laws, namely, pure practical laws given by its own reason.[4]

So, for all of the talk of "emancipating" dissonance, such liberation remains a negative freedom, without sufficient substance to demand the obedience Kant sees as the essence of duty. In other words, the desire for emancipation, or freedom-from, is quite different from the positive logic of freedom-to, realized through an autonomous act of self-legislation, one clearly witnessed in the (post-atonal) life of Schoenberg. Such "independence from the mechanism of nature" results in an aesthetic shorn of its pre- and post-romantic excesses in line with a Kantian perspective that defines genius as the ability to "give the rule to nature" or, as Schoenberg expresses it, "In all circumstances, use force on nature, on the material—sounds: that one must force them to keep to a direction and succession laid down by us."[5] Such self-legislation should not be confused with self-expression, any more than the Kantian person should be confused with the natural human subject. The aesthetic life no longer serves aesthetic pleasure but becomes a task serving the necessary logic of musical progress, where the destiny of art and the artist become one. As Schoenberg remarks, "I was forced by my destiny."[6] He continues:

> While composing for me had been a pleasure, now it became a duty. I knew I had to fulfil a task: I had to express what was necessary to be expressed and I knew I had the duty of developing my ideas for the sake of the progress in music, whether I liked it or not.[7]

Although he is using Kantian language, it is nonetheless here, in accepting this destiny, that Schoenberg parts company with Kant and reveals the essential Hegelianism of his own idealism, one that ultimately eschews the former's infinite dualism for the latter's absolute monism. And, indeed, the problem for Hegel is that Kant's conception of morality is enclosed within an abstract self-consciousness that, while formally coherent, is cut adrift from the substantiality of a genuine ethical community—the difference between morality (*Moralitat*) and ethics (*Sittlichkeit*). As we have seen, the Kantian conception of duty reveals the dualistic self-transcendence of the self to the extent that subjective maxims attain to the universality of moral laws, and principles ("I will") become imperatives ("thou shalt"). This is the classic statement of the categorical imperative: "Act so that the maxim of thy will can always at the same time hold good as a principle of universal legislation."[8] There are, for Hegel, two problems with this: first, the moral law here originates in the contingency of an individual existence rather than the necessity of the universal; second, it is a formal law only, there being no indication as to what the "act" *is*. As Hegel describes it above, it is the "pure direction of activity" rather than actual, substantial acts within a historically specific ethical world. While both Kant and Hegel root their concepts of morality and ethics, respectively, in reason, for the former, this is an eternal abstract principle, whereas for the latter, this describes the revelation of reason within the actuality of history.

Given these fundamental differences, Schoenberg's Hegelian credentials become clearer. As he states, "The method of composing with twelve tones grew out of a necessity"; he then goes on to map out the historical preparation for and prologue of the eventual "emancipation of dissonance" in postromantic music.[9] What is more, his use of the term *method* is significant: he is explicitly not referring to a system, theory, or methodology, and certainly not a law. On the contrary, and here he resembles Descartes in *Discourse on Method*, method is here understood as a singular means of proceeding within the necessary constraints of a specific historical situation—a situation that one finds oneself in rather than a situation that one creates and legislates. In this sense, composing with twelve tones is never promoted as a categorical imperative—as an "ought"—but as a rational response to a necessary moment in the historical becoming of rationality itself. As he writes, "[The composer] "must find, if not laws or rules, at least ways to justify the dissonant character of [the] harmonies and their successions."[10] His duty then is not to legislate but to rationalize and legitimize the given, hence his refusal to play the role of "revolutionary." For Schoenberg, the dialectic is never between the old and the new but between the comprehensible and the incomprehensible—that is to say, between reason and nature. We should also add autonomy and heteronomy to these binaries, if for no other reason than to do so raises some thorny issues regarding the relations between reason and freedom, which might throw some light on the emergence of free improvisation in the post-serialist period: what *is* freedom?

In the Kantian tradition individuals are free to the extent that they are rational, "intelligible" beings able to legislate their irrational, natural, "phenomenal" selves. So, freedom assumes submission, but submission to oneself, enacted as duty. In the Hegelian tradition it is not the individual, but Spirit, or the Absolute, or the Universal, or the Collective that embodies freedom to the extent that it can reveal in actual history, through the casting off of limited forms, the ultimate truth of reason. Individual subjects have a duty not to their own moral selves but to the ethical mores and customs that embody and reveal reason at particular stages of its becoming. For Kant, freedom is the origin; for Hegel, the end: for Kant Freedom is *a priori*;, for Hegel, *a posteriori*.

Returning now to our epigraph, the theological tone, so typical of Schoenberg, is taken up by Carl Dahlhaus in his essay "Schoenberg's Aesthetic Theology."[11] Here he reminds us of how often the composer speaks of "miracles" being revealed for which the artist can take no credit. There is, of course, nothing unusual about such statements, which are only too common in the post-romantic era; but where Dahlhaus registers something more significant is in his identification of what actually counts as a "miracle" for Schoenberg. Commenting on Schoenberg's own claims regarding the "miracles" discovered in the *Op 9 Chamber Symphony*, Dahlhaus makes the following observation:

> It is unusual and characteristic that the inspiration that he felt had been conferred on him did not consist of a theme, but rather of a connection between themes. The inspired idea, in the face of which Schoenberg felt moved to make use of the language of art religion, . . . remained initially latent and manifested itself in a relationship and not a substance. The idea . . . is thus realized less in the musical shapes that make up the surface than in the tissue of relationships which, hidden beneath, connect the ideas with one another.[12]

For all of its theological overtones, this *ex post facto* revelation of the "cunning of reason" hidden beneath the surface or "behind the back" of the composer, is pure Hegel. To dutifully serve the necessity of the idea, then, is by no means the self-enclosed legal abstraction to be found in Kant, which, in Hegel's view, ultimately leads to the dissolution of the Idea in contingency and chance, but neither is it the rigid adherence to the substance of an idea already given. Rather, and analogously, it is not the substance of each individual sense of duty (Hegel calls this "conscience") that is essential (any substance can be the subject of duty), but the shared dutifulness with the other that, on an ethical level, reveals the "tissue of relationships" hidden beneath the differentiated surface of abstract individuality. Hegel expresses it as follows:

> For the essence of the action, duty, consists in conscience's con-
> viction about it; it is just this conviction that is the . . . implicitly
> universal self-consciousness, or the state of being recognized, and
> hence a reality.[13]

Schoenberg does his duty in order to recognize what is there and also be recognized as one who labors under the conviction that there is indeed something there to be revealed. The "miracle" of the work is not the divine but the collective, not the interiority of the unconscious (as he also thinks) but the exteriority of the universal other.

So why this long Schoenbergian/Hegelian preamble in a chapter purporting to be about improvisation? The main reason is to consider the extent to which the task of the improviser, experienced as a duty or obligation to improvise, is comparable to the task of the composer as described by Schoenberg. A subsidiary reason is to consider the above in the light of the questionable claim made by Dahlhaus that it is against the high moral backdrop of Schoenberg's questionable legacy that the emergence of aleatoric compositional strategies and increasingly free improvisation can be best understood: as a backlash. A sub-subsidiary reason is to note that, in spite of the scenario painted by Dahlhaus, Schoenberg himself claims that all composition is, in essence, improvisation.

The Decline of Serialism/Emergence of Improvisation

In his 1972 essay "Composition and Improvisation," Dahlhaus, while placing a question mark above the notion of historical necessity, nonetheless identifies a precise historical moment (1958) when, in his view, circumstances conspired to effect an historical shift or reversal in the fortunes of composed and improvised music. In fact, he offers three rather different (actually, contradictory) reasons for this transformative moment: the first concerns the persistence of chance at the heart of serialism; the second registers a certain fatigue with the deadening strictures of serialist discipline; the third acknowledges the emergence of an emancipatory spirit driven by the desire for spontaneity and freedom. As the first relates to chance rather than improvisation, this will only be touched upon here briefly for the sake of completeness. Here is how Dahlhaus outlines the issues. First,

> the fact that around 1958 chance, under the name of aleatoric tech-
> nique, was elevated into one of the basic principles of music was a
> reaction to inner contradictions in serial music. Serial technique had
> run up against a dilemma: . . . if the details of a musical text were
> serially determined as regards pitch, duration, dynamics and tone
> colour, and the serial mechanics left to their own devices, the overall
> form was a matter of chance.[14]

Second,

> it seems as if around 1958 people were tired of serial discipline and
> musical rationality. . . . Compared to this the movement towards
> aleatoric technique and chance, towards arbitrariness and improvi-
> sation, seems like an attempt to break the shackles.[15]

Third,

> whether the expectations which attached to improvisation and
> aleatoric technique, expectations which revolved around emphatic
> ideas of spontaneity, newness and revolutionary content, were real
> or imagined is difficult to decide at present.[16]

While the internal contradictions of serialism may have become an issue for those already trained in this compositional method (Stockhausen,
Boulez, Berio, Nono, etc.), it is hardly believable that the emerging generation of improvisers coming out of the jazz tradition (Miles, Coltrane,
Ornette Coleman, etc.) would have been in the slightest bit bothered by the
persistence or status of chance within twelve-tone music. In fact, the evidence would suggest the contrary, with many improvisers actively embracing (albeit often very loosely) serial techniques in their own improvisational
strategies: Bill Evans was one of many heavily influenced by Schoenberg,
as is evident in "TTT" ("Twelve Tone Tune") and "TTTT" ("Twelve Tone
Tune Two"), neither of which, incidentally, are serialist in any remotely
strict sense. Ronald Radano writes in his book on Anthony Braxton,

> Arnold Schoenberg and Ornette Coleman were, from Braxton's per-
> spective, musical soulmates, inspired by the same creative muse.[17]

And, anyway, while chance obviously does have an important, even crucial, role to play in improvised music, we should recall here Martin Davidson's above-quoted claim (itself not altogether convincing) that chance music and improvisation are "diametrically opposed." As we have seen, following Deleuze, it is only to the extent that chance is affirmed that it is of any relevance to our discussion of improvisation. Aleatoric music neither affirms nor negates chance: it neutralizes it.

Turning to the "fatigue" Dahlhaus identifies, the tiredness with serialist discipline; again, this does not totally convince if one steps outside of the confines of the "new music." Having said that, the more generalized "shackles" of the conservatoire and the academy, on one side, and the rigid formulas of popular music and jazz, on the other, certainly did contribute to a cultural moment and mood of skepticism, questioning, and critique, which only avoided cynicism and Dadaist destructiveness to the extent that it was transformed into the more positive forces of emancipation and revolution described (quite skeptically, as one might expect) by Dahlhaus.

So, with this somewhat questionable backdrop in place, we can now return to the initial reason for discussing Schoenberg: the question of duty. We can start by immediately relating this to the issue of tiredness and fatigue, and raising the question of how one can retain a sense of conviction and obligation in the face of aesthetic dissolution and the loss of necessity as an historical or cultural principle. Also writing in the fifties, Samuel Beckett famously offers the starkest statement of this predicament in this much-quoted passage: apologies to those who have read it a million times before.

> B.—The expression that there is nothing to express, nothing with which to express, nothing from which to express, no power to express, no desire to express, together with the obligation to express.[18]

And another, slightly lesser-known passage from the same piece:

> B.—The situation is that of him who is helpless, cannot act, in the event cannot paint, since he is obliged to paint. The act is of him who is helpless, unable to act, acts, in the event paints, since he is obliged to paint.
> D.—Why is he obliged to paint?
> B.—I don't know.
> D.—Why is he helpless to paint?
> B.—Because there is nothing to paint and nothing to paint with.[19]

The first and most famous of these two passages is, perhaps not surprisingly, considered to be primarily about the problem of expression. This is true, but it should not obscure the fact that it is equally concerned with the problem of obligation, as brought out more clearly in the second passage. Obviously, if Beckett could answer the question, "Why is he [Bram van Velde] obliged?" there would be no problem, but he cannot, which is why this is interesting. Beckett's repeated deployment of the term "helpless" is also interesting in the way that he manages to articulate both the helplessness of being obliged to act and the loss of the necessary help that would allow one to act: for him, the artist is literally help-less. And we should remember too the final lines of Beckett's *The Unnamable*: "You must go on. I can't go on. I'll go on," where the "must" functions as both a command and the articulation of a helplessness: an inability not to go on. What have these unanswerable questions got to do with improvisation? As the beginning of an answer, we might consider the different ways in which the notion of obligation functions within a Schoenbergian and a Beckettian universe, respectively.

A good starting point would be to return to Schoenberg's claim that all composition is improvisation. He expresses this view in his essay "Brahms the Progressive" as follows (significantly, as part of a discussion of "gifts of grace" and "miracles"):

> There is no doubt that Brahms believed in working out the ideas which he called "gifts of grace." . . . If a mathematician's or a chess player's mind can perform such miracles of the brain, why should a musician's mind not be able to do it? After all, an improviser must anticipate before playing, and composing is a slowed-down improvisation; often one cannot write fast enough to keep up with the stream of ideas.[20]

Once again, it is the stream of relationships between ideas that are at the forefront of this very familiar model of improvisation, one that places the emphasis on speed, flow, and the over-abundance of a gift-bestowing inspiration. But more than this, Schoenberg draws attention to the profundity of the idea as essential to the artist's duty. This is how he arrives at the "must":

> One cannot do this with a shallow idea, but one can, and one can *only*, with a profound idea—and there one *must*.[21]

As already seen, then, for Schoenberg, one's duty is to the given idea, the obligatory task being to excavate the profound depths of musical thought, or the musician's "brain," as he likes to express it, bringing its substance to the surface in an endless stream of variation and difference. Indeed, Schoenberg's view is that the "difficulty" of his music has less to do with dissonance than it does with its difference, the product of an improvisatory process conceived in terms of infinite variation and an almost militant avoidance of repetition. In spite of Dahlhaus's view, this does not sound so different from many of the forms of improvisation that emerged in the fifties and sixties. While a strict adherence to the rationalism of serialism or of other existing ideas of music production might have waned during this period, the underlying improvisatory model of unfixing the fixed clearly remained in place as the one big idea that ensured that Schoenberg and Ornette Coleman did indeed remain "soulmates." And one thing they were both absolutely clear about: *the idea of improvisation itself.*

Beckett's fatigue is radically different. His is not a weariness born of the idea and the weight of responsibility associated with its realization. He is not tired of anything in particular. On the contrary, and in spite of the particular imprisonments and containments of his characters, his thought is absolutely liberated from any such confinement, hence its helplessness and hopelessness. Only here does the improvisatory gesture confront its true enemy: not rigid and restrictive ideas but the *absence* of the idea, and in particular the absence of the idea of improvisation itself. It is not breaking shackles but making shackles, the necessary structures of thought and action, that creates the profound weariness that Beckett identifies as the essential aporia of obligation. To speak of improvisation here (and Beckett rarely, if ever, speaks of improvisation) is not to speak of its "importance" but of its very *possibility*: "You must improvise." "I can't improvise." "I will improvise." "Why?" "I don't know."

The "necessity" Schoenberg speaks of is wedded not to the creation of ideas but to the preservation of the idea. As we have seen, Heidegger recognizes that, while the act of creation fixes the idea in the artwork, it is the unfixing of that idea that preserves it. This fits perfectly with Schoenberg's concept of composition as slowed-down improvisation and infinite variation. With Beckett, however, both creativity and preservation vanish into each other; there is nothing fixed to unfix, nothing given to be re-given as variation (diversity) and/or difference. If we can speak of a model of improvisation at all (or an anti-model, which is too dialectical), it would have to be in terms of the fixing of the unfixed and the eternal recurrence of the same: absolute repetition. The fact that the improvisatory moment in Beckett's radio play *Krapp's Last Tape* is indeed a repeating tape, the repetitive fixing in the endless present of an unfixed past present, suggests that this might be a way forward. Daniel Albright, in his *Beckett and Aesthetics*, seems to sense the same possibility:

> In *Krapp's Last Tape* (1958), the role of script is played by the tapes, which will always deliver exactly the same message no matter how often they are played; but on the other hand, the role of improvisation is also played by the tapes in that the tapes play back a fossil of an extinct improvisation, full of false starts and uncertainties. Here, as elsewhere in Beckett, the distinction between improvisation and script . . . seems to vanish.[22]

Typically, free improvisers have shown very little interest in the taping or recording of improvisations—in the analog or digital freezing of performative flow understood in terms of spontaneity and emancipation. But this is largely because improvisation's big idea is the realization of future possibilities in the unreproducible now of the "in-the-moment" moment. This, the essential futurity of improvisation, bespeaks a profound faith in the emergent substantiality of a "not yet" that can be trusted to pass through the performative present as an infinitely surprising trace. Needless to say, doubt can be cast on the perceived virginity of this infinite becoming, and, as we are drawing on Dahlhaus, we can allow him to do the doubting:

> Improvisations that are repeated are for this reason no longer improvisations.
>
> At the same time it would be bad Romanticism to insist on unbroken spontaneity and immediacy. Analysed soberly, improvisation almost always relies to a large extent on formulas, tricks of the trade and models. . . . The improviser must be able to fall back at a moment's notice on a repertoire of clichés, on a store of prefabricated parts . . . which he or she does not invent on the spur of the moment.
>
> Thus improvisation, under the cloak of aesthetic immediacy, is based on formulas, habits and rules.[23]

In a sense Dahlhaus is trying to have it both ways. He claims (presumably uncontroversially, although Jurij Konjar might have something to say about this) that a repeated improvisation is a contradiction in terms, while at the same time (whether controversially or not depends on the improviser) wishing to alert us to the necessary repetition of formulas and habits typical of virtually everything that counts as improvisation. Either way, tape—the recording and repetition of an improvisation—is deeply problematic, regard-less of where one is situated on the above spectrum. The reproduction and repetition of the unpredictable and surprising quickly renders it predictable and unsurprising, which, evidently, makes for a rather lame listening experi-ence among serious improvisers and improvisation-lovers. Such repetition also risks exposing the clichés, formulas, and tricks secreted within the so-called spontaneity; thus, if it does not undermine the pioneering credentials of free improvisers, then it certainly clips their wings.

Whichever way one looks at this, one thing is incontrovertible: whether reproducible or not, the pure now of the improvised moment can, at that moment, rely on the infinitely rich material resources of an emerging but nevertheless foreseen future and/or the eternal archive of the past. Given this, the duties and obligations of the free improviser are, beneath stylistic surfaces usually linked with "live-ness" (itself a highly unstable concept), not all that different from those of the serialist composer: the obligation to create/preserve the future/past understood as the historical actualization of musical ideas.

Returning to Beckett, the first thing to note is that what would seem to be the least controversial of Dahlhaus's assumptions—the unrepeatabil-ity of improvisation—might be the most questionable of all. In a "world" or predicament such as Beckett describes, without the material resources to sustain life as we know it, let alone a life with sufficient resources to indulge in the luxury of improvisation conceived as infinite variation and differentiation—in such a "world" repetition might turn out to be the only form of improvisation imaginable. In a "world" of duty without du-ties, or obligation without obligations, the improviser has nothing to un-fix except the very concepts of duty or obligation themselves, a destruc-tive and self-contradictory gesture that even Beckett refuses. Within such a predicament—the predicament of the artist for Beckett—the only way to save improvisation and the improviser (assuming we want to) is by consid-ering the idea floated throughout this book that improvisation can be con-ceived as the fixing of the unfixed rather than the unfixing of the fixed. But hasn't a whole generation of free improvisers, having liberated themselves from all given idioms, especially jazz, even in its free-est forms, been engaged in precisely the fixing of the unfixed for a long time now? Well, yes, many of them have, and with significant success, but, it has to said, and this is the essential point, only at the performative rather than what might be called the ontological level.

This difference is implicit in the Beckett passage that begins with the line, "The expression that there is nothing to express," a statement which only escapes self-contradiction by assuming an essential disjuncture between a radically de-subjectivized ontology of expression—*there is* expression—and the existential predicament of subjective expressivity in the face of its perceived impossibility (*I* have no means or desire to express, coupled with the obligation that *I* do so).

In the performative world described by Derek Bailey (and further developed above) as "non-idiomatic free improvisation," where the fixing of the unfixed is commonplace, as is evident in his own work (which was heavily influenced by Beckett, incidentally; see below), the obligation to "go on" as a response to not being able to go on takes on distinctly Kantian overtones, albeit it in a suitably absurd-ized form. Where anything goes because nothing really goes, the duty of the improviser is not primarily to the failing idea of improvisation as an emancipatory strategy in a reified world, but to the formal principle of autonomous self-legislation *itself*. As Hegel suspected, the singular forging of subjective laws, claiming or demanding universal assent, replaces the destiny of "the Idea" with the contingency of mere ideas that are capable only of giving temporary form to the formlessness of the immediate situation: hence the hostility to tape or any form of reproduction: not, as Peggy Phelan thinks, because of an unrepeatable pureness or politically fugitive live-ness, but because of arbitrariness.

But, ontologically, the fixing of the unfixed, thought as an improvisatory event rather than as an improvisatory self-legislative act, points us back in the direction of Hegel and reveals a certain proximity between the destinies of the dutiful Schoenberg and those obligated improvisers who, Dahlhaus believes, reacted against him from the fifties onward.

Consider this paraphrase of Beckett, then:

> The improvisation that there is nothing to improvise, nothing
> with which to improvise, nothing from which to improvise, no
> power to improvise, no desire to improvise, together with the
> obligation to improvise.
> Why is the improviser obliged to improvise?
> We don't know.
> Why is the improviser helpless to improvise?
> Because there is nothing to improvise.

Once again, it is the disjuncture between the ontological and the performative that is crucial.

In the Kantian universe of the self-legislated moral law, it is the impossibility of universalizing the singular that results in the promotion of duty and the infinite striving of the "ought." Hegel's central ambition is to overcome the necessity of the law and the impossibility of universal obedience as understood by Kant through the revelation of a deeper necessity that renders the infinite dialectic of possibility-impossibility redundant: put simply—we obey! And we obey because the very consciousness of obedience dissolves into the substantiality of who we are and how we become who we are within the universality and necessity of Being. For many (and especially improvisers), this is a terrifying vision, with Hegel and the Hegelians being seen as responsible for the imposition of an iron law of history that makes a mockery of individual freedom and the spontaneity associated with creative practice.

But there is another way. Catherine Malabou in her book *The Future of Hegel: Plasticity, Temporality and Dialectic* comments on the frequency of the word "plasticity" (*Plastiche*) in Hegel's oeuvre and uses this concept as a lever to re-locate and re-assess his thinking. The first thing to note here is that "plasticity" is an essentially artistic term, referring to the sculptural act of molding. As she notes, the word can mean both capable of shaping, and capable of being shaped, thus expressing both the active and passive aspects of such shaping.

This is not the occasion to follow Malabou into and through her fascinating re-evaluation of Hegel, and we have already encountered her thoughts on the role of habit in his thought, but in this context it is in fact the relation between plasticity and habit that is of interest. So, we need to reread the following passage:

> "Plastic individuals" are those that synthesize in their very "style" the essence of the genus and the accident which has become habitual. What in the beginning was merely an accidental fact . . . is changed through the continual repetition of the same gestures, through practice, achieving the integrity of a "form." Effected by habit, the singularity of the "plastic individual" becomes an essence a posteriori. . . . The philosopher, the political man or sculptor, are determinations which could not have been anticipated just by the simple generic definition of man: they are destinies contained virtually in the genus "man," but remain there as something unpredictable. By forming themselves, by undergoing repetition and practice, these determinations ultimately construct a state which is habitual and accordingly essential. Habit is the process whereby the contingent becomes essential.[24]

As described earlier, most interesting of all is the way Malabou ends by describing the above as the "canonization of *being's improvisations*," which at a stroke brings us face to face with the *ontology* of improvisation.

Of course, the strictly Hegelian view would be to bury or cast off this con-tingency along the path to the Absolute, but Malabou's Deleuze-inflected reading is keen to retain, as irresolvable, this creative tension between the passive and active dimensions of habit-formation that, through the improvi-sations of Being and beings, offers us the *chance* to become what we become through repetition rather than developing variation.

Take away the Hegelian telos, and you take away the concept of destiny. But, perhaps sacrilegiously, you can take away the end without thereby de-stroying the Hegelian beginning, a beginning that both Schoenberg and the free-est of free improvisers share. The only difference is that, as a "man of destiny," Schoenberg (and those like him) believe that doing one's duty is the necessary means by which the Absolute will miraculously reveal itself to those who are deserving; while those destined to have no destination will remain at that improvised beginning, where the fixing of the unfixed—the ontological moment—can be sensed as the infinite repetition of the molding and remolding of the habitual "plastic" self.

As we have also witnessed, it is the fact that Deleuze always thinks of the contraction and the contemplation of habits together that opens up the pos-sibility of habit having a "mysterious" creative dimension: "Contemplating is creating, the mystery of passive creation."[25] Or, we might say, the mystery of passive improvisation. This brings us back to *Krapp's Last Tape*.

Daniel Albright, while correctly directing us to the tapes as the locus of improvisation, misleads by suggesting that it is the "false starts and un-certainties" that are significant. Perhaps they are, but only at the level of performance. Ontologically, it is not this un-fixity that is essential but the fixing of this un-fixity on tape and the repeated, one might say habitual, contemplation of this decisive moment of fixity. The fact that we can simul-taneously speak of an obligation to improvise while not knowing why there exists such an obligation is, perhaps, because habits form at the point where knowledge is forgotten and becomes an act. Indeed, as Malabou observes, such active forgetting also affects self-knowledge:

> The more closely habit is studied, the more it becomes clear that human subjectivity is constituted in self-forgetting; consciousness and will, under the influence of repeated practice, win their force through a kind of self-absenting.[26]

Thus it is not the actors/performers who can speak of their obligation—their job is to act and perform—no, the *sense* of obligation requires a cer-tain distance from the action/improvisation.

Here is the Deleuze and Guattari passage again:

> The contraction that preserves is always in a state of detachment
> in relation to action or even to movement and appears as a pure
> contemplation without knowledge. It is . . . necessary to discover,
> beneath the noise of actions, those internal creative sensations or
> those silent contemplations.[27]

Thus, it is not Krapp, the faltering and uncertain speaker, who knows why
he is obliged to improvise when there is nothing to improvise, but Krapp the
listener and operator of the tape recorder—the "contracting machine"—
who knows to the extent that he does not or cannot act.

As regards miracles, the miraculous nature of Beckett's work, and the
work of those confronting the same predicament, is not something witnessed as a divine intervention interrupting the continuous flow of a certain
destiny, but the simple fact that the work happens *at all*. It is not doing one's
duty that brings about miracles; the miracle is duty itself: obligation happens; our sense of obligation is secondary.

21 Bits and Scraps: Derek Bailey and the Improvised Situation

It is known that Derek Bailey had a long-term interest in the work of Samuel Beckett. More than that, he was himself only too well aware of the fact that he bore a striking resemblance to the crag-faced writer. Returning for a moment to our anti-improviser-composer Gavin Bryars, he recalls this in an interview in the *Independent* newspaper:

> There are personal connections to Beckett too. I worked as a jazz and improvising bass player with the guitarist Derek Bailey, who looked remarkably like Beckett and even cultivated particular Beckett poses for photographs (and people were unsure [*sic*] whose was the photograph on my mantelpiece).[1]

A silly story no doubt, but then in many ways it captures a very happy accident. As the "inventor" of non-idiomatic improvisation, with all of the visual accoutrements one associates with all of the tabooed idioms (goatees, berets, tattoos, Stetsons, body piercings, shades, excessive leather, impractical trousers, and so on), who better for Bailey to doppelgang than someone not only outside of all musical idioms but, ultimately, outside of all literary ones too. And let us be clear, the reduction of one's body image to the ravaged minimalism of an ill-fed buzzard is much more than empty stylistics, as it is quite distinct from existential posturing. No, here the image, and what Blanchot would call the "fascination" of the image, assumes an ontological significance that extends as far as the objects and even posture of Bailey's performances: everything is image, everything is fascinating, precisely because nothing *is*.

> We do not mean a language containing images . . . or yet again, an imaginary language, one which no one speaks: a language that is, which issues from its own absence, the way the image emerges on the absence of the thing.[2]

Like Beckett, in seeking to go on when there is no means to go on, no idiomatic resources to draw upon, no trans-idiomatic between-ness to cruise and groove along or across, Bailey is obliged to improvise in the absence of the thing: the means, the desire, the power to improvise coupled with the obligation to "go on" in the face of this catalogue of nothingness. Bailey is fascinating (much more so than most people seem to be aware) because both he and we are obliged to enter into the nothingness of fascination in order to properly witness the ontological significance of his apparently throw-away shift of terminology from "free" to "non-idiomatic" improvisation.

> To write is to let fascination rule language, . . . where the image, instead of alluding to some particular feature, becomes an allusion to the featureless, . . . the opaque, empty opening onto that which is when there is no more world, when there is no world yet.[3]

Here Blanchot perfectly captures the predicament shared by both Beckett and Bailey, the fascination with, and produced by, the *absence* of a world of writing and improvising, respectively: the no-more, the not-yet, recalling once again the Deleuzian event.

The subtitle of Ben Watson's book on Derek Bailey is *The Story of Free Improvisation*. In spite of his enthusiastic commitment to Adorno and, one presumes, his "logic of disintegration," he offers a strangely *integrated* account of free improvisation as the historical context for Bailey's own "story." While Bailey himself appears to be a willing ally in the construction of this/his "story," one suspects that his frequently self-confessed skepticism regarding anything remotely resembling the theorization or narrativization of music in general and improvisation in particular would put him somewhat at odds with the heavily theorized/politicized frame that Watson places him within, the latter's anti-academic credentials notwithstanding.

Not one to hold back, Watson wastes no time in nailing his political colors to the mast with "An Introduction: On Freedom," which immediately imports a political purposiveness into the improvisatory stance of Bailey that is at quite some distance from the latter's essentially (no doubt unwitting) Kantian aesthetic, one which famously proclaims that art must be characterized as a purposiveness *without* purpose (political or otherwise). "Getting from A to B with no B," as Bailey describes it.[4] It is precisely the radicalization of this aesthetic in both Bailey and Beckett that disallows in advance the overbearing *presence* of liberatory politics assumed as an infinite resource and unwavering telos. Instead, their ultimate rejection of narrative and idiom respectively, results in an interminable confrontation with *absence* that is the hallmark of their work. Regarding politics (and everything else), Bailey is unambiguous.

> Improvisation is not much use for making statements or presenting concepts. If you have any philosophical, political, religious or racial messages to send, use composition or the post office. Improvisation is its own message.[5]

Needless to say, Bailey would be no less skeptical of the account about to be presented here, but the fact remains that Watson's undisguised contempt for anything smacking of post-structuralism results in his leaving out of account what is most fascinating about his subject—one example being Bailey's own fascination with Beckett.

There are many references to Bailey's interest in Beckett, but this seems not to have excited much or any interest into *why* the writer might be of such interest to the improviser, other than looking a bit or, on occasion, quite a lot like him. So, in light of this, it will be necessary to improvise, speculate, and then improvise some more, just to see what materializes: something will. Unavoidably and unapologetically then, much of what follows will be imagined, if not imaginary.

One can certainly start by imagining that Bailey would have read Beckett's *Texts for Nothing*, given that we know he composed (yes, *composed*) music for *Ping!* first published in the same volume.[6] Reading *Texts for Nothing, IV* is, perhaps a much better place to start than Watson's "Story of Free Improvisation," not least because it problematizes the very idea of a "story."

> There's my life, why not, it is one, if you like, if you must, I don't say no, this evening. There has to be one, it seems, once there is speech,

> no need of a story, a story is not compulsory, just a life, that's the
> mistake I made, one of the mistakes, to have wanted a story for
> myself, whereas life alone is enough.[7]

A life without a "story," and the essential incomprehension this brings with
it, is something that Bailey more openly acknowledges in his 1975 interview
with Henry Kaiser. Bailey prefaces the interview with this very revealing
quotation from Edgar Allen Poe:

> I found it impossible to comprehend him, even in his moral or physi-
> cal relations. Of his family I could obtain no satisfactory account.
> Whence he came I never ascertained, even about his age—there was
> something that perplexed me no little degree.[8]

As Nietzsche famously recognized in his *The Uses and Disadvantages of
History for Life*, it is sometimes necessary to "actively forget" the historical narrative of the past in order to create a space for what is often the incomprehensibility of an improvised life. One can imagine Bailey feeling the
same; certainly, in numerous interviews, he implies that it is his life, rather
than individual performances, that might be conceived as improvisational.
As Mark Wastell and Brian Marley write of Bailey, "He said . . . that he felt
his improvising was continuous, broken only by the moments when he set
down his guitar."[9] Significantly, when he does discuss freedom or (better) the
free-ness of free improvisation, he rarely if ever relates this to the actuality
of the improvisation itself; rather, he relates it to the freedom implicit in
the choices made as to who and who not to improvise with. In this respect
one could say that, for him, as with Lol Coxhill, the concept of free improvisation describes the movement *between* performances (the improvisation
between improvisations), while the concept of non-idiomatic improvisation
describes what takes place *within* the performance. As his long-term commitment to *Company Weeks* attests, as much (if not more) improvisatory
energy was devoted to the construction of collaborative situations than to
what eventually took place *within* those situations; and of course, as Bailey
was aware, the two activities were inextricably entwined. Here he is speaking of Company.

> I like that way of working in free improvisation; forming groups
> that *can't* last long. I like a kind of built-in obsolescence . . . that
> way of working—I think of it as semi ad hoc playing, it's not totally
> ad hoc because these people after five days are certainly not strang-
> ers, and they do have a chance to develop some relationship—it just

stops short of turning into a kind of band, and I think at *that* point, for my tastes, a deterioration sets in.[10]

Bailey often describes himself as "going in" and "coming out" of improvised situations, revealing what might be described as an extraordinary "deterritorializing" agility, one that allowed him to commit absolutely to what might be described (returning to Badiou's vocabulary) as the *evental site* of improvisation (and "fidelity" to this event) without the necessity of an analogous commitment to contingent improvisatory *situations*. When he does talk of being *in* the situation, Bailey rarely if ever uses the favored dialogical language of the communicative community; indeed, for him, improvisation has nothing whatsoever to do with communication, as he emphatically reminds Henry Kaiser:

> People . . . usually drool on about communication. Anyone interested in communication should spend time digging holes for telegraph poles.[11]

And yet, in his quip about Cage having the "copyright on silence,"[12] Bailey makes it clear that a rejection of communicative communicability is by no means proposed in the name of a valorized silence; on the contrary—and here again we can imagine the influence of Beckett—his emphasis is always on keeping things "moving along" (a phrase he often uses), of allowing the music to "carry on."[13] As with Beckett's *Texts for Nothing*, more than anything else, it is nothingness *itself* that needs to be protected from the dumb oblivion and contentment of mere silence. As Bailey explains,

> You can work on those situations where nothing's happening. . . . A device I use sometimes is to play something quite nothing, . . . then try to figure out what it was. . . . And there are quite a lot of things like that where you can't tell exactly what the result is going to be. So you can move into those things. I prefer them to silence.[14]

To which might be added some words from the opening of Beckett's "Enough":

> Such is the silence. When the pen stops I go on. Sometimes it refuses. When it refuses I go on. Too much silence is too much.[15]

Molloy proclaims, "Nothing is more real than nothing," a sentiment echoed in Bailey's recognition that, liberated from the shackles of idiom—jazz and rock in particular—non-idiomatic improvisation is able to improvise noth-ingness in the same way that Beckett is able to express that there is nothing to express.

> There wasn't any question of having to play anything, you see. I mean, the fact that you could go out and play nothing was a great relief. You could go out and play nothing, and someone would say, "*What the fuck was all that?*"[16]

What indeed!

There is no answer: neither Beckett nor Bailey tell stories; they describe situations. And it is only from within the situation that, to use Badiou's terminology again, it is possible to "name the void" that, as evental excess, de-scribes the description or un-writes the writing. Thus, Bailey's stripping-away of the idiomatic has nothing to do with a dialectics of style; rather, it has to do with the free-ing of freedom from the very liberatory discourses that, in nourishing it, render it obese and enslaved to its source. Bailey's conception of improvisation is one that works incessantly to separate or liberate his improvisatory re-sources from any singular source, understand-ing that free improvisation is only free when it needs nothing outside of the improvisation itself; something close to Beckett expressing that there is no desire to express: an improvisation that has no need of improvisation or any of the resources that are there to sustain it. In light of this self-enforced model or predicament, non-idiomatic improvisation must be seen not only as a radical renunciation of all available resources, but also as a task com-mitted to ensuring that the interminable repetition of non-idiomatic impro-visatory acts does not itself create yet another idiom: hence the necessity of an infinite process of de-scription capable of un-writing both the writing and the writer as they emerge within the multiplicitous vanishing points of emergent and contingent situations.

Whether or not Bailey's own nomadic mobility and agility managed to save him and his improvisation from what might be called the idiomatiza-tion of the non-idiomatic itself, while an interesting question, is not the central issue here, but it is worth a moment's thought. Following Christo-pher Small, the drummer Eddie Prevost is at pains to distance himself from Bailey's notion of non-idiomatic improvisation—interestingly, in the name of *habit*, conceived as inherently idiomatic.

> We as a community of musicians have taken a long time to coun-ter . . . the erroneous idea of a "non-idiomatic" form of improvi-sation. Maybe Derek Bailey's book . . . acquired uncritical cred-

ibility because publication gave it the status of "agreed objective." As Christopher Small noted, habits and thereby conventions attend each and every performance—even of "free" improvisation—and habit becomes idiom.[17]

Ben Watson is quite right to cast some doubt on the efficacy of this attack, and he is correct to remind us that Bailey himself "recognizes that improvisers get stuck in their ways,"[18] but he himself seriously misrepresents Bailey when suggesting that the latter sees habit as a "loss of nerve, a decay in the musician's ability to play inventively in the here and now."[19] In fact, the opposite would be closer to the truth: Bailey has absolutely no problem with habits at all, as long as (one assumes) they are "good" habits. And why would he? His own playing is habitual through and through, full of tics and personal clichés, as he openly acknowledges:

> Habits—technical habits and musical habits (clichés)—are quite consciously utilized by some performers [including himself]. And there is a type of creative impetus which can come from playing well technically which can't be achieved in any other way.[20]

Watson is also unpersuasive when he claims that, contra Prevost, the non-idiomatic should be understood as a *process* rather than a *product*, the repetition of an argument already directed at the music critic/philosopher Andy Hamilton, who claimed that non-idiomatic improvisation was immediately recognizable as a style. This is Watson:

> One should interpret Bailey's "non-idiomatic" not as a claim about a finished piece of music—a product—but as a practical programme for effective improvisation—a process.[21]

In what follows there will be no fetishization of either the product or the process. Much more to the point is the task of trying to imagine a form of free improvisation that is true to the realities of Bailey's lived experience as an improviser (habits and all) while remaining faithful to the radical consequences of the non-idiomatic when taken to its logical, and thus extreme, conclusions. In this way it is hoped that the status of the above dialectic will be properly contextualized and rendered, ontologically at least, secondary to a more essential interrogation of the *decisiveness* of *resoluteness* and *obligation*.

Bailey's commitment to improvised music is impressive, admirable, and undeniable, and we have now used the term *commitment* a number of times in this discussion: but what do we mean? Clearly, to risk being trite, Bailey is not committed to non-idiomatic improvisation in the same way that Ben Watson is committed to what he perceives as the political ideals of free improvisation. In fact, it would probably be more accurate, and certainly more fruitful, to say that, rather than being committed to improvisation, Bailey recognizes and accepts the *obligation* to improvise, whether or not there are the idiomatic resources available to sustain such improvisation. Commitment is an exigency that can be accepted or refused; obligation is a sense that is ontologically *decisive* and thus not subject to the freedom of *choice* associated with it. This, it will be remembered, is precisely the distinction made by Heidegger, one that will help us here to hold Beckett and Bailey together in our imaginary embrace.

Our terminology thus far has also made liberal use of Beckett's conception of obligation as that which remains when everything else has been stripped away. Badiou was an avid reader of Beckett, and his concept of "fidelity" shares a great deal with this anti-nihilistic minimalism, as we shall discuss below. But before doing so, let us keep Heidegger in the frame and introduce his own notion of "resoluteness," as he considers it in *Being and Time*,[22] with a view to enriching our account of the creation, de-scription, and repetition-differentiation of improvised situations.

At the outset it should be made clear that the discussion of resoluteness in *Being and Time* is the culmination of a phenomenological interrogation of *Dasein* (being-there) that, unlike Heidegger's "later" work, is still embroiled in a thinking of "authenticity" that remains attached to the existential experience of subjectivity: the being of the "ontic" self rather than an ontology of Being. As long as we remain mindful of this and remember to what extent Heidegger, Badiou, and Beckett (and we imagine Bailey) ultimately deconstruct any possibility of the authentic self, then there is still something to be gained from an excursion into Heidegger's "earlier" thinking, especially if his insights are deployed in the service of the anti-humanism that ultimately characterized his thought, along with all those we are now considering.

Taking up the issue of freedom again, as one might expect, Heidegger is keen to distinguish the freedom he associates with resoluteness from the negative freedom, or freedom-from, that characterizes most liberatory discourses, including, it has to be said, those associated with improvisation.

> Resoluteness, as *authentic Being-one's-self*, does not detach Dasein from its world, nor does it isolate it so that it becomes a free-floating "I." (344)

Heidegger's evident skepticism regarding the liberatory claims of the free self is compounded by the quotation marks temporarily protecting the "I" from its inevitable dissolution and disappearance into the "loneliness" of existential singularity: clearly his deconstruction of the transcendental ego is already well underway here, in spite of the residue of the ontic that still clings to his thinking. Anyway, although resisting such negative freedom, Heidegger characteristically avoids entering into a dialectic and thus resists counterposing a freedom-to as an alternative. The reason is that neither of the above models of freedom sufficiently acknowledge the essential fact that, for Heidegger, being is always being-with (*Mitsein*) within a "world." There is no question of being free-from the world or free-to create a world: being is always already and essentially "*Being-in the world*." Instead of freedom-from and freedom-to then, Heidegger proposes a freedom-for that is "authentic" to the degree that it discloses and acknowledges the co-presence of the other: *Mitsein*.

> Resolute Dasein *frees itself for the world*. Dasein's resoluteness towards itself is what first makes it possible to let the Others who are with it "be" in their ownmost potentiality-for-Being, and to co-disclose this potentiality in the solicitude which leaps forth and *liberates*. (344)

Although the language might be unfamiliar (especially for those fortunate enough not to have become hooked on Heidegger), there is a message here that has much to offer those improvisers who, like Bailey, are simultaneously committed to collaborative practice while suspicious of what Heidegger calls the "talkative fraternizing" (345) of communicative communities—improvisers, like Bailey, who are committed to freedom while skeptical of liberatory politics and "activist" art. The strength and relevance of Heidegger's perspective is that it allows the improviser to conceive of the world (of improvisation) not as a fixed context *within which* the prowess of improvisational unfixing can take place—he describes this as an "empty *habitus*" (347)—but as an emergent space where both self and other are summoned into their shared potentiality and possibility. In other words, to be resolute is not the same as committing to a pre-existent "world" to which one would want to belong and show allegiance (the hallmark of idiomatic improvisation); no, it is the very resolve of resoluteness that, so to speak, brings the "world" into existence. In these terms improvisation would be more about the improvisation *of* "worlds" than about the improvisation *within* and *with the things* of an existing world, the latter always being ontologically secondary.

> One would completely misunderstand the phenomenon of resolute-
> ness if one should want to suppose that this consists simply in tak-
> ing up possibilities which have been proposed and recommended,
> and seizing hold of them. *The resolution is precisely the disclosive
> projection and determination of what is factically possible at the
> time.* (347: Heidegger's emphasis)

As can be seen, Heidegger draws attention to the temporal specificity
of resoluteness, thus repeating an earlier statement: "resoluteness, by its
ontological essence, is always resoluteness of some factical Dasein *at a particular time*" (347; emphasis added). So, engaging in some sub-Heideggerian
wordplay, resolve might be understood as the interminable *re-solution* of the
problem of being-in-the-world. And what is the problem? In Heidegger's
view resoluteness responds to three existential predicaments: "thrown-
ness," "lostness," and "indefiniteness." We will reference the last of these
first:

> To resoluteness, the *indefiniteness* characteristic of every potentiality-
> for-Being into which Dasein has been factically thrown, is some-
> thing that necessarily *belongs*. Only in a resolution is resoluteness
> *sure of itself.* The *existentiell indefiniteness* of resoluteness never
> makes itself definite except in a resolution: yet it has, all the same,
> its existential definiteness. (347)

Picking up the other two: the "I" only has being (*Dasein*) to the extent that
it finds it-self "thrown" into an already given "world" of brute and indefinite facticity (very Beckettian). Although "thrown," the "I" is not "lost"
in the "world" but "lost" in the "They" that, through the "empty talk" of
communicative community, replaces the task of thinking with the dialogical
pleasures of the group—thus *preventing* the dis-closure of the authenticity
and "unsociability" of being-in-the-world. In earlier humanist times the reception of Heidegger latched onto the existential angst created by the above
scenario, ignoring the philosophical reserve of the original in favor of an exaggerated celebration of the tragic/romantic hero hell-bent on self-discovery.
In our own post-humanist days we are more inclined to take a different message from this way of thinking. Particularly for our purposes here, it is the
question of "indefiniteness-definiteness" that will be of primary interest,
particularly as it fits so well into the earlier discussions of Hegelian "severity" and Kantian "certainty."

When lost, or in "lostness," the "world" lacks definition, is merely a
"general situation" that is "accidental" in nature (346–47). As we have seen,

resoluteness interrupts this, the bland continuum of the "They," with the temporal particularity of resolve: for us, the time of the improvisation. At a "particular time," in a particular place, the resolute self and (by implication and by virtue of *Mitsein*) the resolute other disclose together the *definite* spatiality of the "Situation:" Heidegger describes this as "making room" (346).

> The Situation is the "there" which is disclosed in resoluteness—the "there" as which the existent entity is there. It is not a framework present-at-hand in which Dasein occurs, or into which it might even just bring itself. Far removed from any present-at-hand mixture of circumstances and accidents which we encounter, the Situation *is* only through resoluteness. (346)

One can compare this to Eugene Chadbourne's description of Bailey's *Company Weeks*, of which he was a sometime participant:

> It is interesting when Derek creates situations in which he might not even be playing. He is not only creating situations for himself to get involved with, he is creating it for the situation where he can sit back and hear something new or special.[23]

Looking at improvisation through this lens is transformative, not least because it inverts the accepted image of improvisers as intrepid seekers after the accidental, chance, surprise, and the unpredictable: un-fixers of the fixed. The latter view or *doxa* is completely reliant on the assumed existence of frameworks (idioms) present-to-hand that can be the subject of improvisational *action*, whether or not in the name of freedom and/or liberation. Heidegger's view recognizes that the *decisive* act, as opposed to the active *choices* made within existing frameworks, is the resolute disclosure of the Situation. And, contrary to the emphasis of Chadbourne above, the "new" and the "special" are less qualities of the improvised action *within* the situation; they have more to do with the resolute act of disclosing the situation. It is this *a priori* moment of improvisation that Bailey's activities draw attention to—what might be called an "expanded field" of improvisation, one that requires a rethinking of action and the decisive act.

> Resoluteness does not first take cognizance of a Situation and put the Situation before itself; it has put itself into that Situation already. As resolute, Dasein is already *taking action*. The term "take action" is one which we are purposely avoiding . . . [because] . . . it

suggests a misunderstanding in the ontology of Dasein, as if resoluteness were a *special way of behaviour* belonging to the *practical*
faculty as contrasted with one that is theoretical.[24]

If we must speak of freedom and liberation, then here might be the time
and place to do it. What Heidegger holds out here is nothing less than the
possibility of liberating ourselves (as improvisers, thinkers about improvisation, and perhaps *even* critics of improvisation) from the utterly misguided
view that improvisation can only be understood and engaged with as a *practice*, as the direct experience of a series of improvised *actions* within a particular situation. Even Bailey is guilty of this, although luckily for him (and
us), his statements on the theory and practice of improvisation, and their
relative merit, bear little resemblance to his actual improvisatory activity,
which, as resoluteness, is, in Heidegger's terms, "theoretical" through and
through. But here is a flavor of his pronouncements on the subject, drawn
from his highly influential book *Improvisation: Its Nature and Practice in
Music*. No mention of theory there, then!

> I couldn't imagine a meaningful consideration of improvisation
> from anything other than a practical and personal point of view. For
> there is no widely held theory of improvisation, and I would have
> thought it self-evident that improvisation has no existence outside
> of its practice.[25]

> Under these conditions the player performs not according to the
> "theory of practice," but intuitively, according to the "practice of
> practice." . . . I hope it will be adequate if I refer to the "practice of
> practice" as practice.[26]

> Learning improvisation is a practical matter: there is no exclusively
> theoretical side to improvisation. Appreciating and understanding
> how improvisation works is achieved through the successes and fail-
> ures involved in attempting to do it.[27]

Such statements have, of course, become gospel, both within the generally
anti-theoretical improvising community, as well as among the host of journalists and critics, most of whom are drawn from the very academic world
they are quick to trash in the name of an imagined, pure, intuitive practice
untrammeled by the leaden weight of thought and philosophizing. Ben Watson describes Bailey's improvisation as "counter-theory,"[28] which, if true,
would make the current chapter redundant.

Continuing with Heidegger, from his perspective, the discussion of the relative merits of theory and practice and the heated debates that ensue are, for all of the commitment on display, little more than "lovers quarrels" of limited relevance to the decisive issue. In this regard, resoluteness—the primordial obligation or "care," as he would describe it—is neither theoretical nor practical, but *prior* to both.

> Care . . . as concernful solicitude, so primordially and wholly envelops Dasein's being that it must *already be presupposed* as a whole when we distinguish between theoretical and practical behaviour; it cannot first be built up out of these faculties by a dialectic. (348; emphasis added)

In an indirect way Bailey seems to recognize this *a-priority* at the very outset of his improvisation book. Having, as we have seen, already rejected the possibility of a theory of improvisation, he is also (and quite rightly) dismissive of more technical approaches to the capture of improvised practice through transcription. That said, what is revealing is Bailey's observation that, when it comes to discussing improvisation with practitioners, which of course is how he put together his book and the subsequent TV programs, they tend to speak in "abstract terms" rather than dwelling on the "practice of practice" apparently promoted by Bailey himself.

> Almost all the musicians I spoke to chose to discuss improvisation mainly in "abstract" terms.[29]

> It became clear that, whatever its deficiencies, this is the best method available. An abstract description of improvisation can achieve, perhaps, a *sighting*. Close, technical analysis leads elsewhere.[30]

Of course, even more than *theoretical* or *technical*, the term *abstract* is itself hopelessly abstract and thus hardly the most promising "method" imaginable. Nevertheless, there is something here worth noting. The very fact that he uses the term *method* rather than methodology indicates that, stripped of any theoretical pretensions, method, unlike methodology, does not claim to account-for, speak-of or speak-about an objective externality; rather it speaks *from out of* the experience of a practice and the *life* that is, thus, experienced. Method is not a means of explaining but, as Blanchot describes it, a "mode of progressing": keeping things "going along" as Bailey would say. This is Blanchot:

As for Descartes, if the *Discourse on Method* is important, be it only in its freedom of form, it is because this form is no longer that of a simple exposition . . . but rather describes the very movement of a research that joins thought and existence in a fundamental experience: this being the search for a *mode of progressing*, that is a method; this method being the bearing, the mode of holding oneself and of advancing of one who questions.[31]

Indeed, Descartes himself admits that his method, unlike methodology, has no universal ambitions; it is not a "grand narrative" but just one articulation of a singular "life."

I shall be delighted to show in this Discourse what paths I have followed, and to represent *my life* as it were in a picture; in order that everybody may be able to judge of my methods for himself. . . .

My design . . . is not to teach here the method everybody ought to follow in order to direct his reason rightly, but only to show how I tried to direct my own. . . . I offer this work only as a history, or, if you like, a fable, in which there may perhaps be found, besides some examples that may be imitated, many others that it will be well not to follow.[32]

How does "abstract" thought and talk keep things progressing or moving along? What does Bailey mean when he suggests that such abstraction might offer a "sighting:" a sighting of what? And why the visual metaphor rather than an aural one? What does discussing improvisation in such terms allow us to "see?" Presumably not the improvisation itself but that which underpins or originates such improvisation. Obviously, Heidegger's view would be that both language and art practice can allow us to "see" (or "hear") the dis-closure of Being. Needless to say, Bailey wouldn't be comfortable with the language of Being and Truth but, in an indirect way again, he does suggest something not altogether dissimilar. For example, another way he uses to describe abstraction is "intuitive description," before quoting with obvious approval the following passage from Thomas Clifton's work on intuition and music.

The question is . . . whether or not the [intuitive] description says something significant about the intuited experience so that the experience itself becomes something from which we can learn and in so doing learn about the object of that experience as well.[33]

Admittedly, in common parlance "intuition" can be, and usually is, every bit as vague and abstract as abstraction; but thought with more care and precision, the nature of intuition might offer some real insights into the Baileyite/Beckettian model of improvisation we are working so hard to imagine here.

So, intuition, if thought along quasi-Kantian lines more closely aligned with our discussion here, is not referring to an immediate, non-rational (usually "embodied") knowingness quite distinct from the rational structures of conceptual knowledge, but to the *a priori* conditions of both knowingness and knowledge. As Clifton suggests above, it is not the intuitive experience of music that is primary, but the *experience of experience itself* prior to gaining knowledge ("learning") of the object of that experience. For Kant, and here he is followed in a radicalized/ontologized form by Heidegger, intuition refers to the *a-priority* of space and time: the only things not *in* space and time being space and time. We can see how this resonates with the above discussion of the "Situation," which is not primarily concerned with what takes place *within* the situation but with the *decisive moment* and *act* of resoluteness that discloses the situation *prior* to all subsequent action and activism. In a sense what we can see at play here is a fundamental (and unresolved) paradox in Kant's thinking: that while an intuited space/time is a condition of objective knowledge, such an intuition is only activated by the experience of things *in* space and time. Here one is reminded of the influence of Kant's thought on Deleuze who, it will be recalled, conceives of art as the creation of different space/times. The danger of "intuition" in the crude sense is that it can too easily pose as a shortcut to knowledge without the necessity of thinking—especially of thinking about intuition itself. Such an outrage to what Heidegger calls the "task of thinking," in the name of a resonant but inexplicable immediacy, effectively restricts thought and discussion to the interiority of contingent situations rather than opening out onto an exteriority—the "Outside," as Blanchot and Foucault call it—that gives a "sighting" of the coming into being of situatedness itself: its beginning.

In spite of Bailey's public image as an improviser unconcerned and unconvinced by the "theoretical," it could be argued that there is a lot more at stake in his playing, organizing, and broadcasting than the promotion and celebration of improvising for its own sake. In fact the shift from the emergence of situations to the emergence of a "scene" is something he bemoans.

> The fact that [free improvisation] has continued and turned into a kind of scene is nothing that I anticipated. I don't even feel that it's anything to celebrate.[34]

The spatial/temporal particularity of emergent situations and the intuition of what conditions this and what it opens out to are the first casualties of a "scene," so one can understand Bailey's concerns. And, by way of emphasis, Dominic Lash in his research on Bailey has uncovered interesting material that confirms the latter's interest in Husserl's phenomenology and, more specifically, the Husserlian account of improvisation offered by his some-time collaborator George Lewis. Here is the relevant section from Lash's unpublished PhD thesis.

> Bailey's description of time-consciousness here seems clearly influenced by that of Edmund Husserl, perhaps influenced by George Lewis's essay on the phenomenology of improvisation. . . . Bailey was possibly also interested in Lewis's adaptation of the Husserlian idea of the phenomenological reduction. . . . Accompanying Lewis' typescript is a note by Bailey, which reads: "George's 'musical ep-och.' P21—23 as a description of PLAYING (No adequate description of "playing" for an improviser. Not same as playing for musicians who don't imp[rovise]. etc etc—George's as one (best?) description." (Handwritten note inserted in Lewis 1974.) This implies that Bailey may have read Lewis's work in preparation for the first edition of *Improvisation*; he perhaps decided against including his concept of the "epoché" because he felt it to be too philosophically technical for his purposes.[35]

Not unlike Beckett's denial of any interest in philosophy, only to discover, as Simon Critchley has observed, that he has already out-philosophized the philosophers,[36] Bailey's "anti-theoretical" stance should be treated with some caution. Whatever Bailey's actual thoughts on phenomenology, it is clear that the severity of his own improvisatory practice represents a form of reduction and renunciation that, *first and foremost*, sets about stripping away as much of the idiomatic substance from the "musical world" as is humanly and performatively possible. In so doing, his ambition is not to reveal the pure noematic essence of music or improvisation but, at least as we are imagining it here, the void at the epicenter of the incessantly repeated situation—remembering that the epicenter is *not* the center but the focal point of the greatest instability. As Bailey knows well, there are an infinite number of ways to "name" this void (to return to Badiou's language)—he is by no means *against* idioms—it is just that his own way of de-scribing the situation (as non-idiomatic improvisation) is committed to a form of un-writing that reduces everything to what Beckett repeatedly calls (throughout *How It Is*) "bits and scraps" and Bailey similarly refers to as "bits."[37] This, at last, might allow us to hazard some guesses as to the likely or imagined influence Beckett might have had on Bailey's thinking and practice.

What are these bits and scraps? They are, it would seem, something like the minimal resources necessary to continue to make work—to write, to improvise—as an obligatory rather than expressive enterprise. And it is not just that there is no means to express or no desire to express, but that there is no substantial self or "I" to engage in such expression or, indeed, an it-self to express: *everything* has been reduced to bits and scraps, not just the "musical world." Also, before leaving phenomenology, recall that the biggest problem for Husserl is not nihilism but *solipsism*, thus leading him, famously, to strive in vain throughout the fifth of his *Cartesian Meditations* to arrive at a convincing model of intersubjectivity, one that could underpin the self-other transaction that is assumed in most accounts of improvisation—except Bailey's. So, before turning in earnest to the Bailey-Beckett conjunction being imagined here, I offer a brief, but more detailed immersion in Husserl's thinking on intersubjectivity as a way into the peculiar "unsociability" of their "worlds."

Husserlian phenomenology is intent on disclosing the symmetrical structure of the life-world as constituted by the transcendental ego—the "I"—through a phenomenological "reduction" that removes alienation (the otherness of the "natural world") from experience. The achievement of a pure sphere of "ownness" thus requires a form of experiential "cleansing" that "frees" the horizon of "everything that is at all alien."[38] The price paid for the strict reciprocity between "ownness" and "otherness" is that the figure of the other can only appear within the sphere of "ownness" as an "alter-ego" that "mirrors" the self. This constitution of intersubjectivity through a process of "pairing" ensures that "separate pluralities," "not in communion," are rendered inconceivable by Husserl, allowing him to assume a "single universal community" validated by "empathy" as the key moment.[39] However, in spite of his sustained effort to constitute a symmetrical and harmonious intersubjective lifeworld, Husserl is forced to acknowledge that "closer inspection would further show that two streams of experience (spheres of consciousness for two pure egos) cannot be conceived as having an essential content that are identically the same; . . . no fully determinate experience of one could ever belong to the other."[40] Further inspection reveals that the asymmetry of Husserl's "monadic community" is also a consequence of the "prominence" of each solitary ego within its "sphere of ownness,"[41] a prominence which, when introduced into the intentionality of empathic intersubjectivity, threatens to produce the inorganic (or "pseudo-organic") "discord" that Husserlian phenomenology strives (ultimately in vain) to overcome.

To remain faithful to the phenomenological project in the face of the above would require us to turn our philosophical attention to "fixing" the problem through a prolonged engagement with issues surrounding the constitution of the self as an inherently dialectical, dialogical, performative entity. We would need to enter into these ongoing debates and find ways to *speak about*, discuss, and resolve such problems to the satisfaction of our own intersubjective lifeworld, our peer group: such are the requirements of being an academic. That, of course, would miss the point. It is precisely when it falters—its moment of "failure"—that phenomenology has most to offer those (e.g., writers, improvisers) who have no interest in *speaking about* or indeed doing anything about the "unsociability" of being-with—the windowless incarceration of the monad, the "essential solitude" of the writer—but who are compelled or *obliged* to *speak out of* the "inorganic discord" that constitutes the self, the other, and the asymmetrical space-time between the two. We have already seen how, in *Being and Time*, Heidegger rejects the promotion of empathy as a solution to the problem of intersubjectivity with a reminder that such a desire for sociability obscures the more essential "unsociability" of being-with. But, and this is the point, it is not just a question of speaking philosophically *about* this confusion (as he does in *Being and Time*) but *from out of* this "unsociability" (as he does in his later writing). Heidegger himself recognizes the issue in *The Fundamental Concepts of Metaphysics: World, Finitude, Solitude*, where he begins to signpost his own future as a thinker:

> We must concede: Although we dealt directly with philosophy itself, . . . we have shirked in the face of philosophy. We have not spoken of other things, of science, art, or religion, but of philosophy—yet not directly and concretely *from out of it*, but *about* it. We are speaking *from out of it* only when we move in advance within a *metaphysical questioning*. Yet precisely this has not happened. . . . No matter how extensively we are concerned *about* it, everything remains a misunderstanding unless we are *gripped* by such questioning. . . . We have indeed dealt *with* philosophy, but not taken action *within* philosophy itself. What is decisive, however, is that we emerge from this dealing with . . . and *take action within metaphysics itself*. This means nothing other than the fact that we must now really and properly question.[42]

And, to be clear, it is not simply a matter of re-positioning philosophy and the philosopher: Heidegger is not simply offering a new and novel perspective. On the contrary, to question *from out of* philosophy is intended to render both philosophy and the philosopher themselves questionable: "a questioning that . . . takes the questioner himself into the question as well, puts him into question."[43] It should also not escape our attention that Heidegger's call to *action* has nothing in common with post-romantic striving or voluntaristic activism; rather, it is cognizant of the questionable nature of action itself. In particular, it is his recognition that the *act* of questioning must be displaced by the more essential "act" of being *gripped* not by particular questions but by questioning itself. The fact that being gripped suggests passivity more than it does activity reminds us that, like Nietzsche, Heidegger is aware of the need for new *habits* of thinking and, like Deleuze, reveals the possibility of a passive creativity that contemplates and responds to that which questions or grips us: the affirmation of chance again.

Without pursuing this any further, we can simply say this: the thinking, writing, and acting *from out of* the essential "unsociability" of being-with produces something that is quite unlike any of the forms (or idioms) that precede it. After his famous "turn" away from the unquestioning questions of philosophical discourse, Heidegger quickly and increasingly speaks in a strange "thinking-saying" that, if nothing else, radically questions the communicative efficacy of language and the communicative communities that are constructed upon the sharing of what, for Heidegger, is incapable of being owned or shared. The following passages from *Contributions to Philosophy* will give a taste of this while also acting as a bridge back to Beckett and Bailey. This is from his "Preview":

> We must attempt the thinking-saying of philosophy which comes from another beginning. This saying does not describe or explain, does not proclaim or teach. This saying does not stand over against what is said. Rather the saying *is* the "to be said," as the essential swaying of be-ing. . . . What is said . . . is a questioning that belongs neither to the purposeful activity of an individual nor to the limited calculation of a community. Rather, it is above all the further hinting of a hint which comes from what is most question-worthy and remains referred to it. Disengaging from all "personal" fabrication succeeds only in its intimacy to the earliest belonging. No grounding will be granted to us that is not warranted by such a disengagement.[44]

This is from the last page:

> *Language*, whether *spoken or held in silence*, [is] the primary and broadest humanization of beings. So it seems. But *it* [is] precisely the most non-humanization of man as an *extant living-being*

and "subject" and the heretofore—and thereby the grounding of Da-sein and of the possibility of non-humanization of beings. Language is grounded in silence.[45]

It would be neat if this read like Beckett, but, sadly, that isn't the case. No matter. For all of their differences, there are things that they share, and in particular it is the mutual recognition that even when "speaking-saying" has nothing more to describe, explain, proclaim, or teach, the *task* (as Heidegger often calls it) of thinking remains. The *task* of thinking has less to do with the thinking of thoughts or the re-presentation of ideas than it does with the *preserving* of thinking *itself*. As we have seen before, Heidegger understands preservation as the counterpart to creativity; where the latter "fixes" in the form of created "works," the essential role of preservation is the unfixing of the "work" in order to disclose what might be called the *working* of the work. Thus the task of thinking is to preserve thinking by separating it both from *what* is thought and from *who* is doing the thinking. What remains is not the thinking-saying of the human subject nor the "calculation of a community" but the neutral, "non-humanized" incessance of language itself: the *decisive event* of language.

Just as the *task* of thinking-saying is understood by Heidegger as a form of "disengagement" from both the human subject and the communicative community, so Beckett's *obligation* to express in writing the absence of all expression results in a similar disengagement which, as writing, amounts to something like a dramatization of the non-humanized situation that is described but not fully articulated or inhabited by Heidegger in the language of philosophy. What would a non-humanized language be like? Who would speak it? Whose voice is it? Where, if anywhere, is the subject situated within a language that is unowned? How can one "dwell in one's homelessness" as Heidegger suggests? Thankfully, Beckett does not answer these questions: he (or his characters) enact/s them. Here is a typical passage from Beckett's *Company*. It is a pity it wasn't written until 1980, four years after Bailey's establishment of the *Company Weeks*, but, then, they did continue until 1994, so perhaps we are at liberty to imagine that he did read Beckett's novella. Anyway, the passage:

> If the voice is not speaking to him, it must be speaking to another. . . . To another of that another. Or of him. Or of another still. To another of that other or of him or of another still. . . . For were the voice speaking not to him but to another then it must be of that other it is speaking and not of him or another still. Since it speaks in the second person. Were it not of him to whom it is speak-

ing speaking but of another it would not speak in the second person but in the third . . . It is clear therefore that it is not to him the voice is speaking but another it is not of him either but of that other and none other to that other.[46]

If Husserl has trouble convincingly articulating an intersubjective lifeworld by means of an empathic model of ego and alter-ego, then it is precisely this "failure" that is both preserved and unfixed as writing in passages such as this. If Heidegger, in his "strange tongue," somewhere between the philosophical and the poetic, has trouble thinking-speaking the event that is prior to all speech and thought, then Beckett's radical dislocation of the existential subject, subject-to the ontological instability of the narrative voice, expresses the obligation to express this predicament in the face of its own impossibility: he literally de-scribes the situation.

But, lest we forget, this is supposed to be a case study of Derek Bailey, not Beckett or Heidegger. So maybe it is time to start imagining in earnest how he can become a meaningful (if imaginary) part of this philosophical/literary thought experiment.

For a start, let us imagine that Bailey really *did* read Beckett's *Company*. What is clear throughout the dis-located "narrative/s" of the novella is that the very concept of company, of the experience of existential intersubjectivity, is not assumed and/or expressed but "*devised*" as a function of language and speaking. Here are some more examples:

> Deviser of the voice and of its hearer and of himself. Deviser of himself for company. Leave it at that. He speaks of himself as of another. He says speaking of himself, He speaks of himself as of another. Himself he devises too for company. Leave it at that. Confusion too is company up to a point.[47]

> Another devising it all for company.[48]

> Wearied by such stretch of imagination he ceases and all ceases. Till feeling the need for company again he tells himself to call the hearer M at least. For readier reference. Himself some other character. W. Devising it all himself included for company.[49]

> What visions in the dark of light! Who exclaims thus? Who asks who exclaims, What visions in the shadeless dark of light and shade! Yet another still? Devising it all for company. What a further addition to company that would be! Yet another still devising it all for company.[50]

Reading Beckett (and Heidegger) is the perfect antidote to the valorization of all those things so celebrated within the "world" of improvisation:
community, dialogue, intersubjectivity, communication, *company*. Let us
imagine, then, that Derek Bailey really did consciously *devise* the *Company
Weeks* not as a means of promoting the familiar collectivist ideology of
togetherness but as a way of disclosing the fundamental singularity, "unsociability," and "essential solitude" of not only the creative act but, more
specifically for us, the collectively improvised creative or performative act.
As such, the final words of *Company* should be noted:

> And how better in the end labour lost and silence. And you as you
> always were.
> Alone.[51]

It might be an insignificant aside (and imaginary thinking certainly needs
such things), but Bailey's comment on *Company Week* speaks volumes, as
long as one reads it in a particular way, admittedly one seduced by Heidegger, Beckett, and the imaginary:

> Playing and improvising solo has certain usefulnesses [*sic*] to do
> with language and working things out, but after that it is ridiculous.
> So a lot of it [organizing *Company Week*] is to do with me playing
> *in the company of* other musicians. If I didn't do Company gigs I'd
> be playing solo again.[52]

But, let us be absolutely clear, playing "in the company" of others must
be rigorously distinguished from the improvisatory collectivism that dominates the field, the "community of improvisers" that Eddie Prevost assumes
in his critique of Bailey. While playing solo within the group is undoubtedly
frowned upon in the world of collective improvisation, the essential *solitude*
of being does in fact acknowledge the "voice" of the other, thus distinguishing it from "loneliness" (Arendt). But it is the *nature* of this otherness and
the *dis-location* of this voice that is key to an understanding of Bailey's
improvisation. Where he differs radically from his contemporaries is his lack
of interest in the substantial *presence* of otherness in the shape of the other
person, other improvisers, collaborators, listeners, respondents involved
in the construction of a communicative community. For Bailey, the orga-
nization of *Company Weeks* (possibly his most significant improvisatory
act) was precisely intended to problematize all of the above. Repeatedly,
Bailey has spoken of his fascination with the emergence of an improvised
situation in the early formative stages of bands, a fascination that quickly

evaporates once the band is properly formed and ceases becoming in order
to *be* a *"band."* For him, the fascination is not with the other band members
as such but with the ways in which such formative situations present the
players with a void that needs to be filled (or "named"). It is the otherness
of the void that is key here, not the otherness of the other player. In that
sense, then, the creation of situations amounts to a persistent need or desire
to present oneself and others with the void that, while ontologically shared
(being-with), is performatively alienating and thus incapable of sustaining
an assumed empathic community of players. In fact, it was precisely Bailey's
awareness of the ease with which improvisers were able fill the voids that he
attempted to confront them with that led him to invite non-improvisers into
the situations he devised.

> There is, after all, some very basic idea behind "improvisation":
> it means getting from A to C when there is no B; it implies a void
> which has to be filled. Sometimes, in improvising circles, that ab-
> sence is missing. One way of retaining it was to introduce non-
> improvisers.[53]

The idea of improvising as a means of *retaining absence* is remarkable
and once again reveals the logic of promoting the *absence* of idioms above
the *presence* of "freedom," or whatever terminology Prevost and his "community of improvisers" would prefer to the "non-idiomatic." Retaining absence is the *task* of the improviser, a task which recognizes that the "void" is
not absolute but situated: the creation of situations is the creation of spatial/
temporal voids, thus requiring us to completely re-conceive of improvisation
as the *a-voidance* (sorry, couldn't resist) of imagining, making, and inhabiting temporary structures. It is true that the 1993 *Company Week* program
contains the following statement: "Company Week is a building site; we get
together and make something that wasn't there before," to which Ben Watson rightly adds, "Of course, without a score, what's played won't be there
afterwards either."[54] But, we might pose the question, What is it that is made
that wasn't there before? As Watson implies, it is better conceived as the
flaring-up of something vanishing rather than the performative construction
of a shared dwelling no matter how *ad hoc*. Strictly speaking, a building
site is the material *situation* that emerges in the *absence* of a building yet to
come. The danger, for Bailey, is that in an improvised situation the material
resources brought to bear by the individual collaborators (co-laborers) can
too quickly fill in the void with a workable *habitus*. Devising situations, or
different "companies," that might introduce some delay into this process
is one strategy used by Bailey to protect the void before it is stripped of its

alterity and given a "name." Another strategy, and certainly one learned from Beckett (we imagine), is the reduction of one's material resources to the bare minimum, to the point where—as "bits" or "bits and scraps"—the construction of improvised abodes loses all viability. Comparing Bailey to Arnold Schoenberg, Watson quotes from Adorno's *Philosophy of Modern Music* as follows:

> There is perhaps no single factor which distinguishes Schoenberg so basically from all other composers as his ability to discard and reject what has previously been possessed.[55]

This passage is drawn from a chapter entitled "The Renunciation of Material," and it is this power of renunciation that Adorno believes is responsible for "the process by which material becomes no more than a matter of indifference."[56] Such indifference is the mark of an aesthetic language that has become completely liberated from the expressive duties necessary to represent, and thus sustain, not only the artist but the idioms, genres, and structures that "house" the artist. In this regard, Adorno's account of Schoenberg's and Stravinsky's music resonates both with Beckett (of whom Adorno was a great supporter) and Bailey (who was certainly influenced by Schoenberg).

> Expression, which has always proceeded from the subject and the object, is scorned because a contact is no longer established. . . .
>
> All responsible music today has in common a critical relationship to expression. . . . There are passages in Stravinsky which, in their melancholy indifference or unrelenting harshness, do more honor to expression and its vanishing subject; . . . the empty eyes of his music have at times more expression than does expressionism itself.[57]

"Melancholy indifference," "unrelenting harshness"; yes, it is easy to hear this in Bailey's playing too, and tempting to honor it with an expressive value, as does Adorno here in a dialectical reversal so characteristic of his thought. That is to say, the Adorno who never truly liberated himself from expressionism, which is why, contra Simon Critchley, we cannot accept that he is "the philosopher who has come closest to describing the difficulties of interpreting Beckett and gone furthest in taking up the challenge that he poses to philosophy."[58] Let us take this indifference and harshness at face value and for what it is, indeed, "*how it is.*" Bailey's self-deprecating irony, anti-intellectualism and ridicule of the "wet eye"[59] should be enough to convince us that, for him, the resoluteness to improvise outside of all idioms and, indeed, outside of all community-based collectives is not something that should be trivialized by the familiar narratives and stories—especially his own story and the "story of improvisation." For him, there is no story, only situations, endlessly repeating and endlessly different to the extent that they confront the void that they were created to reveal.

One thing we don't need to imagine is that Bailey not only read Beckett's *Ping* but, strange for a life-long improviser, set it to music, one of the very few extant compositions in his archive. While an inherent "musicality" has been identified by numerous commentators on *Ping*,[60] a somewhat obvious and rather banal attempt to offer an alternative way into what is, and is no doubt intended to be, an incomprehensible piece, we might imagine that this was not the primary attraction for Bailey, even though the "ping" of harmonics is one of his own trademarks. But then we can only imagine where the fascination lay. One possibility might be this: Beckett's *Ping* utilizes a very limited set of words which are deployed in what appears to be a random order, constantly repeating and shifting. The effect has much in common with Earle Brown's method of indeterminate composition, where the content is predetermined but is formally mobile. As is well known, he developed this method having witnessed the effect of Alexander Calder's mobiles. Interestingly, Bailey interviewed Brown for his improvisation book, where the latter concludes,

> I thought that it would be fantastic to have a piece of music which would have a basic character always, but by virtue of aspects of improvisation or notational flexibility, the piece could take on subtly different kinds of character.[61]

Clearly, "aspects of improvisation" would link to Bailey, while "notational flexibility" would link to Beckett's *Ping*, but it is Bailey's comments on this that are both interesting and significant:

> The main difference that occurs to me between your methods and Jackson Pollock's is that you are using other people's sensibilities, other people's spontaneity, and with Jackson Pollock, of course, his involvement was direct. You are accepting *the effect of the situation* on other people's sensibilities.

Brown replies:

The writing of music involves an aspect of projection, I would say, projecting your imagination into a situation you are not going to be present in, and in that sense it's not so strange for me to try to project one stage further, which is to project the conditions that I hope, with good will, the musicians will enter into.[62]

What both *Ping* and Earle Brown's work do then is to place the reader, the musician, into a set but shifting *situation*, where the negotiation of the emerging and evolving space is not "read" as a story or score in the usual sense but improvised both in the moment but also (and this is the fascinating thing) outside of that moment and the situation, to the extent that the writer/composer/deviser projects himself into that situation. In other words, what we witness here is a method of improvising that takes place across the boundaries of the improvised situation, a form of improvisation that would suggest once again that Bailey's devising of *Company Week* is a performance that is *a priori*, absent while at the same time being ever-present in the situation as an imagined project. One might say this chapter has been exactly that: the projection of imagination into a situation you are not going to be present in—pure Derek Bailey.

Derek Bailey and Evan Parker: London, April 22, 1985[63]

Pure Derek Bailey, yes, and that's much more than a lame metaphor in his case. To be more accurate, at the level of performance as witnessed here, there *is* no purity as such. Purity is not given; rather, it is an infinite work of purification, coupled with the obligation to purify: pure Bailey, pure Beckett. But even before the performance starts, this purification is underway: the removal of all *emotional* involvement from and in the improvisatory act, the removal of any communicative and communal claims from the improvisatory act, the removal of any extra-improvisatory significance or meaning from the improvisatory act: the absolute affirmation of renunciation. One might go as far as to say that here we witness a profound paradox: the projection of Bailey's improvisatory imagination into a situation that he is not going to be in, even though he is in fact in it—there he is, he's the one playing the guitar! Yes, but remember, this solo performance (we'll ignore his duet with Evan Parker) took place around the same time that Bailey was saying, as we've seen above, that solo playing was only "useful" as a way of developing a language and "working things out," but as improvisation proper it was "ridiculous." Come to think of it, it was also around the same time that an audience member in London felt conned enough to rip up his ticket, throw it in Bailey's face, and storm out; which only goes to confirm the earlier suggestion that practicing has to stop before the performance starts, otherwise there's likely to be trouble.

But back to the performance: Bailey is there all right, yet strangely absent, exuding a subtle but unmistakable disinterestedness (almost as if he'd just finished reading Kant's *Critique of Judgment* where, of course, "disinterestedness" is the very hallmark of the aesthetic: maybe he had!). The stage looks a bit of a mess, guitar case cluttering things up, more like a *practise* space. Bailey looks reasonably smart in a dowdy, rather careless (almost disinterested?) kind of way, but hardly dressed to impress! Somewhere between a geography teacher and a carpet-fitter on vacation: clearly not straight from one of his Beckett look-alike photo shoots, more's the pity. Anyway, distracted by this and that, but apparently not by the audience (although at least there is one for a change), he adopts his familiar posture, sitting, bent over his guitar, the trusty Gibson ES 175. A word about this before we start, before he starts: first the posture.

Occasionally, although rarely, one sees photos of Bailey playing standing up, but they inevitably look wrong, like a boy who has been told to stand up by a bullying teacher (is there any other kind?) or just someone who can't find anywhere to sit and is starting to get desperate. With or without his guitar, performing or not, Bailey never looked like the kind of person who should be standing up:[64] Beckett was the same (Parisian café, coffee, seated, *voila!*). But this is not just sitting; what we are describing is the adoption of a *posture*, and, as Deleuze and Guattari indicated earlier, posture, is one element of the "refrain" which, it will be remembered, plays its part—an essential part—in the creation of territory, or what we have been calling the "devising" of improvised "situations." Here's the quotation from Deleuze and Guattari again, still the same, but now strangely different:

> There are also refrains of posture and color, and postures and colors are always being introduced into refrains: bowing low, straightening up, dancing in a circle and lines of color.[65]

But, to be clear, Bailey's posture is inextricably linked to the very jazz "refrain" he is intent on, not critiquing or negating (that would require another idiom as critical lever) but *avoiding/a-voiding*: his is the jazz-guitarist posture *par excellence*!

And the Gibson ES 175: the jazz guitar *par excellence*! But then is there an idiom-neutral guitar worth having? Tele (country/rock), Strat (blues/rock), Les Paul (rock/punk), Flying V (metal), Rickenbacker (pop), ES 335/345/355 (jazz rock/jazz funk/blues), Gretsch (rockabilly/country), ES 175 (jazz).

This is a deeply ironic dimension of Bailey's work that has been largely ignored (probably because the non-improvising critics don't see this as an important part of the practice): the look, the posture, the equipment (it looks like he is using an Orange amp too, a mainstay of the jazz guitarist) create, visually at least, the one situation he most wants to avoid (jazz is the only music he is openly critical of in interviews). But, as we have seen, irony has to be situated to allow the necessary "mental reservation" to deconstruct the structure from the *inside*: avoiding by voiding, to labor the wordplay.

But back to the performance: Bailey's disinterestedness extends to the start of the improvisation itself. For a few moments it is not even clear if he *has* started. A cursory strum to make sure the amp is working, a couple of tentative plucked notes, rubs his hand up and down his trouser leg to warm it up (his hand not his leg!), a few more phrases, a couple of beautiful ringing harmonics, then he decides to remove his spectacles: starts again. A few runs, not yet up to speed on the control front, but almost immediately some incredibly delicate transitions, clusters of notes and harmonics, and then falters, sits back, inspects his plectrum (a sure sign that he risked something and it hasn't quite come off: it's always the plectrum's fault—a glimmer of irony).

As with Lol Coxhill, the hands are mesmerizing. Bailey must have practiced long and hard in front of a mirror,[66] and, again, if you turn off the sound, most of what he is doing *looks* like it is jazz, but then, turn the sound up and it isn't.[67] Apart from the trademark harmonics that glitter on the surface like jewels, Bailey goes in for a pretty harsh palette, devoid of any emotional affectation, clunky, abrasive, and studiously mechanical. Yes, as he himself admits, he is a very "technical" player, the "bits" that he refers to as the building blocks of his improvisations are undoubtedly in evidence here; they are often very tricky to play, and he doesn't always pull them off: "fail, fail better." He often plays at speed (a weakness of all good guitarists, analogous to the loudness of saxophonists, which, ironically, Bailey often bemoans), but the rapidity and difficulty, indeed *virtuosity*, are peculiarly unimpressive, largely because of the scrabbling and scurrying cacophony that such technique ultimately produces.

As any guitarist knows, putting a brand new set of strings on just before a performance or recording is usually a bad idea, they sound metallic, tinny, the bottom drops out of the frequency range and every movement of the fingers produces (usually unwanted) squeaks and scrapes. Strings need to be played-in for a couple of hours, or a couple of weeks, even months if you are a jazz guitarist looking for the idiomatic "warmth" that one associates with jazz: flat wound strings being one shortcut to this suffocating dullness. It sounds (and looks) like Bailey has a brand new set of strings on. Of course, this allows his harmonics to chime like bells and it also allows him to obsessively monitor the tuning of his guitar, (another trademark), but the overall sound takes some getting used to and is, let's be honest, not for the faint-hearted. And it's not just the new strings: it is noticeable that Bailey has selected the central position on the guitar's pick-up switch. A jazz player would normally select the neck pick-up, while a rock or country guitarist would most likely go for the bridge pick-up, certainly when playing a solo. But quite apart from such idiomatic predilections, the fact is that unlike these two positions, which directly link the sound to the specific characteristics of the pick-ups, the central position mixes the sound of both without, however, being either: a kind of sonic in-betweenness. The result is a neutrality that very effectively undermines or obstructs the production of a character-ful or recognizable sound, one that most other guitarists devote so much of their energy pursuing. Bailey simply switches all of that off and enters into "the neutral." Perhaps it is the neutrality rather than the harshness of Bailey that is so hard to take.

For all of the emotional disengagement, there are nevertheless some "moments" here, beginnings if you like, often when the improvisation seems to be faltering, a sudden pause, stasis, repetition, one almost witnesses the rehearsal of the contraction of a habit. Bailey's attitude changes slightly, yes, his head is beginning to sway, he's "getting into it," then it passes. Things start "moving along" again, and his improvisations do move along at quite a pace, which, incidentally, distinguishes him from those guitarists, and there are a few out there, who play in the "Bailey-style." They shall remain nameless, but any direct comparison will reveal the difference and, in particular, the incredible agility and dynamism of his playing: deterritorialization at work.

The improvisation ends, no "sense of an ending," no ceremony, no self-satisfaction, just the momentary recognition of a chance to stop, which he snatches. More disinterestedness, even some discomfort at the applause, and then straight into a rather formal—indeed, ludicrously formal—announcement: all part of the improvisation?

Beginnings and endings do not coincide with the start and the finish; they occur throughout, and sometimes (most times?) it is only Bailey who senses them—we might catch a fleeting sign, a shift in posture, a glance—but the most important thing is to be in the situation, in the company of Bailey, witness to the "ridiculousness" of solo improvisation. Ridiculous or not, there he is improvising solo: he can't go on, he goes on.

22 Memoir: Miles Davis, Royal Festival Hall, July 1984

This, I'm sad to say, will be a very short memoir indeed. No videos (bootleg or not) to jog or confirm my failing memory; my only significant recollection of the performance was his rendition of Cyndi Lauper's pop classic "Time After Time." Of course, like everyone else in the audience, I expected the jazz/funk/rock outings that had come to characterize the "late" Miles after the "return" from his six-year cocaine and drink-induced interlude of paranoia and epic promiscuity; but one could sense the initial disbelief—even collective heart-sinking—when the first chords of Lauper's poignantly pretty little song began encircling us. A sucker for poignancy and prettiness (not the same thing at all) and a huge admirer of Cyndi Lauper, I was immediately fascinated. Of course, Miles himself, his extraordinary charisma, was and remains endlessly fascinating—charisma and fascination go together—as is Cyndi Lauper, who similarly fascinates through a powerful juxtaposition of image and voice— seeing and hearing—that confirms both Blanchot's and my own younger self's thoughts on the subject. Blanchot first:

> Whoever is fascinated doesn't see, properly speaking, what they see. Rather it touches them in an immediate proximity: it ceases and ceaselessly draws them close, even though it leaves them absolutely at a distance.[1]

And me, from my book on aesthetic education, although the terminology would need to be changed in the current context: teacher would need to become performer/singer/player; student would become viewer/listener—but the point remains the same:

> To be fascinating, the teacher must present an image to the student. To present an image, the teacher must be constituted as a body, one that takes on presence in the student's "sphere of ownness" [Husserl] and which draws the other out of this sphere through such fascination. It is however, not the body of the teacher that is fascinating . . . but the voice that, as speech [here we would say music or song], is mediated there. . . . In fact, it is precisely this splitting of the body, between sight and sound, that renders the teacher fascinating. . . . Here the mediating role of the body introduces the strange and estranging incessance of language that speaks through the speaker from an absolute distance.[2]

Putting aside the fact that virtually everyone who ever played with Miles considered him a "teacher," the issue here is that Miles himself was utterly, and very openly, obsessed with his own *image*. Indeed, the end of his marriage to Cicely Tyson came when she, in the course of an argument that got ugly, pulled out his hair extensions—he was appalled by his "motherfucking" hair loss: what is it with men and hair? But I digress.

Miles is on stage, and he's playing a pop song. Now, the endless fascination of Miles is directly related to his ability to forget, to renounce his own past for the sake of a future always yet to come. From playing with Charlie Parker to *Birth of the Cool*; from *Kind of Blue* to *Miles Smiles*; and from there to *Bitches Brew*, the trajectory (in retrospect) is obvious and compelling: but Cyndi Lauper! What kind of "yet to come" was this? Worse still, there seemed no desire on his part to disguise the at times almost (although not quite) saccharine sentimentality of the song; if anything, luxuriating in this much more than Lauper herself does: the swirling orchestral synthesizers, the (now horribly dated) chorus guitar and tinkling percussion, all so Eighties—such a difficult decade.

Anyway, at that time, with the release of *Decoy*, much of Miles's repertoire was up-tempo, with very tight and somewhat slick arrangements, funky and often high-octane, especially during the improvised stretches. Within this context, one of headlong and Hell-bound linearity, *Time After Time* (and we should take note of the title) was something like a stopping of time—what Augustine describes as "stilling"—a moment of *ekstasis* that suggested a time outside of time and, indeed, a space outside of the ongoing space of performance witnessed at that moment by the audience. Removing the lyrics (which are actually rather touching), Miles revealed the insistent repetition of the song's structure. Rather than using the space to explore the melodic lines of the original or in anyway mimic the ebb and flow of the singing voice, it was noticeable that Miles chose instead to simply shadow the rotating chords, adding almost nothing as regards obvious improvised content—indeed, I remember him repeatedly laying out at key moments of the melodic line, leaving only the backing groove beneath his own silence. Strangely, unlike almost all of the other material in the set, Miles completely dominated the improvisation in this piece, actually playing over others if they made any attempt to interject or get a solo off the ground. This was strange because, although Miles's playing had yet to return to something close to his best (1985 onwards), he was in very good form that night, playing straight with less of the tell-tale mute; punchy and precise in the tight ensemble playing and looking confident; yet in "Time After Time" the fragility was only too evident. The strangeness was that it was as if Miles wanted to *emphasize* this fragility, to draw attention to his inability to reach the notes he was seeking, or sustain the voice much beyond short and uncertain utterances. It was at times almost painful to watch, and *would* have been painful to watch if the rest of the set hadn't been so assured: leaving the impression then that this was precisely the intention of the piece. Bill Frisell says somewhere that his whole career has been the search for a particular sound that he has never quite managed to produce; and, as already mentioned, Miles spent his own life never quite recapturing the experience of witnessing Parker and Gillespie for the first time. For me, such a hopeless hope was never more in evidence than during "Time After Time" on that night in 1984. It was as if Miles wanted us all to confront with him the vulnerability normally concealed behind the image of Miles: "king of cool." As Blanchot explains, we are not fascinated by the image itself but by the absence that the image conceals. As I remember it, the almost wanton desire to expose that which he had spent his life concealing, not only through cracking notes and fumbled riffs and runs, but also through his blatant exposure to the cameras in the front row as he did so—he literally posed for them—made this the most moving, indeed, shattering performance I have ever seen from Miles.

It is well known that Jimi Hendrix heavily influenced Miles, both musically and visually. That said, there is little if any attention paid to their respective approaches to improvisation that, on the face of it, look quite different, notwithstanding the dreaded wah-wah pedal. My own view is that, for the most part, their approaches to improvisation have very little in common and that the planned collaboration, interrupted by Hendrix's untimely death, would have been interesting, no doubt, but probably futile. However, and strange though it may sound, Miles's "Time After Time" is the one moment where a fascinating common ground opens up between himself and what turned out to be the "late" Jimi Hendrix: this shared improvisatory space is one of essential solitude, and thus not shared in the usual sense. But as regards Miles, what I experienced at the Royal Festival Hall in 1984 was a performance where, contrary to most of his history, a real openness to the other seemed to be in evidence, even exaggerated. The camaraderie with his band, the physicality, his arms around their necks; his openness to the audience, facing them, acknowledging them, even speaking to them during the pieces (rather than between them); this was all very different and, of course, universally applauded by the critics who love to feel like they're part of something (even if, in reality, they're not). Personally, I found it slightly disconcerting and, probably quite unfairly, rather stage-managed. Having since looked at a great deal of live footage of that period, in a fruitless attempt to witness again the actual performance I attended, I can confirm that this indeed was Miles's style/attitude at that time, and I still find it simultaneously both charming and rather tragic. If ever one needed evidence to support Heidegger's paradoxical claim that being-with (*Mitsein*) is the epitome of "unsociableness," then this would be it. Alongside Hendrix's improvisation in "Machine Gun," Miles's "Time After Time," as I witnessed it, takes improvisation into a realm or, perhaps, uses improvisation to open up a realm of utter solitude. To repeat: the "essential solitude" for Blanchot has nothing to do with intersubjective loneliness, but is the moment when the artist/writer/performer/improviser is "cast aside" by the work (or working) itself. What I saw (and continue to see) in Miles's "Time After Time" was a form of improvisation that, through an almost exaggerated "failure" to fully engage with and take ownership of the work, dramatized this moment of being "cast aside," leaving the work, in all its "incessance," unworked and, thus, endlessly fascinating.

Improvisers routinely reference and, perhaps, exaggerate the risks involved in improvising. In truth the "failure" rate is very low, and anyway, not to play one's best is not to "fail"; it is to underachieve, and a lot of improvisers manage that, just like everybody else (especially those on the checkouts at my local supermarket). Real "failure" can be painful to experience: as a guitarist, I simply cannot watch the "late" playing of my one-time hero Tal Farlow: it is excruciating—plain sad. With Miles though, to witness someone reaching out again and again for something that they cannot attain—that is unattainable—is not only fascinating and tragic in equal measure: it is, as are all great tragedies, sublime.

23 Case Study: Cyndi Lauper, "Time After Time"

The Sirens: evidently they really sang, but in a way that was not satisfying, that only implied in which direction lay the true sources of the song, the true happiness of the song. Nevertheless, through their imperfect songs, songs which were only a song still to come, they guided the sailor towards that space where singing would really begin.

Maurice Blanchot[1]

You know, you can copy yourself until you're blue in the face, but I don't wanna be a re-run, like a tired old thing. How many people live in the past and are successful in the present? I don't wanna live there.[2]

Cyndi Lauper

George Cole, in his book *The Last Miles*,[3] acknowledges that the adoption of "Time After Time" in 1984 "marked the beginning of a new musical direction for Miles, which would see more pop songs creeping into his repertoire over the next year or so. "Time After Time" would remain in Miles's set right up until his final concert seven years later."[4] Yes, but why? We know, as the above quote is intended to emphasize, that neither Cyndi Lauper nor Miles were the kind of artists who moved into the future facing backwards (Keith Johnstone's definition of improvisation, remember), but *why* pop music, and why does "Time After Time" figure so prominently in this pop-orientation, whether new (for Miles) or old (for Lauper)?

One answer, already floated, is that it is precisely the fixity of the standardized idiomatic pop song that suggests, no matter how allusively and illusively, a form of improvisation that has remained more or less completely unacknowledged in the literature on both popular music and improvisation: obviously something of a worry—does it even exist? Hopefully, maybe, who knows, let's see.

"Time After Time" is, to say again, a classic pop song, which means, if we return to Hegel's typology of symbolic, classical, and romantic art, that it no longer has need of the "severity" necessary to galvanize an incomprehensible objective meaning, nor has it descended into the mere "pleasing," where it is an incomprehensible subjective meaning that renders all external form ironic and inauthentic. Needless to say, much pop music and (more so) rock music can easily be fitted into the romantic "pleasing" form, but such music is, sad to say, incapable of producing a *classic*; something that Green Gartside of Scritti Politti admits he spent much of his early life trying to achieve; and maybe he did with "Perfect Way" which, of course, Miles recorded on *Tutu*.

For Hegel, the classical is that which aesthetically presents the universality of spirit within a sensuous particular form, such that the infinite receives finite expression and the Absolute speaks through the singular. Thought thus, to achieve classic status (within the world of Hegelian pop at least), a pop song would have to bring form and content into harmony in such a way that the individual sentiments of the singer are capable of being *freely* expressed in a "language" (thought extra-linguistically) rooted in, substantiated by, and constrained by the universal, rendering it universally communicable. In this way, the classic pop song has to be, at the very least, both unique and universal at the same time. In other words, Cyndi Lauper's famed "unusualness" (her first album: *She's So Unusual*) only achieves classical status, by transcending the idiosyncratic mannerisms of the/her "romantic" form and exemplifying an archetype of individualism that has *universal* appeal. She is the one who "speaks" to us *all* because it is precisely the All that we hear speaking though the One: and on this occasion Cyndi is the One and All.

By definition, pop music is intended to be popular, and popularity depends upon repetition: the repetition necessary to "hook" the listener in the first place, and then the repetition necessary for this moment of seduction to be endlessly rehearsed as nostalgia, happiness, regret, and so on. Obviously, all of the above can be achieved by the original record/CD/cassette, played to death on whatever format is technologically current. While, as already discussed at length, repetition and difference are anything but contraries, in the world of pop, where Hegel and Deleuze are notable by their absence, such repetition is almost exclusively placed in the service of sameness: an eternal recurrence of the same that is as far removed from Nietzsche's eternal return as is imaginable. But of course, and here we need to recall Hegel in the different context of "self-certainty," the same is *not* the same, any more than the "this" is always the same "this." In other words, the "then" associated with the pop song in question (let's call this song "Time After Time") is not the same as the "now" in which we (the lovers of pop) re-hear and rehearse this song time after time. But, then again, if we really *are* lovers of pop music and, more specifically, lovers of classic pop songs (rather than the trivial, personal, extra-aesthetic associations such songs might evoke) then the "then" and the "now" have to be mediated in a way that allows the "fidelity" (Badiou again) to the event of the original song to be actualized and re-actualized repeatedly: this is Cyndi Lauper's problem, one that is hardly unique. Nevertheless, her response is exemplary and—the point—it demands a very particular improvisatory imagination and skill: one that is fixed and idiomatic and, thus, "secret."

It is highly likely that the majority of Lauper's fans (probably now in their fifties) attend her gigs to relive the eighties and the trials, tribulations, and triumphs of their youth: that's what they/we do. But "Time After Time" is a classic pop song precisely because, while articulating that moment at the level of individual or what Hegel would call phenomenological experience, it also and more essentially brings into view a shared spiritual universality that, while experienced in solitude, has universal resonance. Thought in these Hegelian terms, "Time After Time" is emphatically *not* a typical eighties song: eternity has no typology. Lauper acknowledges as much when she suggests to her manager (in no uncertain terms), during an argument over whether or not to replicate exactly the original version of the song in a recording session for a film, that if the fans want to relive their past, they should "go and buy the friggin record."[5] Quite.

As Kierkegaard recognized in *Either/Or*, the nostalgic are "unhappy" people because the lost past that they so long for is, in truth, not a past at all but a future still to come.[6] Nostalgia is not a memory of past events but of past *hopes*, what Husserl would call the "retention" of "protentions,"[7] or, more expansively, the recollection of expectations. To understand this is to understand why (to reverse Johnstone) Lauper, to the extent that she is obliged to repeat her past work, might be described as an artist moving backward into the past facing forward to the future. What is *really* "unusual" about Cyndi Lauper is not her weird hairdos, crazy, doll-like clothes, or her grittily charming Queens accent (fabricated wackiness), but her uncanny ability to return to her own past *without* turning toward that past, without losing sight of the unfulfilled hopes and yet-to-be attained futures that are both responsible for the original work and remain responsible for its repeated origination (or re-novation) in the "now." To try and imagine a form of improvisation that fits this temporal model is the challenge.

Keith Johnstone's description of the improviser as one moving forward facing backward has considerable currency because it captures so much of what counts as improvisation in so many different areas of practice. Once again, it exemplifies the process of unfixing the fixed that has already been discussed at length. Here the past is fixed and retained but then progressively unfixed as it is fed into a future that, because behind the improviser's back, is "protended" as anticipation, uncertainty, and unpredictability: what Heidegger describes as "certain but indefinite"[8]—but then he's speaking of death! This, of course, is the very essence of the jazz standard (certainty and indefiniteness, that is, not death . . . that's more of a junkie jazz musician thing), but in the realms of pop music, such an approach is responsible for a whole industry of re-vamping and re-packaging that, in the name of bringing things "up to date" and "keeping current," introduces moments of uncertainty through such novelties as spontaneous, unscored repetitions, extended solos, audience involvement (hand-clapping, foot-stamping, singing along, "co-creation," etc.), impassioned variations and additions "in the moment," and so on: all as a way of keeping the nostalgia alive and kicking. Admittedly, something similar can also be achieved without the introduction of such exuberant uncertainty, where the re-packaging and re-vamping is carefully (albeit with an improvisatory component) fixed in advance of the performance. But regardless of the transformations made possible by such an approach, it is, at the end of the day, the facing-backward element of the process that undoes it: the result—diversity without difference.

Listen to and watch Cyndi Lauper's many performances of "Time After Time," such as, for instance, the one she argues with her manager about above, or the one on the *Martha Stewart Show*,[9] or on *Australian Idol* (my favorite),[10] or on *Good Morning America*,[11] and these just for starters. If you get quickly bored with this, then by all means turn her and her squawking off, but also stop reading this book immediately; there will be nothing of interest for you here: bye! But seriously (for those few still reading), these performances are indeed "unusual," remarkable even, in their sheer concentration, intensity, conviction, and (dare we use such a compromised word? . . . maybe just this once) *authenticity*. Just compare these performances to the quietly cynical regurgitations of James Taylor, or the hyper-re-authenticated blasts of Bruce Springsteen, ever more desperately trying to re-connect with his roots:[12] the difference is absolute.

Why?

Returning to our earlier distinction between practising and rehearsing, we might propose that JT and The Boss, as renowned perfectionists, practise and practise and practise in order to perform, and then perform at the highest level imaginable. Let us also propose then that Lauper rehearses in order, at the point of performance, to rehearse *again* where, as before, *re-hear-sing* allows her and her audience to re-hear her song and its singing as if for the first time.

> There was something marvellous about the song: it actually existed, it was ordinary and at the same time secret, a simple, everyday song which they were suddenly forced to recognize, sung in an unreal way by strange powers.[13]

As already discussed, rehearsing is a form of improvisation that, unlike practising, is primarily concerned with preserving the past rather than preparing for the future—remembering, with Heidegger, that the creation of artworks fixes them, while preservation necessarily unfixes them. But this unfixing is very different from that which predominates in the world of improvisation, where such unfixing is played out processually on the surface of the performance: here, instead, it is invisible and *secret*.

How So?

Part of the secret (not her secret, *the* secret) is that there is a way of turning to the past without *re-turning* to face what is there ready and waiting to have "new life" given to it by the rejuvenating breath of the improviser's song (nice though that sounds). Improvisers do not perform miracles. Yes, of course, past works are there in the past; but the secret form of improvisation imagined here is not concerned with the work as such, has no interest whatsoever in tampering with its form or content: the return is, to say again, the re-turning *away* from the work. Such a way of returning recognizes that it is not the original work but the originary *working*, or the work of origination, that must be re-turned to as that which originates the origin, so to speak. Without this "other beginning," which, as Heidegger says, "leaps away" from the dead matter of the historical into the historicity of that which is "still to come," there would be no work in the first place.

So, Cyndi Lauper, as pop star, has to repeat "Time After Time" time after time: that's her job. Does this mean that each time she is required to do this, she must in her heart and mind return to the eighties and find ways of rekindling the happiness and sadness of those days long gone? Of course not: what fans and critics forget is that it is only *they* who periodize the music they love; for the creator, the work is essentially outside of time, neither new nor old, neither contemporary nor dated: the reason being that from inception to reception, the work, for them, is always "still to come." Only by returning to the past facing the future can this, the essential futurity of the work, be preserved. If we locate our secret improvisation here, we will not need to concern ourselves with the diversification of an existent work in endless improvisatory gestures designed to keep it "alive" and endlessly entertaining but can, instead, accept its fixity as the necessary correlative of a primary, anticipatory consciousness that, in actualizing in singular/particular songs, the event of song itself sings through the individual song to the absolute or universal song "still to come." It is this singularity-universality that, if achieved, delivers to us the classics we so desire.

> This song . . . was a form of navigation too: it was a distance, and what it revealed was the possibility of travelling that distance, of making the song into a movement towards the song and of making this movement into the expression of the greatest desire.[14]

The acceptance of the fixity of the work means that the only movement available to the improviser is not within the work but, as Blanchot suggests (to repeat his beautiful phrase), "a movement towards the song and of making this movement into the expression of the greatest desire."

It is very noticeable that in all of Cyndi Lauper's performances of "Time After Time," there is no significant improvisation evident whatsoever; there are barely perceivable hints of looseness here and there from her accompanists, perhaps (which is what they are . . . certainly *not* a "band"), but *never* from Lauper herself. She is the epitome and embodiment of fixation and fixity: the rigid and businesslike stance behind her dulcimer speaks volumes. The song begins, it is sung, and it ends. During the song, there is no give and take with her fellow musicians, no (Heaven forbid) camaraderie with the audience, who, as always, are all too desperate for just such an opportunity to reduce the sublime to the ridiculous: that's what we do. While the musicians are listening to each other and to Cyndi, always with great enjoyment and pleasure written all over their faces (and why not?), *she* is listening exclusively to the song as the song yet to be sung, not as some eighties relic or some "some old thing," but as the eternal desire to reach out and capture the universal within the singular voice which is singing "now." There is no movement *within* the song, no opening up of localized dialogical spaces to satisfy the short-term desires of immediate communicative and expressive gratification; there is only a movement *through* the song, not in order to get it over and done with but, perhaps, to transcend or (better) exceed it. For all of her goofy celebrity and wisecracking façade, she sings as if a woman possessed, with absolutely no concessions to the culture she is a product of: now that *is* unusual.

But Back to Improvisation: Where Is It?

Having proposed that her improvisation is both idiomatic and fixed, we (OK, I) now need to nail it once and for all.

Normally, improvisations take place *within* situations, whether idiomatic or non-idiomatic, whether fixed, semi-fixed, or unfixed. We have also tried to imagine a form of improvisation that takes place outside of or between situations, where the improvisation is either the choice of a situation (Lol Coxhill) or the construction of a situation (Derek Bailey). First, Cyndi Lauper, the improviser, does not operate at the level of the situation. Within the situation, there is no space for or, indeed, need for improvisation. Second, although every musician in preparation for a gig has to create the situation within which the performance can take place, there is no sense in which, for Lauper, this has any great improvisational or creative value: it doesn't really matter that much who plays her songs with her; she has no interest in how they can interact and communicate as a "band," as long as the song is sung—that's the priority. This, sorry to say, brings us back to the philosophy of the event and again to Alain Badiou's distinction between the "site" of the event and its localized actualization within multiple "situations" or, for us, performances. For Badiou, the event only has a presence within any situation to the extent that we become aware of its absence: what he calls "naming" it as a "void." The kind of example he gives is that, for instance, classicism is an event in music whose "site" exceeds every "situation" that actualizes itself locally after the event. The "name" or "names" we give this event are "Haydn," "Mozart" and "Beethoven," all of whom are ever-present within the "classical" situation and yet absent as a virtual multiplicity that exceeds all situations but remains a reality that can be actualized in all work "still to come:" this is the retrospectivity and futurity of the event. The same might be said for Duchamp, Schoenberg, Dylan, Parker, Joyce, Beckett, Eliot, Cunningham, Paxton, Kant, Hegel, Nietzsche, Heidegger, Deleuze, Marx, Freud, Fanon, Mao, . . . and so on.

So, to come back to the problem, and the problem of Cyndi Lauper as improviser: is it possible to imagine a form of improvisation that operates at the level of the event? Or if not that, somewhere between the "site" of the event and the "situation" of, in this case, the pop song?

The event has to be actualized, but not all actualizations are improvised; in fact few of them are, although perhaps we should recall again here Malabou's mind-blowing claim that all being has an improvisatory essence (hold that thought). Anyway, what would an improvised actualization of the event look or sound like, and, more to the point, is this what Cyndi Lauper manages to achieve?

A proposition running throughout this book (and throughout my last book) is that improvisation has a particular way of *dramatizing* the beginning, the beginning understood as the moment where the swarming multiplicity of contingent being is fixed as this or that form: habit, work, subject, improvisation, and so on—a coming into being, if you like. Somewhat controversially, Peter Gabriel, in some of his recent concerts, has performed/composed/improvised some unfinished pieces alone on the piano, literally dramatizing the creative process before an audience. Such an enactment of the entanglement of composition and improvisation is certainly thought-provoking and in many ways quite brave, but it is not quite what it is being grasped for here. First, the drama revolves around precisely the un-fixedness of the compositional situation; second, it is overly intentional, smacking too much of the "master at work," improvising choices until the "right" one comes along and then—*voila!* Nevertheless, this is still helpful, in that it raises the question of what, inversely, a fixed, non-intentional improvisation might be, which very much brings us back to Catherine Malabou and the notion of being itself as improvisational.

What if we are posing the wrong question, and instead of asking how Cyndi Lauper might somehow improvise outside of the "situation," we consider the possibility that she is herself (and her work) the *subject of* improvisation rather than its intentional perpetrator; that *she* is improvised rather than that she is an improviser. Certainly Badiou's "theory of the subject" would claim that it is the situated actualization of the event that *creates* or *produces* subjectivity rather than itself being the creation or product *of* a given subject. Here are two examples to give a flavor; the first is from his *Being and Event*; the second, from the more recent *Logic of Worlds*.

> Grasped in its being, the subject is solely the finitude of the generic procedure, *the local effects of an evental fidelity*. What it "produces" is the truth itself, an indiscernible part of the situation, but the infinity of the truth transcends it. It is abusive to say that truth is a subjective production. A subject is rather *taken up* in the fidelity to the event, and *suspended* from truth; from which it is forever separated by chance.[15]

> There are truths, and there must be an active and identifiable form
> of their production. . . . The name of this form is *subject*. Saying
> "subject" or saying "subject with regard to truth" is redundant. For
> there is a subject only as the subject of truth, at the service of this
> truth.[16]

For Badiou truth is not singular, nor is it related to the *facts*; no, truth is
multiple and can only be actualized locally through what he calls "truth procedures." It is these procedures that produce subjects to the extent that they
are faithful to ("faithful subjects") or show "fidelity" to the infinite event
of truth. Badiou enumerates four, and only four, truth procedures: science,
politics, art, and love. Fidelity to one or more of these events both actualizes
(or preserves, for Heidegger) the truth, while also *constituting the subject*
as a scientific, political, artistic, or amorous being: there is neither truth nor
subjectivity outside of these four domains/procedures.

In light of this we might say that Cyndi Lauper is not the cause but an
"effect" of her fidelity to the event of, in this case, artistic and amorous
truth: "Time After Time" is a love song, an amorous art-truth/and artistic
love-truth. She and her work are the "identifiable forms" of truth within
the amorous/artistic situation that *produces* singers capable of love and the
songs that are true to that love. The only thing missing here is improvisation, and, truth to tell, one doesn't get much of an improvisatory buzz from
Badiou's work (maybe the set theory gets in the way). That said, his recognition that the subject is eternally separated from truth "by chance" does
suggest a way of bringing improvisation back into play. In order to attempt
this, we will need to revisit (yet again, sorry) the necessary passage in Malabou's *The Future of Hegel*:

> "Plastic individuals" are those that synthesize in their very "style"
> the essence of the genus and the accident which has become ha-
> bitual. What in the beginning was merely an accidental fact—
> Plato's commitment to philosophy, Pericles' to politics, Phidias to
> sculpture—is changed through the continual repetition of the same
> gestures, through practice, achieving the integrity of a "form." . . .
> The process of habit ends by canonizing being's improvisation on
> its own themes.[17]

This time around, it is the accidental and the improvisational that will
concern us rather than the habitual. As has been said on a number of occasions, chance and improvisation have little to do with each other unless,
following Deleuze, such chance is *affirmed*, thus transforming the passive

reception of fate, or the aleatoric, into a creative practice ("passive creativity"). What the Malabou passage suggests is that *prior* to our constitution as singular subjects, our potential or virtual being is *already* in a state
of improvisational flux or fluidity—what she calls, as we have seen before,
"plasticity." We, as subjects, are molded by (subjected to) such plasticity, but
we are also capable of *molding ourselves*, once we recognize and affirm who
we have become. It is this process or act of "canonizing being's improvisations" that conceals such *a priori* improvisation within the apparent fixity
of our consequent identity and the apparent fixity of our work: therein is
the secret. But, and this is the key, the improvisation doesn't stop there at
the moment of "canonization." As Badiou notes, the "chance" finitude of
the subject, while necessary for the production of truth, is also "forever"
separated and "suspended from" the infinity of truth, and this word "forever" is loaded: truth is not simply separate; we *yearn* for it eternally, we
become subjects to the extent that we desire infinitely. Which returns us first
to Blanchot—"making the song into a movement towards the song and of
making this movement into the expression of the greatest desire"—and then
to Cyndi Lauper, the secret improviser.

   And the secret is this: as Kierkegaard knew, the "essential secret" is only
essential if it cannot be betrayed, never, ever, to anyone.[18] Yet we are obliged
to write, knowing that writing can only aid in the concealment of what it
is we are searching for: what Kierkegaard calls "indirect communication."[19]

But Some Clues

"Time After Time" is one finite, chance actualization of the truth: of art
and love. Forever separated from the event of artistic and amorous love,
the "procedure" it (the subject of art and love) is obliged to follow moves
through the situation of the work toward the event which is marked or
"named" as a "void" or the work "still to come." Unlike Descartes's trajectory through the woods when lost, this movement is not "severe," but strict:
the destination is in view, no one is lost: only the distance cannot be reduced
by such movement. Heidegger calls this "erring," where, unlike error, the
truth is seen and heard but only as it endlessly withdraws. Improvisers, as
we know them, can devise ever new ways to approach or, indeed, ignore,
reject, or flee from the truth; and they can also make the journey, whichever
direction it takes, more interesting, more exciting, more surprising, more
boring, . . . and so on.

   Our secret improvisers, while appearing to leave improvisation to the
improvisers, actually touch upon something that all improvisers would do
well to remember: the improvisational nature of *being itself*. For the secret

improviser, *every* performance is an improvisation, whether or not it contains the improvisational gestures necessary to identify it as such. All performances are improvised because they are literally de-void of truth; that *is* their truth: their separation from the truth. Nothing *is* true, there are only "procedures" or "movements" that, at a distance from the truth, could always be absolutely other than they are, in every detail except for one: the movement itself. If everything could be different, then everything is subject to improvisation, including the improviser as the "identifiable form" of the event of improvisation—another way of saying the event of being. If this is the case, why is it that no one appears to be aware of the fact that all performance is improvised? Because it takes a secret improviser to give us an "inkling" of the fact that there is a secret. Not one that they can or will betray, but one that, Deleuze would say, can be *sensed*, although Badiou doesn't like this word, but then Deleuze doesn't like the word *truth*, so they're even. But the thing about secret improvisers is that not only are they very secretive, but they are also very rare: "unusual." One reason for their rarity is the extraordinary allure of improvisation as an overt and celebrated art form: everyone wants everyone else to believe that they can improvise; not to be able to seems so uptight, rigid, and anal. As a consequence, secret improvisers must take the risk of being lumped together with all of these non-improvising saddos and suffer the ridicule that awaits them: hence the rarity. That's why secret improvisers tend to be the kind of people who, like Cyndi Lauper, couldn't give a shit about what people think of them. And while we're back on the subject of Cyndi Lauper, let us conclude, or at least go for a cut: this needs to end.

Perhaps Miles Davis is the only one to have sensed the secret improvisation in "Time After Time," which would explain why he left it well alone, resisting the urge to interrupt its own originary movement with unnecessary and inessential improvised gestures, detours, and distractions. Thanks to him, we can return to the original song with a different set of ears, ones attuned to the event of art and love rather than the singular situation of a young woman from Queens wearing silly clothes in the eighties. With this new set of ears, we can hear the song within the song, the universal within the singular, the eventual site within the actual situation; hence, the song's classic status becomes undeniable: just listen. But to hear this song within/ beyond the song is not to sense its presence but its absence, as that which the song is moving toward. Cyndi Lauper improvises to the extent that she allows herself to be subjected to (molded by) the improvisation of being that endlessly churns beneath the chance fixity of the song. She does not have to *actually* improvise to allow us to hear any of this, but she does nevertheless actualize one thing that Badiou ignores or has little or no sense of: the improvisatory nature of actualization itself—that means everything.

> It remains questionable when we are in such a way that our being is song, and indeed a song whose singing does not just resound anywhere but is truly a singing, a song whose sound does not cling to something that is eventually attained, but which has already shattered itself even in the sounding . . .[20]

Conclusion

Somewhere in this book I say that improvisations do not end—they simply stop beginning. So this book is about to stop rather than end. Trouble is, in trying to improvise a conclusion, everything starts beginning again: will it ever end? Of course, I could simply write a conclusion rather than improvise one; simply go back over the key points in the text, draw some conclusions, make a few claims (ready to be shot down in flames), and then wave goodbye. But I'm not going to do that, as it would be a betrayal of everything this book is supposed to stand for: I have my reputation to consider (that was a joke, by the way).

But, all joking aside, if the readers of this book have reached this point, they will have guessed already that the text has no proper beginning (discussing beginnings is hardly a beginning), middle, or end, and so cannot be concluded in any meaningful sense. This is not because I am engaged in some infinite mega-improvisation that—in its pure becoming-ness—exceeds the parameters of any one text, rendering all introductions and conclusions meaningless; on the contrary, the real difficulty is that there has not really been any significant journey *at all*: and it is journeys that reach their conclusion and are thus concluded. Yes, but you have to go somewhere first. Of course, as I often mention, one of my favorite Deleuze quotations is the one about journeys taking place "on the spot," "journeys of intensity," and it would be nice to think that this book was just such a journey; not from start to finish, here to there, beginning to end, but eternally returning to the same place: "from to from," as we described it earlier. Or perhaps the concept of place is itself misplaced; should we not be thinking of a non-place, in fact two non-places: from the "decentered center," from the "displaced periphery?" But the real issue and difficulty, at least as far as conclusions are concerned, is, to repeat, the conceptualization of a journey as from-from. Thought along these lines, each improvisation in this book might be considered a departure, albeit a departure without an arrival: imagine an airport with only a departure lounge, this book is the textual equivalent of that—all take-offs, no landings, or certainly more take-offs than landings.

I suppose each of the improvisations/chapters has an ending of sorts; maybe that is the place to look for the elements of a genuine conclusion. Perhaps, but I must confess, my favorite by far is the "conclusion" to the Del McCoury case study, which ends with, "It is actually quite exhausting watching the Del McCoury Band for any length of time, as it is writing about them—so I'll stop." So, that doesn't really help much.

Actually, I *am* exhausted, and I do want to just stop but, like Beckett, I also feel the obligation to go on . . . I can't go on . . . I must go on, . . . etc. What makes this all so exhausting is not the distance traveled—there is no distance—but the effort required just to stand still: not forgetting that "going on" usually *is* standing still in Beckett. Meaning, more precisely, the effort necessary to resist the habitual thinking on improvisation—not as defiance or provocation, not in the name of "originality" or academic acumen, and certainly not in the name of critical debate, but (taking Deleuze's advice) in my own name: the "contemplation" of my *own* habits of thinking and doing, my *own* automatic acts of embodied memory. Just like tonality and idioms, the dominant patterns of habitual thought on improvisation and, indeed, on habit itself are deeply attractive and, like chocolate, extraordinarily hard to resist, but resist them we must. Yes, this is the demand, the obligation, the responsibility to think, even when there is no means, no desire, no power to think: exhausting.

If I were brave enough to make a claim, it would be this: that probably the only way to loosen habitual thought's stranglehold on improvisation is to think *from out of* improvisation itself; only improvisation itself can offer any real insight into its own predicament, but first it has to find ways of doing just that—writing this book is my contribution to that task; getting people to read it is the next challenge; convincing them that that this is the *one* book they really *had* to read—utterly essential—well that's probably getting a little ahead and above ourselves.

To start each chapter (sorry, improvisation) with absolutely nothing to say, no insights, no theories, and no "position," combined with the obligation to write, was tiresome as well as tiring, and yet the writing still happened; actually quite a lot of it in the end, and still it goes on. What is beyond question is that none of this writing would have been written without entering into the predicament of improvisation alongside whoever was the subject of this writing (Lol, Del, Bernard, Jurij, Jimi, Miles, Cyndi . . . the "dazzling names"). But throughout, it is the predicament or the event of improvisation that is the real focus, rather than the "names" under discussion. I assume that any reader would be little the wiser regarding the actual improvisation of this book's "chosen ones"; Derek Bailey looked a bit like Samuel Beckett; Jimi Hendrix simulated sex with things; Gato Barbieri got drunk; Bernard Purdie talks a lot—so what? The real issue is where a certain "fascination" with each of them can take you if you keep thinking, even when you've got nothing to think about, if you keep moving when you've nowhere to go: from nowhere to nowhere—from to from.

But, to repeat, it was *the* (not their) predicament, what Blanchot might call the space of improvisation, that the writing of this book was trying to both open up and occupy, while knowing at the same time that this space—as evental—cannot be owned.

In his preface to *Being and Event*, Badiou begins with the following statement:

> Soon it will have been twenty years since I published this book in France. At that moment I was quite aware of having written a "great" book of philosophy. I felt that I had actually achieved what I had set out to do. Not without pride, I thought that I had inscribed my name in the history of philosophy.[1]

On the CD sleeve of his *Vienna Concert* (ECM, 1992), Keith Jarrett makes the following comment:

> I have courted the fire for a very long time, and many sparks have flown in the past, but the music on this recording speaks, finally, the language of the flame itself.

Who wouldn't want to conclude a book like this? The arrogance is breathtaking!

> Peters's *Improvising Improvisation*, sure to become the standard work on improvisation for many generations to come: insanely in-

genious, innovative, and altogether incredible—certain to become a timeless classic.

Who wouldn't want to write a "great" book? Who wouldn't want to speak "the language of the flame itself" (if I knew what that meant: it sounds both dangerous and painful; don't try it at home)? But, then again, what does such arrogance signify? As a psychosocial attitude, it is of course deeply unattractive, denoting a sense of superiority accompanied by contempt and insensitivity to the relative worth of others. But that's not the issue; there are far too many not very nice people in the world to lose any sleep over them and their overweening pride, which is why all of the personal attacks on them (Jarrett included) are so pointless and beside the point. The real issue is not their overbearing self-importance but the act or process of arrogation itself—that is to say, the act of taking over or taking possession of that which is not rightfully theirs: the assumption of proprietal entitlement and *ownership*.

To be written *into* the history of philosophy—an eternal inscription or mark in the space opened by philosophizing—is to arrogate to oneself a "dwelling" place or *habitus* that the very event Badiou speaks of should *deny* him and everyone else access to—unless, of course, Badiou considers *himself* an event, which no doubt he does. To arrive at an improvisational language that speaks the language of the "flame itself" is to take possession of the originary ground in an illusory fusion of one's "sphere of ownness" (Husserl) with the source and the assumed ownership of the source. This, to me, sounds like a death knell for any further improvisation, a return to a mystified starting-point parading as a beginning, one which brings everything to an end before it can even begin.

Needless to say, then, this book could never be a "great" book, because throughout its course I have singularly *failed* to find a way to the source, essence, origin, or even meaning of improvisation: I have simply improvised in the hope that the distance between the "situation" thereby created and the absent "site" of the event of improvisation is at least brought to life—becomes a live rather than a dead space.

Perhaps my main ambition was to write a "good" book.

In the chapter entitled "Why I Write Such Good Books" in *Ecce Homo*, Nietzsche writes,

> Let us imagine an extreme case: that a book speaks of nothing but events that lie altogether beyond the possibility of any frequent or even rare experience—that it is the first language for a new series

of experiences. In that case, simply nothing will be heard, but there will be the acoustic illusion that where nothing is heard, nothing is there.[2]

Unlike speaking the "language of the flame itself," there is no arrogance attached to the desire to speak "from out of" improvisation. Improvisation is not the flame itself; it is, as Jarrett both rightly and unwittingly acknowledges, the "sparks" that fly around the burning "void" or "nowhere" of the event, the trace of invisible and unheard-of presence. If this book even *begins* to indicate the presence of an unheard-of language, silently signifying a "new series of experiences," then, as far as I'm concerned, it will have turned out to be a "good" book or, at least, good enough.

Notes

PREFACE

1. Samuel Beckett, "Three Dialogues," in *Disjecta* (London: John Calder, 1983), 139.

2. The distinction between *practise* and *practice* will be taken up again later in the book.

3. Belated apologies to those who bought my previous book.

CHAPTER 1

1. Martin Heidegger, *Contributions to Philosophy (From Enowning)*, trans. Parvis Emad and Kenneth Maly (Bloomington: Indiana University Press, 1999), 39.

2. See, for example, Derek Bailey, *Improvisation: Its Nature and Practice in Music* (New York: Da Capo Press, 1993), where Jerry Garcia offers the following observations: "A magic of one sort or another . . . that has been part of what has kept us going all this time. . . . It's something that breaks out every now and again. We can't make it happen either. It defies analysis, but it's certainly something to wonder about" (43).

3. Hans Georg Gadamer, *Truth and Method*, trans. Joel Weinsheimer and Donald Marshall (London: Sheed and Ward, 1989), 370.

CHAPTER 2

1. G. W. F. Hegel, *Science of Logic*, trans. A. V. Miller (London: Allen and Unwin, 1969), 67–78.

2. Ibid., 68–69 (first and final emphases added).

3. Ibid., 69.

4. Ibid., 82–83.

5. G. W. F Hegel, *The Phenomenology of Mind*, trans. James Baillie (London: Allen and Unwin, 1977), 83–84.

6. Immanuel Kant, *Critique of Judgment*, trans. Werner S. Pluhar (Indianapolis: Hackett, 1987), 64–65. (I have used the Pluhar on this one unique occasion rather than my preferred Meredith translation because the latter translates *Zweck* as "finality" rather than "purpose," which doesn't help my discussion.)

7. Immanuel Kant, *Critique of Judgement*, trans. James Creed Meredith (Oxford: Clarendon Press, 1952),174.

8. Ibid., 204.

9. Ibid., 205.

10. Ibid., 137.

11. René Descartes, "Discourse on Method," in *Philosophical Writings,* trans. E. Anscombe and P. T. Leach (London: Nelson, 1970), 25.

12. G. W .F. Hegel, *Aesthetics*, trans. T. M. Knox (Oxford: Oxford University Press, 1970), 356.

13. Ibid., 894 (emphases added).

14. Ibid., 616.

15. Ibid., 315.

16. *The Other Side of Nowhere: Jazz, Improvisation, and Communities in Dialogue*, ed. Daniel Fischlin and Ajay Heble (Middletown, CT: Wesleyan University Press, 2004).

17. Dana Reason, "Navigable Structures and Transforming Mirrors: Improvisation and Interactivity," in Fischlin and Heble, *Other Side of Nowhere*, 71.

18. Eddie Prevost, "The Discourse of a Dysfunctional Drummer: Collaborative Dissonances, Improvisation, and Cultural Theory," in Fischlin and Heble, *Other Side of Nowhere*, 359.

19. Hegel, *Aesthetics*, 619.

20. Ibid., 620.

21. Kant, *Critique of Judgement*, 152.

22. Ibid., 151 (last two emphases added).

23. Ronald Beiner, "Hannah Arendt on Judging," in *Lectures on Kant's Political Philosophy*, by Hannah Arendt (Brighton, UK: Harvester Press, 1982), 92.

24. Kant, quoted in Hannah Arendt, *The Life of the Mind* (New York: Harcourt, 1978), 186.

25. Ibid., 185.

26. Ibid., 186.

27. See Kant, *Critique of Judgement*, 153. Here Kant states that works "involving intensity" require the "enlarged mind" resulting from obedience to the second maxim.

28. J. M. Bernstein, *The Fate of Art: Aesthetic Alienation from Kant to Derrida and Adorno* (Cambridge: Polity Press, 1992), 60–61.

29. Martin Heidegger, "On the Essence of Truth," trans. John Sallis, in *Martin Heidegger: Basic Writings*, ed. David Farrell Krell (New York: Harper & Row, 1977), 136. "Man errs. Man does not merely stray into errancy, because as ek-sistent he in-sists and so already is caught in errancy. . . . By leading him astray, errancy dominates man through and through."

30. Scott Thomson, "The Pedagogical Imperative of Musical Improvisation," *Critical Studies in Improvisation* 3, no. 2 (2007).

31. Pierre Boulez, *Conversations with Célestin Deliège* (London: Eulenburg Books, 1976), 115. "We were listening to a group improvising, and I amused myself by describing what was going to come next; it is very obvious."

32. John Cage, *For the Birds* (Boston: Marion Boyers, 1981), 36.

33. Antonin Artaud, *The Theatre of Cruelty*, trans. Victor Corti (London: Calder and Boyers, 1974), 83–84.

34. Niklas Luhmann, *Art as a Social System*, trans. Eva Knodt (Stanford, CA: Stanford University Press, 2000), 309.

35. Ibid., 117–18.

36. Heidegger, *Contributions to Philosophy*, 40-41.

37. Susan Leigh Foster, "Taken by Surprise: Improvisation in Dance and Mind," in *Taken by Surprise: A Dance Improvisation Reader*, ed. Ann Cooper Albright and David Gere (Middletown, CT: Wesleyan University Press, 2003), 4.

CHAPTER 3

1. Lol Coxhill, quoted in a private e-mail from Mike Cooper.

2. For an excellent illustration, follow this link: https://www.youtube.com/watch?v=RzxzkOBRvoM. Lol Coxhill: Solo at Powis Terrace, for reference.

3. Gilles Deleuze, "Nomad Thought," in *The New Nietzsche: Contemporary Styles of Interpretation*, ed. David B. Allison (Cambridge, MA: MIT Press, 1985), 149.

4. Remember that, for Heidegger, "being-with" (*Mitsein*) is essentially "unsociability," hence his disinterest in "empathy," something awarded regal status in improvisation. I return to this later.

5. Howard S. Becker, "The Work Itself," in *Art from Start to Finish: Jazz, Painting, Writing and Other Improvisations*, ed. Howard Becker, Robert Faulkner, and Barbara Kirstenblatt-Gimblett (Chicago: University of Chicago Press, 2006), 26.

6. Vincent Descombes, *Modern French Philosophy*, trans. L. Scott-Fox and J. M. Harding (Cambridge: Cambridge University Press, 1980), 139.

7. Gary Peters, *The Philosophy of Improvisation* (Chicago: University of Chicago Press, 2009), 167–70.

8. Kuhn, of course, distinguished "normal" science from "revolutionary" science, which constituted a break with the dominant paradigm. Lol was no more a revolutionary than he was normal. He undoubtedly worked within the dominant paradigms but with a "mental reservation" that introduced something abnormal into otherwise normal situations: that was his genius and his irony. See Thomas Kuhn, *The Structure of Scientific Revolutions* (Chicago: University of Chicago Press, 1970), 23.

CHAPTER 4

1. Jacques Derrida, *Writing and Difference*, trans. Alan Bass (London: Routledge, 1978,) 252–53.

2. http://www.youtube.com/watch?v=Ok1YBDohvgQ.

3. *Lol Coxhill Sings*: https://www.youtube.com/watch?v=QSktAuDpV8A.

4. http://www.youtube.com/watch?v=kFP15LIVoiM.

5. A reference to Alain Badiou' s book title, *The Clamor of Being*, trans. Louise Burchill (Minneapolis: University of Minnesota Press, 1999).

6. Maurice Blanchot, *The Infinite Conversation*, trans. Susan Hanson (Minneapolis: University of Minnesota Press, 1993), 26.

7. Foster, "Taken by Surprise," 4 (emphasis added).

8. Frank Kermode, *The Sense of an Ending: Studies in the Theory of Fiction* (Oxford: Oxford University Press, 1967).

9. *Lol Coxhill Sings!,* http://www.youtube.com/watch?v=QSktAuDpV8A.

10. Arendt, *Life of the Mind*, 185.

CHAPTER 5

1. Arendt, *Life of the Mind*, 185.

2. Arendt, *Lectures on Kant's Political Philosophy*, 45.

3. I hope this begins to address the observation (made by an anonymous peer reviewer) that my own writing on improvisation is better fitted to solitary rather than collective improvisation—indeed, that I promote one above the other. For me, following Kant, Arendt, and Heidegger, solitude and collectivity cannot be so easily separated and opposed: they are interdependent.

4. From the same review of my article.

5. Heidegger, *Contributions to Philosophy*, xx.

CHAPTER 6

1. Gilles Deleuze, *Difference and Repetition*, trans. Bruce Patton (London: Continuum, 2001), xxi.

2. Keith Johnstone, *Impro for Storytellers* (New York: Routledge, 1999), 94.

3. Martin Heidegger, *The Fundamental Concepts of Metaphysics: World, Finitude, Solitude*, trans. William McNeill and Nicholas Walker (Bloomington: Indiana University Press, 1995), 78-164.

4. Deleuze, *Difference and Repetition*, xxi.

5. Ibid., 84.

6. Miles Davis, *Miles: The Autobiography* (London: Picador, 1990), v–viii.

7. Deleuze, *Difference and Repetition*, 24.

8. See Theodor Adorno, *Aesthetic Theory*, trans. C. Lenhardt (London: Routledge & Kegan Paul, 1984), 303, where he understands "technique" as the mastery of artistic materials.

9. Deleuze, *Difference and Repetition*, 19.

CHAPTER 7

1. Peters, *Philosophy of Improvisation*, 51–53.

2. Veryan Weston: Piano; Gary Peters: Guitar; Simon Picard: Saxophones; Dan Brown: Electric Bass; Cliff Venner: Drums.

3. And, lest we forget, one of Jim Hall's albums is called *The Winner!* (Fontana,

1964) The cover has an image of an incongruously glamorous woman holding a nice shiny trophy.

4. Private e-mail, 13 March 2016.

5. *El Pais*, 29 July 1980.

6. Lincoln Goines, the bass player in Barbieri's band, has since informed me that they arrived ahead of Gato; they were on the bus, while he was traveling in a limo with his wife Michelle. Private e-mail. 13 March 2016.

7. Bill Washer, the guitarist in the band, states that he doesn't remember Gato being "wasted" (although he accepts I might have a better memory of it than he) and that he never saw Gato in that state when touring with him. Clearly, this might have been an exception, but the contemporary news reports do confirm that he was exceedingly drunk. Private e-mail, 13 March 2016

8. Private e-mail, 13 March 2016.

9. Alan Lewens (director), *Classic Albums: Steely Dan—Aja*, music/documentary film, 1999. Series Producers, Nick de Grunewald and Martin Smith. Made by Isis Productions. Distributed by, Eagle Rock Entertainment.

CHAPTER 8

1. Peggy Phelan, *Unmarked* (London: Routledge, 1993).

2. Phillip Auslander, *Liveness: Performance in a Mediatized Culture* (London: Routledge, 1999).

3. Gilles Deleuze, *The Logic of Sense*, trans. Mark Lester (London: Continuum, 2004) 73.

4. https://www.youtube.com/watch?v=KG6z2_Kbqzk

5. Bernard Purdie in Performance: https://www.youtube.com/watch?v= YYfWpUvtJhs

6. https://www.youtube.com/watch?v=aLHQG20Xsyg.

CHAPTER 9

1. Theodor Adorno, "On Popular Music," in *Essays on Music*, ed. Richard Leppert. (Berkeley: University of California Press, 2002), 445.

2. Berthold Brecht, *Mother Courage and Her Children*, trans. John Willett (London: Methuen, 1980), 144.

3. Davis, *Miles: The Autobiography*, 59.

4. Ibid., 92.

5. Jacques Derrida, "Tympan," trans. Alan Bass, in *Margins of Philosophy*. Chicago: University of Chicago Press, 1982.

6. Badiou, *Handbook of Inaesthetics*, 13.

7. Georges Bataille, *Eroticism*, trans. Mary Dalwood (London: Marion Boyars, 1987), 65: "The barriers are not merely raised, for it may even be necessary at the moment of transgression to assert their solidity. Concern over a rule is sometimes at its most acute when the rule is being broken."

8. Taken from the sleeve notes for *The Complete Jack Johnson Sessions*, Sony Music, 2003.

9. Derek Bailey describes such modal improvisation as "blandness"; see Bailey, *Improvisation*, 88.

10. George Lewis, "Afterword to 'Improvised Music after 1950': The Changing Same," in Fischlin and Heble, *Other Side of Nowhere*, 163.

11. George Lewis, "Improvised Music after 1950," in Fischlin and Heble, *Other Side of Nowhere*, 151.

12. Isaiah Berlin, *Two Concepts of Liberty* (Oxford: Clarendon Press, 1957).

13. Arnold Schoenberg, *Style and Idea*, trans. Leo Black (London: Faber and Faber, 1975), 216–17. For an excellent discussion of this, see Charles Rosen, *Schoenberg* (London: Fontana, 1976), chap. 2.

14. Schoenberg, *Style and Idea*, 217 (second emphasis added).

15. Arnold Schoenberg, *Theory of Harmony (Harmonielehre)*, trans. Robert Adams (New York: New Philosophical Library), 1948.

16. Hegel, *Aesthetics*, 616.

17. Deleuze, *Difference and Repetition*, 24.

18. Jorge Luis Borges, "Pierre Menard, Author of Quixote," in *Labyrinths* (Harmondsworth: Penguin Books, 1970), 69.

CHAPTER 10

1. Borges, "Pierre Menard," 65–66.

2. Ibid., 67.

3. Ibid., 68.

4. Deleuze, *Difference and Repetition*, 84.

5. This is precisely what Borges's fictional character Funes the Memorious, in the story of the same name, cannot do. See *Labyrinths*, 87.

6. Borges, "Pierre Menard," 66.

7. Deleuze, *Difference and Repetition*, 212 (emphases added).

8. Borges, "Pierre Menard," 69.

9. Ibid., 70.

10. Paul Ricoeur, *Hermeneutics and the Human Sciences*, trans. John Thompson (Cambridge: Cambridge University Press, 1981), 182.

11. Ibid., 192.

12. Ibid., 191.

13. Borges, "Pierre Menard," 71.

14. See Andre Maurois's introduction to Borges, *Labyrinths*, 9.

15. Ricoeur, *Hermeneutics and the Human Sciences*, 182–83.

CHAPTER 12

1. Howard Caygill, "Benjamin, Heidegger and the Destruction of Tradition," in *Walter Benjamin's Philosophy: Destruction and Experience*, ed. Andrew Benjamin and Peter Osborne (London: Routledge, 1994), 12.

2. http://www.youtube.com/watch?v=rdT18n79SFY.

CHAPTER 13
    1. Deleuze, *Difference and Repetition*, 211.
    2. Ibid., 209.
    3. Ibid., 212.

CHAPTER 14
    1. Gilles Deleuze and Felix Guattari, *A Thousand Plateaus*, trans. Brian Massumi (London: Athlone Press, 1988), 311–12.
    2. Deleuze, *Difference and Repetition*, 129.
    3. Ibid., 132.
    4. Ibid., 199.
    5. Deleuze and Guattari, *A Thousand Plateaus*, 315.
    6. Martin Davidson, quoted online at http://www.emanemdisc.com/addenda/newmusic.html.
    7. Deleuze, *Difference and Repetition*, 198.
    8. Ibid.
    9. Ibid., 199.

CHAPTER 15
    1. Friedrich Nietzsche, "The Uses and Disadvantages of History for Life," trans. R. J. Hollingdale, in *Untimely Meditations* (Cambridge: Cambridge University Press, 1983), 76.
    2. Paul Ricoeur, *Freud and Philosophy: An Essay on Interpretation*, trans. Denis Savage (New Haven, CT: Yale University Press, 1970), 32.
    3. Ibid., 33.
    4. Ibid., 34 (Ricoeur's emphases).
    5. Richard Kostelanetz, ed., *Conversing with Cage* (London: Omnibus Press, 1989), 91.

CHAPTER 16
    1. Jurij Konjar, "The Goldberg Observations: Unwritable Notes on an Unthinkable Practice," *Contact Quarterly* 36, no. 2 (Summer/Fall 2011): chapbook 2; hereafter cited parenthetically by page number in this chapter.
    2. Martin Heidegger, "The Origin of the Work of Art, in *Poetry, Language, Thought* (New York: Harper & Row, 1971), 71. "Art is the fixing in place of a self-establishing truth in the figure. This happens in creation as the bringing forth of the unconcealedness of what is. Setting-into-work, however, also means: the bringing of work-being into movement and happening. This happens as preservation."
    3. Foster, "Taken by Surprise," 7.
    4. Ibid., 11.
    5. Badiou, *Handbook of Inaesthetics*, 60–61.
    6. Ibid., 60.
    7. Nietzsche, "Uses and Disadvantages of History for Life," 62.
    8. Badiou, *Handbook of Inaesthetics*, 60.

9. For both of them restraint, as with Heidegger's notion of reserve, is ontologically undialectical.

10. Ibid.

11. Friedrich Nietzsche, *Ecce Homo*, trans. Walter Kaufmann, in *Basic Writings of Nietzsche* (New York: Random House, 1968), 756.

12. Badiou, *Handbook of Inaesthetics*, 61.

13. Badiou himself conjoins undecidability and surprise in *The Adventures of French Philosophy*, trans. Bruno Bosteels (London: Verso, 2012), where he specifically writes of "the undecidable surprise of the event" (292).

14. Jacques Derrida, "A Certain Impossible Possibility of Saying the Event," trans. Gila Walker, in *The Late Derrida*, ed. W. J. T. Mitchell and Arnold I. Davidson (Chicago: University of Chicago Press, 2007).

15. Ibid., 223, 225, 228, 233, 238.

16. Jean-Luc Nancy, "The Surprise of the Event," trans. Robert Richardson and Ann O' Byrne, in *Hegel after Derrida*, ed. Stuart Barnett (London: Routledge, 1998).

17. Ibid., 91.

18. Felix Ravaisson, *Of Habit*, trans. Clare Carlisle and Mark Sinclair (London: Continuum, 2008), 25 (emphases added).

19. Catherine Malabou, "Addiction and Grace: Preface to Felix Ravaisson's *of Habit*," in Ravaisson, *Of Habit*, vii.

20. Ibid., viii (emphasis added).

21. Catherine Malabou, *The Future of Hegel: Plasticity, Temporality and Dialectic*, trans. Lisabeth During (London: Routledge, 2005).

22. Ibid., 37.

23. Ibid.

24. Martin Heidegger, *The Event*, trans. Richard Rojcewicz (Bloomington: Indiana University Press, 2013).

25. Ibid., 127. The full list follows: event, appropriation, expropriation, consignment, arrogation, adoption, properness, eventuation, appropriateness, dispropriation, the domain of what is proper.

26. Like Deleuze after him, Heidegger had very little time or respect for academic shadow-boxing, which he often described as "lovers quarrels."

27. Henri Bergson, *Matter and Memory*, trans. Nancy Paul and W. Scott Palmer (London: George Allen and Unwin, 1911), 93.

28. Martin Heidegger, *Discourse on Thinking*, trans. John Anderson and E. Hans Freund (New York: Harper and Row, 1966), 74.

29. Ibid., 79.

30. Nancy, "Surprise of the Event," 101–102.

31. Heidegger, *Contributions to Philosophy*, 69.

32. Heidegger, *Fundamental Concepts of Metaphysics*, 78–164.

33. Ibid., 158 (last emphasis added).

34. Johnstone, *Impro for Storytellers*, 19.

35. Jean-Luc Nancy, "Philosophy as Chance: An Interview with Jean-Luc Nancy," trans. Pascale-Anne Brault and Michael Naas, in *The Late Derrida*, 209.

36. Ibid., 221.

37. Walter Benjamin, "On the Concept of History," trans. Harry Zohn. In

Walter Benjamin: Selected Writings: Volume 4, 1938–1940, ed. Howard Eiland and Michael W. Jennings (Cambridge, MA: The Belknap Press of Harvard University Press, 2003), 392.

38. Alain Badiou, *Being and Event*, trans. Oliver Feltham (London, Continuum, 2005), 179.

39. Malabou, *Future of Hegel,* 74.

40. Ibid (Malabou's emphases).

41. Deleuze, *Difference and Repetition*, 222.

42. Ibid., 23–24.

43. Nietzsche, quoted in Deleuze, *Difference and Repetition*, 200; from, Friedrich Nietzsche, *Beyond Good and Evil*, trans. R. J. Hollingdale (Harmondsworth: Penguin Books, 1973, 231(emphasis added).

44. Deleuze, *Difference and Repetition*, 198.

CHAPTER 17

1. Deleuze, *Logic of Sense*, 73.

2. Deleuze and Guattari, *A Thousand Plateaus*, 311–12.

3. Phelan, *Unmarked*: "Performance's only life is in the present. Performance cannot be saved, recorded, documented, or otherwise participate in the circulation of representations *of* representations: once it does so, it becomes something other than performance. To the degree that performance attempts to enter the economy of reproduction, it betrays and lessens the promise its own ontology" (146).

4. Perhaps it is significant that the cover of the English translation of the *Logic of Sense* is bedecked with playing cards.

5. Konjar, "Goldberg Observations," 14.

6. Deleuze, *Repetition and Difference*, 79.

7. Ibid., 78–79 (emphases added).

8. *Gilles Deleuze from A to Z*, (DVD) with Claire Parnet, directed by Pierre-Andre Boutang, trans. Charles J. Stivale, Semiotext(e), 2012.

9. Deleuze, *Difference and Repetition*, 79.

10. Malabou, *Of Habit*, xx.

11. Konjar, "Goldberg Observations," 30.

12. Mike Cooper, "Hail the Happy Accident," *Critical Studies in Improvisation* 7, no. 2 (2011).

13. Bailey, *Improvisation*, 110–11.

14. Ibid., 10 (emphasis added).

15. Heidegger, "Origin of the Work of Art," 17.

16. Ibid., 138.

17. Ibid., 71.

18. Ibid., 54.

19. Martin Heidegger, "Building, Dwelling, Thinking," in *Poetry, Language, Thought*, trans. Albert Hofstadter (New York: Harper & Row, 1971), 161 (emphases in original).

20. "Practice makes perfect. But nobody's perfect, so why practice?" Kurt Cobain.

21. Heidegger, "Origin of the Work of Art," 59 (emphases in original).

22. Martin Heidegger, "The Question Concerning Technology," trans. William

Lovitt, in *The Question Concerning Technology and Other Essays* (New York: Harper and Row, 1977), 13 (emphases added).

23. Heidegger, "Origin of the Work of Art," 59.

24. Gilles Deleuze, "What Is a Creative Act," trans. Ames Hodges and Mike Taormina, in *Two Regimes of Madness: Texts and Interviews 1975–1995* (Cambridge, MA: Semiotext(e), 2006), 315.

25. Gilles Deleuze, *Empiricism and Subjectivity: An Essay on Hume's Theory of Human Nature,* trans. Constantin V. Boundas (New York: Columbia University Press, 1989), x.

26. Derrida, "A Certain Impossible Possibility," 239.

27. *Derrida,* (DVD) directed by Kirby Dick and Amy Ziering Kofman, Jane Doe Films, 2002.

28. Jacques Derrida, *Points . . . : Interviews, 1974–1994,* trans. Peggy Kamuf and Elizabeth Weber (Stanford, CA: Stanford University Press, 1995), 49.

29. Derrida, "A Certain Impossible Possibility," 233.

30. Nancy, "Surprise of the Event," 101.

31. Deleuze, *Difference and Repetition,* 211.

32. Ibid., 212.

33. Ibid.

34. Ibid.

35. Ibid.

36. Deleuze and Guattari, *What Is Philosophy?* 183. Hereafter cited parenthetically by page number in this chapter.

37. Ronald Bogue, *Deleuze on Music, Painting and the Arts* (New York: Routledge, 2003), 181.

38. Bogue, *Deleuze on Music,* 180 (emphases added).

39. Andre Lepecki, "From Partaking to Initiating: Leading Following as Dance's (a-personal) Political Singularity," in *Dance, Politics and Co-Immunity*, ed. Gerald Siegmund and Stefan Holscher (Zurich: Diaphanes, 2013), 35.

40. See, Bailey, *Improvisation,* where Bryars remarks, "One of the reasons I am against improvisation now is that in any improvising position the person creating the music is identified with the music. The two things are seen to be synonymous. The creator is there making the music and is identified with the music and the music with the person. It's like standing a painter next to his painting so that every time you see the painting you see the painter as well and you can't see it without him." 115.

CHAPTER 18

1. Alain Badiou, *In Praise of Love*, trans. Peter Bush (London: Serpent's Tail, 2012), 29.

2. Ibid., 28.

3. Ibid., 30.

4. www.ukrockfestivals.com

5. https://www.youtube.com/watch?v=pRg9h-XCHKs.

6. See, for example, http://crosstowntorrents.org/archive/index.php/t-1511.html.

7. Badiou, *In Praise of Love*, 44–45.

CHAPTER 19

1. Hegel, *Aesthetics*, 518, 574–75.

2. Jimi Hendrix, *Voodoo Chile*.

3. Hegel, *Aesthetics*, 66.

4. Maurice Blanchot, *The Space of Literature*, trans. Ann Smock (Lincoln: University of Nebraska Press, 1982), 53.

5. Blanchot, *Infinite Conversation*, 300.

6. Ibid., 303.

CHAPTER 20

1. Schoenberg, *Style and Idea*, 87.

2. Ibid., 67.

3. Ibid., 123 (emphasis in original).

4. Immanuel Kant, *Critique of Practical Reason*, trans. Thomas Kingsmill Abbott (London: Dover Press, 2004), 92.

5. Schoenberg, *Style and Idea*, 253.

6. Ibid., 78.

7. Ibid., 53.

8. Kant, *Critique of Practical Reason*, 31.

9. Schoenberg, *Style and Idea*, 216.

10. Ibid., 218.

11. Carl Dahlhaus, "Schoenberg's Aesthetic Theology," in *Schoenberg and the New Music*, trans. Derek Puffett and Alfred Clayton (Cambridge: Cambridge University Press, 1990).

12. Ibid., 81.

13. Hegel, *Phenomenology of Mind*, 388.

14. Dahlhaus, "On the Decline of the Concept of the Musical Work," in *Schoenberg and the New Music*, 266.

15. Ibid., 267.

16. Ibid.

17. Ronald M. Radano, *New Musical Figurations: Anthony Braxton's Cultural Critique* (Chicago: University of Chicago Press, 1993), 74.

18. Samuel Beckett, "Three Dialogues," in *Disjecta* (London: John Calder, 1983), 139.

19. Ibid., 142.

20. Schoenberg, *Style and Idea*, 439.

21. Ibid. (Schoenberg's emphases).

22. Daniel Albright, *Beckett and Aesthetics* (Cambridge: Cambridge University Press, 2003), 5.

23. Dahlhaus, "Composition and Improvisation," in *Schoenberg and the New Music*, 268.

24. Malabou, *Future of Hegel*, 74.

25. Deleuze and Guattari, *What Is Philosophy?* 212.

26. Malabou, *Future of Hegel*, 75.

27. Deleuze and Guattari, *What Is Philosophy?* 213.

CHAPTER 21

1. *Independent*, Friday, 18 July 2014.

2. Blanchot, *Space of Literature*, 34.

3. Ibid., 33.

4. Derek Bailey, quoted in "Forum–Improvisation," *Perspectives of New Music* 21, nos. 1–2 (Autumn 1982–Summer 1983), 50.

5. Henry Kaiser, interview with Derek Bailey, *Interview 1975*, http://metropolis .free-jazz.net/derek-bailey-the-interview-london-1975/artist-portraits/4648/.

6. Samuel Beckett, *No's Knife: Collected Shorter Prose, 1947–1966* (London: Calder and Boyers, 1967).

7. Ibid., 89.

8. Bailey, quoted in Kaiser, *Interview 1975*.

9. Brian Marley and Mark Wastell, *Blocks of Consciousness and the Unbroken Continuum* (London: Sound, 2005), 6.

10. "Forum–Improvisation," 52.

11. Bailey, quoted in Kaiser, *Interview 1975*.

12. Ibid.

13. Ibid.

14. Ibid.

15. Samuel Beckett, "Enough," in *No's Knife*, 153.

16. Bailey, quoted in Kaiser, *Interview 1975*.

17. Eddie Prevost, quoted in Ben Watson, *Derek Bailey: The Story of Free Improvisation* (London: Verso, 2004), 265.

18. Ibid., 266.

19. Ibid.

20. Bailey, *Improvisation*, 100.

21. Watson, *Derek Bailey*, 251.

22. Martin Heidegger, *Being and Time*, trans. John Macquarrie and Edward Robinson (Oxford: Basil Blackwell, 1962), 343–47. Hereafter cited parenthetically by page number in this chapter.

23. Eugene Chadbourne, quoted in Watson, *Derek Bailey*, 215.

24. Ibid., 347 (latter two emphases added).

25. Bailey, *Improvisation*, x.

26. Ibid., xi.

27. Ibid., 8.

28. Watson, *Derek Bailey*, 2.

29. Bailey, *Improvisation*, xi.

30. Ibid., 16 (emphasis added).

31. Blanchot, *Infinite Conversation*, 4 (emphasis added).

32. Descartes, "Discourse on Method," 8–9.

33. Thomas Clifton, quoted in Bailey, *Improvisation*, xi.

34. Bailey, quoted in Watson, *Derek Bailey*, 224.

35. Dominic Lash, *Metonymy as a Creative Constructive Principle in the work of J. H. Prynne, Derek Bailey and Helmut Lachenmann. with a Creative Component*, Unpublished PhD diss. (Brunel University, 2010), 94–95.

36. Simon Critchley, *Very Little . . . Almost Nothing: Death, Philosophy and Literature* (London: Routledge, 1997), 141. "His texts continually seem to pull the

rug from under the feet of the philosopher by showing themselves to be conscious of the possibility of such interpretations, or, better, such interpretations seem to lag behind the text which they are trying to interpret."

37. Dominic Lash, "Derek Bailey's Practice/Practise," *Perspectives of New Music* 49, no. 1 (Winter 2011): 2.

38. Edmund Husserl, *Cartesian Meditations: An Introduction to Phenomenology*, trans. Dorion Cairns (Dordrecht: Kluwer, 1995), 95.

39. Ibid., 140.

40. Edmund Husserl, *Ideas 1*, trans. W. R. Boyce Gibson (London: Allen and Unwin, 1969), 241.

41. Husserl, *Cartesian Meditations*, 113.

42. Heidegger, *Fundamental Concepts of Metaphysics*, 56–57 (emphases in original).

43. Ibid., 57.

44. Heidegger, *Contributions to Philosophy*, 4.

45. Ibid., 359.

46. Samuel Beckett, *Company* (London: John Calder, 1980), 14–15.

47. Ibid., 34.

48. Ibid., 45.

49. Ibid., 59.

50. Ibid., 84.

51. Ibid., 89.

52. Bailey, quoted in Watson, *Derek Bailey*, 206–7.

53. Bailey, *Improvisation*, 136.

54. Watson, *Derek Bailey*, 208.

55. Adorno, quoted in Watson, *Derek Bailey*, 225.

56. Adorno, *Philosophy of Modern Music*, 120.

57. Ibid., 176, 177.

58. Critchley, *Very Little . . . Almost Nothing*, 147.

59. Bailey, quoted in Kaiser, *Interview, 1975*.

60. For example, the following has a discussion of Beckett's *Ping*: Werner Wolf, *The Musicalization of Fiction: A Study in the History and Theory of Intermediality* (Amsterdam: Rodopi, 1999).

61. Bailey, *Improvisation*, 60 (emphasis in the original).

62. Ibid., 62 (first emphasis added).

63. https://www.youtube.com/watch?v=2lQnwqnEHDE.

64. Guitarists normally look like they can't sit down, lying down, flat out maybe, but not sitting down. They strut, they duck-walk, they leap, slide across the stage on their knees even, but no sitting.

65. Deleuze and Guattari, *What Is Philosophy?* 184.

66. I believe that beautiful playing must look beautiful—the visual aspect of improvisation discussed earlier.

67. "What the Hell are you listening to?" My twenty-one-year-old daughter shouts from another room. More difficult to answer than she knows! What *is* it exactly? "What a din!" she adds, turning up the volume on *Keeping Up with the Kardashians* in retaliation. I relent and go back to Barry Manilow. Family life!

CHAPTER 22

1. Blanchot, *Space of Literature*, 33 (gendered translation adjusted).

2. Gary Peters, *Irony and Singularity: Aesthetic Education from Kant to Levinas* (Aldershot: Ashgate, 2005), 165–66.

CHAPTER 23

1. Maurice Blanchot, "The Song of the Sirens: Encountering the Imaginary," in *The Gaze of Orpheus*, trans. Lydia Davis (New York: Station Hill Press, 1981), 105.

2. Cyndi Lauper, *Still So Unusual: A Memoir* (TV series). We TV, executive producers, Anabelle McDonald, Mark Burnett and Cyndi Lauper; production company, One Three Media; screened, 2013. Online at https://www.youtube.com/watch?v=YqfeSSspNGU.

3. George Cole, *The Last Miles: The Music of Miles Davis, 1980–1991* (Ann Arbor: University of Michigan Press, 2005).

4. Ibid., 350.

5. Cyndi Lauper, *Still So Unusual*.

6. Soren Kierkegaard, *Either/Or*, Vol. 1, trans. David Swenson and Lillian Swenson (Princeton NJ: Princeton University Press, 1959), 220–28.

7. Edmund Husserl, *The Phenomenology of Internal Time Consciousness*. For a more detailed account of this as it relates to improvisation, see my chapter "Improvisation and Time Consciousness," in *The Oxford Handbook of Critical Improvisation Studies*, ed. George Lewis and Ben Piekut (Oxford: Oxford University Press, 2016).

8. Heidegger, *Being and Time*, 302–3.

9. https://www.youtube.com/watch?v=m73dZFTgzXo.

10. https://www.youtube.com/watch?v=E-I7—qUy5Y.

11. https://www.youtube.com/watch?v=dxuAende7jQ.

12. Don't get me wrong, I'm an absolute sucker for both of them: a confession.

13. Blanchot, "The Song of the Sirens," in *The Gaze of Orpheus*, 106.

14. Ibid.

15. Badiou, *Being and Event*, 406 (first emphasis added).

16. Alain Badiou, *Logic of Worlds: Being and Event*, 2, trans. Alberto Toscano (London: Continuum, 2009), 50.

17. Malabou, *Future of Hegel*, 74.

18. Soren Kierkegaard, *Concluding Unscientific Postscript*, trans. David Swenson and Walter Lowrie (Princeton NJ: Princeton University Press, 1968), 74.

19. Ibid.

20. Martin Heidegger, "What Are Poets For?" in *Poetry, Language, Thought*, 138–39.

CONCLUSION

1. Badiou, *Being and Event*, xi.

2. Nietzsche, *Ecce Homo*, 717.

Bibliography

Adorno, Theodor. *Aesthetic Theory*. Translated by C. Lenhardt. London: Routledge & Kegan Paul, 1984.

———. "On Popular Music." In *Essays on Music*, edited by Richard Leppert. Berkeley: University of California Press, 2002.

Albright, Daniel. *Beckett and Aesthetics*. Cambridge: Cambridge University Press, 2003.

Arendt, Hannah. *The Life of the Mind*. New York: Harcourt, 1978.

Artaud, Antonin. *The Theatre of Cruelty*. Translated by Victor Corti. London: Calder and Boyers, 1974.

Auslander, Phillip. *Liveness: Performance in a Mediatized Culture*. London: Routledge, 1999.

Badiou, Alain. *The Adventures of French Philosophy*. Translated by Bruno Bosteels. London: Verso, 2012.

———. *Being and Event*. Translated by Oliver Feltham. London: Continuum, 2005.

———. *Handbook of Inaesthetics*. Translated by Alberto Toscano. Stanford, CA: Stanford University Press, 2005.

———. *Logic of Worlds: Being and Event, 2*. Translated by Alberto Toscano. London: Continuum, 2009.

Bailey, Derek. *Improvisation: Its Nature and Practice in Music*. New York: Da Capo Press, 1993.

Bataille, Georges. *Eroticism*. Translated by Mary Dalwood. London: Marion Boyars, 1987.

Becker, Howard S. "The Work Itself." In *Art from Start to Finish: Jazz, Painting, Writing and Other Improvisations*, edited by Howard S. Becker, Robert Faulkner, and Barbara Kirstenblatt-Gimblett. Chicago: University of Chicago Press, 2006.

Beckett, Samuel. *As The Story Was Told*. London: John Calder, 1990.

———. *Company*. London: John Calder, 1980.

———. *How It Is*, London: Calder and Boyers, 1964.

———. *Molloy: Malone Dies: The Unnamable*. London: Calder and Boyers, 1966.

———. *No's Knife: Collected Shorter Prose, 1947–1966*. London: Calder and Boyers, 1967.

———. "Three Dialogues." In *Disjecta*. London: John Calder, 1983.

Beiner, Ronald. "Hannah Arendt on Judging." In Hannah Arendt, *Lectures on Kant's Political Philosophy*. Brighton, UK: Harvester Press, 1982.

Benjamin, Walter. "On the Concept of History." Translated by Harry Zohn. In *Walter Benjamin Selected Writings: Volume 4, 1938–1940*, edited by Howard Eiland and Michael W. Jennings. Cambridge, MA: The Belknap Press of Harvard University Press, 2003.

———. *The Origin of German Tragic Drama*. Translated by John Osborne. London: Verso, 1985.

Bergson, Henri. *Matter and Memory*, Translated by Nancy Paul and W. Scott Palmer. London: George Allen and Unwin, 1911.

Berlin, Isaiah. *Two Concepts of Liberty*, Oxford: Clarendon Press, 1957.

Bernstein, J. M. *The Fate of Art: Aesthetic Alienation from Kant to Derrida and Adorno*. Cambridge: Polity Press, 1992.

Blanchot, Maurice. *The Infinite Conversation*. Translated by Susan Hanson. Minneapolis: University of Minnesota Press, 1993.

———. "Song of the Sirens: Encountering the Imaginary." Translated by Lydia Davis. In *The Gaze of Orpheus*. New York: Station Hill Press, 1981.

———. *The Space of Literature*. Translated by Ann Smock. Lincoln: University of Nebraska Press. 1982.

Borges, Jorge Luis. "Pierre Menard, Author of Quixote." In *Labyrinths*. Harmondsworth: Penguin Books, 1970.

Bogue, Ronald. *Deleuze on Music, Painting and the Arts*. New York: Routledge, 2003.

Boulez, Pierre. *Conversations with Célestin Deliège*. London: Eulenberg Books, 1976.

Brecht, Berthold. *Mother Courage and Her Children*. Translated by John Willett. London: Methuen, 1980.

Cage, John. *For the Birds*. Boston: Marion Boyers, 1981.

Caygill, Howard. "Benjamin, Heidegger and the Destruction of Tradition." In *Walter Benjamin's Philosophy: Destruction and Experience*, edited by Andrew Benjamin and Peter Osborne. London: Routledge, 1994.

Cole, George. *The Last Miles: The Music of Miles Davis, 1980–1991*. Ann Arbor: University of Michigan Press, 2005.

Cooper, Mike. "Hail the Happy Accident: An Interview with Mike Cooper." *Critical Studies in Improvisation* 7, no. 2 (2011).

Critchley, Simon. *Very Little . . . Almost Nothing: Death, Philosophy and Literature*. London: Routledge, 1997.

Davis, Miles. *Miles, the Autobiography*. New York: Picador Books, 1990.

Deleuze, Gilles. *Difference and Repetition*. Translated by Bruce Patton. London: Continuum, 2001.

————. *Empiricism and Subjectivity: An Essay on Hume's Theory of Human Nature*. Translated by Constantin V. Boundas. New York: Columbia University Press, 1989.

————. *The Fold: Leibniz and the Baroque*. Translated by Tom Conley. London: Continuum, 2006.

————. *The Logic of Sense*. Translated by Mark Lester. London: Continuum, 2004.

————. "Nomad Thought." In *The New Nietzsche: Contemporary Styles of Interpretation*, edited by David B. Allison. Cambridge, MA: MIT Press, 1985.

————. "What Is a Creative Act?" Translated by Ames Hodges and Mike Taomina. In *Two Regimes of Madness: Texts and Interviews 1975–1995*. Cambridge, MA: Semiotext(e), 2006.

Deleuze, Gilles and Felix Guattari. *A Thousand Plateaus*. Translated by Brian Massumi. London: Athlone Press, 1988.

————. *What Is Philosophy?* Translated by Graham Burchell and Hugh Tomlinson. London: Verso, 1994.

Dahlhaus, Carl. "Composition and Improvisation." In *Schoenberg and the New Music*. Translated by Derek Puffett and Alfred Clayton. Cambridge: Cambridge University Press, 1990.

————. "On the Decline of the Concept of the Musical Work." In *Schoenberg and the New Music*.

————. "Schoenberg's Aesthetic Theology." In *Schoenberg and the New Music*.

Derrida, Jacques. "A Certain Impossible Possibility of Saying the Event." Translated by Gila Walker. In *The Late Derrida*, edited by W. J. T. Mitchell and Arnold I. Davidson. Chicago: University of Chicago Press, 2007.

————. *Points . . . : Interviews 1974–1994*. Translated by Peggy Kamuf and Elizabeth Weber. Stanford, CA: Stanford University Press, 1995.

————. "Tympan." Translated by Alan Bass. In *Margins of Philosophy*. Chicago: University of Chicago Press, 1982.

————. *Writing and Difference*. Translated by Alan Bass. London: Routledge, 1978.

Descartes, René. "Discourse on Method." In *Philosophical Writings*. Translated by E. Anscombe and P. T. Leach. London: Nelson, 1970.

Descombes, Vincent. *Modern French Philosophy*. Translated by L. Scott-Fox and J. M. Harding. Cambridge: Cambridge University Press, 1980.

Eliot, T. S. *Four Quartets*. London: Faber and Faber, 1979.

Fischlin, Daniel, and Ajay Heble, eds. *The Other Side of Nowhere: Jazz, Improvisation, and Communities in Dialogue*. Middletown, CT: Wesleyan University Press, 2004.

Foster, Susan Leigh "Taken by Surprise: Improvisation in Dance and Mind." In *Taken by Surprise: A Dance Improvisation Reader*, edited by Ann Cooper Albright and David Gere. Middletown, CT: Wesleyan University Press, 2003.

"Forum: Improvisation." *Perspectives of New Music* 21, nos. 1–2 (Autumn 1982–Summer 1983).

Gadamer, Hans Georg. *Truth and Method*. Translated by Joel Weinsheimer and Donald Marshall. London: Sheed and Ward, 1989.

Hegel, G. W. F. *Aesthetics*. Translated by T. M. Knox. Oxford: Oxford University Press, 1970.

———. *The Phenomenology of Mind*. Translated by James Baillie. London: Allen and Unwin, 1971.

———. *Science of Logic*. Translated by A. V. Miller. London: Allen and Unwin, 1969.

Heidegger, Martin. *Being and Time*. Translated by John Macquarrie and Edward Robinson. Oxford: Basil Blackwell, 1962.

———. "Building, Dwelling, Thinking." Translated by Albert Hofstadter. In *Poetry, Language, Thought*. New York: Harper & Row, 1971.

———. *Contributions to Philosophy (From Enowning)*. Translated by Parvis Emad and Kenneth Maly. Bloomington: Indiana University Press, 1999.

———. *Discourse on Thinking*. Translated by John Anderson and E. Hans Freund. New York: Harper & Row, 1966.

———. *The Event*. Translated by Richard Rojcewicz. Bloomington: Indiana University Press, 2013.

———. *The Fundamental Concepts of Metaphysics: World, Finitude, Solitude*. Translated by William McNeill and Nicholas Walker. Bloomington: Indiana University Press, 1995.

———. "On the Essence of Truth." Translated by John Sallis. In *Martin Heidegger: Basic Writings*, edited by David Farrell Krell. New York: Harper & Row, 1977.

———. "The Origin of the Work of Art." Translated by Albert Hofstadter. In *Poetry, Language, Thought*. New York: Harper & Row, 1971.

———. "The Question Concerning Technology." Translated by William Lovitt. In *The Question Concerning Technology and Other Essays*. New York: Harper & Row, 1977.

———. "What Are Poets For?" Translated by Albert Hofstadter. In *Poetry, Language Thought*. New York: Harper Row, 1971.

Husserl, Edmund. *Cartesian Meditations: An Introduction to Phenomenology*. Translated by Dorion Cairns. Dordrecht: Kluwer, 1995.

———. *Ideas 1*. Translated by W. R. Boyce Gibson. London: Allen and Unwin, 1969.

———. *The Phenomenology of Internal Time Consciousness*. Translated by James Churchill. The Hague: Martinus Nijhoff, 1964.

Johnstone, Keith. *Impro for Storytellers*. New York: Routledge, 1999.

Kant, Immanuel. *Critique of Judgement*. Translated by James Creed Meredith. Oxford: Clarendon Press, 1952.

———. *Critique of Judgment*. Translated by Werner S. Pluhar. Indianapolis: Hackett Publishing Company, 1987.

———. *Critique of Practical Reason*. Translated by Thomas Kingsmill Abbott. London: Dover Press, 2004.

———. *Critique of Pure Reason*. Translated by Norman Kemp Smith. London: Macmillan, 1933.

Kermode, Frank. *The Sense of an Ending: Studies in the Theory of Fiction*. Oxford: Oxford University Press, 1967.

Kierkegaard, Soren. *Concluding Unscientific Postscript*. Translated by David Swenson and Walter Lowrie. Princeton, NJ: Princeton University Press, 1968.

———. *Either/Or*. Vol. 1. Translated by David Swenson and Lillian Swenson. Princeton, NJ: Princeton University Press, 1959.

Konjar, Jurij. "The Goldberg Observations: Unwritable Notes on an Unthinkable Practice." In *Contact Quarterly* 36, no. 2 (Summer/Fall 2011): chapbook 2.

Kostelanetz, Richard, ed. *Conversing with Cage*. London: Omnibus Press, 1989.

Kuhn, Thomas. *The Structure of Scientific Revolutions*. Chicago: University of Chicago Press, 1970.

Lash, Dominic. "Derek Bailey's Practice/Practise." In *Perspectives of New Music* 49, no.1 (Winter 2011).

———. *Metonymy as a Creative Constructive Principle in the work of J. H. Prynne, Derek Bailey and Helmut Lachenmann*. Unpublished PhD diss. Brunel University, 2010.

Lepecki, Andre. "From Partaking to Initiating: Leading Following as Dance's (a-personal) Political Singularity." In *Dance, Politics and Co-Immunity*, edited by Gerald Siegmund and Stefan Holscher. Zurich: Diaphanes, 2013.

Lewis, George. "Afterword to 'Improvised Music after 1950': The Changing Same." In Fischlin and Heble, *Other Side of Nowhere*.

———. "Improvised Music after 1950." In Fischlin and Heble, *Other Side of Nowhere*.

Luhmann, Niklas. *Art as a Social System*. Translated by Eva Knodt. Stanford, CA: Stanford University Press, 2000.

Malabou, Catherine. "Addiction and Grace: Preface to Felix Ravaisson's *Of Habit*." London: Continuum, 2008.

———. *The Future of Hegel: Plasticity, Temporality and Dialectic*. Translated by Lisabeth During. London: Routledge, 2005.

Marley, Brian and Mark Wastell. *Blocks of Consciousness and the Unbroken Continuum*. London: Sound, 2005.

Nancy, Jean-Luc. "Philosophy as Chance: An Interview with Jean-Luc Nancy." Translated by Pascale-Anne Brault and Michael Naas. In *The Late Derrida*, edited by W. J. T Mitchell and Arnold I. Davidson. Chicago: University of Chicago Press, 2007.

———. "The Surprise of the Event." Translated by Robert Richardson and Ann O'Byrne. In *Hegel after Derrida*, edited by Stuart Barnett. London: Routledge, 1998.

Nietzsche, Friedrich. *Ecce Homo*. Translated by Walter Kaufmann. In *Basic Writings of Nietzsche*, edited by Walter Kaufmann. New York: Random House, 1968.

———. *Thus Spoke Zarathustra*. Translated by Walter Kaufmann. In *The Portable Nietzsche*, edited by Walter Kaufmann. New York: Viking Press, 1954.

———. "The Uses and Disadvantages of History for Life." Translated by R. J. Hollingdale. In *Untimely Meditations*. Cambridge: Cambridge University Press, 1983.

Peters, Gary. "Improvisation and Time Consciousness." In *The Oxford Handbook of Critical Improvisation Studies*, edited by George Lewis and Benjamin Piekut. Oxford: Oxford University Press, 2016.

———. *Irony and Singularity: Aesthetic Education from Kant to Levinas*. Aldershot: Ashgate, 2005.

———. *The Philosophy of Improvisation*. Chicago: University of Chicago Press, 2009.

Phelan, Peggy. *Unmarked*. London: Routledge, 1993.

Prevost, Eddie. "The Discourse of a Dysfunctional Drummer: Collaborative Dissonances, Improvisation, and Cultural Theory." In Fischlin and Heble, *Other Side of Nowhere*.

Radano, Ronald M. *New Musical Figurations: Anthony Braxton's Cultural Critique.* Chicago: University of Chicago Press, 1993.

Ravaisson, Felix. *Of Habit.* Translated by Claire Carlisle and Mark Sinclair. London: Continuum, 2008.

Reason, Dana. "Navigable Structures and Transforming Mirrors: Improvisation and Interactivity." In Fischlin and Heble, *Other Side of Nowhere.*

Ricoeur, Paul. *Freud and Philosophy: An Essay on Interpretation.* Translated by Denis Savage. New Haven, CT: Yale University Press, 1970.

———. *Hermeneutics and the Human Sciences.* Translated by John Thompson. Cambridge: Cambridge University Press, 1981.

Rosen, Charles. *Schoenberg.* London: Fontana, 1976.

Schoenberg, Arnold. *Style and Idea.* Translated by Leo Black. London: Faber and Faber, 1975.

———. *Theory of Harmony (Harmonielehre).* Translated by Robert Adams. New York: New Philosophical Library, 1948.

Thomson, Scott. "The Pedagogical Imperative of Musical Improvisation." *Critical Studies in Improvisation* 3, no. 2 (2007).

Watson, Ben. *Derek Bailey: The Story of Free Improvisation.* London: Verso, 2004.

Wolf, Werner. *The Musicalization of Fiction: A Study in the History and Theory of Intermediality.* Amsterdam: Rodopi, 1999.

Young, Julian. *Heidegger, Philosophy, Nazism.* Cambridge: Cambridge University Press, 1998.

Index